Same-Sex Marriage and the Constitution

Does the Constitution protect the right to same-sex marriage? Much of the writing on this subject has been highly one-sided. This book takes a careful second look at the issue. Not only does it carefully look at the legal debate, but it also asks whether, in a democratic society, the courts should settle this question rather than the voters and it takes on the issue of whether such a court-created law could be effective in the face of public opposition. The book argues that this issue is one of the most significant constitutional issues facing society because it challenges society's commitment to the promise of true legal equality.

Evan Gerstmann is an Associate Professor at Loyola Marymount University. He received his Ph.D. from the University of Wisconsin–Madison after receiving his undergraduate degree from Oberlin College and his law degree from the University of Michigan Law School. His publications include *The Constitutional Underclass: Gays, Lesbians, and the Failure of Class-Based Equal Protection.*

"Evan Gerstmann has here presented a carefully crafted, highly nuanced, and important argument about same-sex marriage. His conclusion will be controversial, but in the best sense: People will be forced to reckon with his powerful argument."

– H. N. Hirsch, *Macalester College*

"This book does the best job I have seen in relating the constitutional law and theory of equal protection and the implied fundamental right of privacy to the politics of whether the Supreme Court should decide the important question of the right to same-sex marriage. This well-written, sensitive, and original book will be of invaluable use in undergraduate and law school classrooms. Evan Gerstmann demonstrates the tautological nature of arguments against gay marriage, while still being respectful to alternative arguments such as Sunstein's call for Supreme Court minimalism on this matter."

– Ronald Kahn, *Oberlin College*

"In *Same-Sex Marriage and the Constitution*, Evan Gerstmann once again applies his considerable analytical scalpel to an issue of constitutional and moral importance. Showing due regard for competing normative and legal arguments, Gerstmann exposes the weaknesses in existing positions on both sides of the debate. He then presents an illuminating and convincing case on behalf of same-sex marriage rights based on a conception of equal protection that is applicable to all citizens, regardless of their sexual orientation. The book will enlighten not only those concerned with the issue of same-sex marriage, but also those interested in jurisprudence, constitutional law, and the relationship between constitutional law and citizenship. Gerstmann's innovative approach points us toward a more productive understanding of equal protection."

– Donald A. Downs, *University of Wisconsin-Madison*

Same-Sex Marriage and the Constitution

EVAN GERSTMANN

Loyola Marymount University

CAMBRIDGE
UNIVERSITY PRESS

PUBLISHED BY THE PRESS SYNDICATE OF THE UNIVERSITY OF CAMBRIDGE
The Pitt Building, Trumpington Street, Cambridge, United Kingdom

CAMBRIDGE UNIVERSITY PRESS
The Edinburgh Building, Cambridge CB2 2RU, UK
40 West 20th Street, New York, NY 10011-4211, USA
477 Williamstown Road, Port Melbourne, VIC 3207, Australia
Ruiz de Alarcón 13, 28014 Madrid, Spain
Dock House, The Waterfront, Cape Town 8001, South Africa

http://www.cambridge.org

First published 2004

Printed in the United States of America

Typeface Sabon 10/13.5 pt.   *System* LaTeX 2_ε [TB]

A catalog record for this book is available from the British Library.

Library of Congress Cataloging in Publication Data

Gerstmann, Evan.
Same-sex marriage and the Constitution / Evan Gerstmann.
    p.   cm.
Includes bibliographical references and index.
ISBN 0-521-81100-7 (HB) – ISBN 0-521-00952-9 (PB)
    1. Same-sex marriage – Law and legislation – United States.   2. Constitutional
law – United States.   I. Title.
KF539.G47   2003
346.7301'6–dc21   2002041537

ISBN 0521 81100 7 hardback
ISBN 0521 00952 9 paperback

For Lauren, who reaffirms my faith in marriage every day, and, of course, for Isaac.

Contents

Preface   *page* ix

Acknowledgments   xv

PART I   THE CHALLENGE OF SAME-SEX MARRIAGE

1   Introduction   3

2   Reason and Prejudice: Is the Heterosexual Monopoly
    on Marriage Rational?   13

3   Looking for Stricter Scrutiny: Sexism, Heterosexism,
    and Class-Based Equal Protection   41

PART II   MARRIAGE AS A FUNDAMENTAL CONSTITUTIONAL RIGHT

4   The Fundamental Right to Marry   67

5   Same-Sex Marriage and the Fundamental Right
    to Marry   85

PART III   RIGHTS AND EQUALITY

6   Should Courts Create New Rights?   115

7   Identifying Fundamental Rights   134

PART IV   RIGHTS IN A DEMOCRATIC SOCIETY

8   Democracy, Neutrality, and Consistency of Principle   159

9   Principles and Practicalities   194

Bibliography   211

Index   219

Revised Preface

Just as this book was being published, the Supreme Court handed down its decision in *Lawrence v. Texas*, striking down the Texas anti-sodomy law. Shortly afterwards, a tidal wave of change swept over the landscape, in Massachusetts, California, New York, Canada, and elsewhere, altering the debate over same-sex marriage with dramatic speed. This revised preface takes into account these new developments.

Lawrence is an enormously important decision that supports the central arguments of this book. Most constitutional experts had thought the Court would strike down the law on the relatively narrow ground that it targeted only gays and lesbians. Instead, the Court unexpectedly issued a much more radical decision, overturning *Bowers v. Hardwick* (1986), the constitutional *bête noire* of gays and lesbians. *Bowers* not only had upheld Georgia's broadly defined sodomy law, but also contained language that was widely viewed as vilifying gays and lesbians. The rejection of *Bowers* was further noteworthy because the Court rarely overturns its own decisions, and because a Court with a conservative majority overruled a decision that many conservative commentators viewed favorably.

When I was writing this book, a great many experts who were sympathetic to the idea of same-sex marriage believed it was too aggressive to call for federal courts to recognize a right to these unions under the Constitution. Many averred that the idea of same-sex marriage was too unpopular and the arguments for it were too radical. It was better that advocates for same-sex marriage set their sights on more limited goals, including civil unions or domestic partnerships, they argued. This book rejects such a cautious approach, and *Lawrence* suggests the Court well might recognize the right to same-sex marriage.

First, *Lawrence* disposes of the argument that same-sex marriage is not a real marriage because it cannot legally be sexually consummated, an argument that has been central to the case against same-sex marriage. Second, *Lawrence* appears to indicate that the Justices have a new appreciation of the complexities of history and of the daunting challenges of interpreting its lessons. A simplistic, one-sided account of how Western society has always condemned homosexuality dominated *Bowers*; historians have widely condemned this view for its lack of balance and rigor. Such simplistic history has also been at the core of opposition to same-sex marriage. Even people who rightly regard themselves as tolerant and sympathetic to equal rights for gays and lesbians are hesitant to endorse same-sex marriage because of their overwhelming intuition that marriage has *always* been between a man and a woman, and that same-sex marriage is contrary to the weight and lessons of history. These arguments are problematic, and a more sophisticated Court is more likely to understand those problems. *Lawrence* presents a far more nuanced view of history and of the complexities that, in the Court's words, "counsel against adopting the definitive conclusions upon which *Bowers* placed such reliance."

Lawrence is also notable for the Court's attention to the legal views of other Western nations. Generally, the Court has been extremely parochial, ignoring the legal world beyond the United States. But in *Lawrence*, the Justices paid careful attention to the views of the European Court of Human Rights, which has held repeatedly that the right of sexual privacy extends to gays and lesbians. In fact, in the Court's most recent term, it referred to the laws and legal decisions of other Western nations in several cases. This increasing global awareness bodes well for advocates of same-sex marriage. While I was writing this book, only the Netherlands recognized same-sex marriages. Now, just a year later, Belgium recognizes them and, apparently Canada, is about to do so. A great many Western nations recognize the kinds of legal rights of same-sex partners that, until very recently, only the tiny State of Vermont recognized in this country. The growing recognition of same-sex marriage around the world should help make the Court more receptive to the idea of such unions.

Internationally, the situation in Canada is likely to have an especially great impact here in the United States. In 2003, courts in Ontario, British Columbia, and Quebec all ruled that Canada's common law definition of marriage – one man, one woman – violates Canada's Charter of Rights and Freedoms. In Ontario, same-sex couples, including American couples that travel to Ontario, are free to marry. At the time of this writing, it appears that the Canadian government is likely to ratify same-sex marriage for the entire country. A bill allowing same-sex marriage was sent to the Supreme Court of Canada to be vetted prior to being returned to the legislature.

While it is far from guaranteed, the Supreme Court might follow Canada's lead. *Lawrence* represents a new judicial recognition of, and respect for, the human dignity of gays and lesbians. The Court bluntly stated that its decision in *Bowers* "demeans the lives of homosexual persons," an admission that is critical to the debate over same-sex marriage. Also, *Lawrence* recognizes the crucial link between substantive rights and legal equality. "Equality of treatment and the due process right to demand respect for conduct protected by the substantive guarantee of liberty are linked in important respects, and a decision on the latter point advances both interests," the Court said. In attempting to protect legal equality, federal courts have focused much of their energy on dividing people into "classes" that receive different levels of constitutional protection against governmental discrimination. "Suspect classes" are protected by "strict scrutiny," "quasi-suspect classes" are protected by "intermediate scrutiny," and others, such as gays and lesbians, are protected by the lowest level of scrutiny, which is called "rational basis scrutiny". A discriminatory law will pass rational basis scrutiny if the State can show that it is rationally related to a legitimate governmental interest. I argue in other writings that this approach is a misguided dead end that should be abandoned. *Lawrence* could represent an important step toward recognizing that the key to legal equality is to protect substantive rights at the same level for everybody.

Finally, *Lawrence*, like other recent decisions, indicates that the Court might not be the rigidly ideological institution it is often portrayed to be. Among social scientists, the overwhelming view of the Court is that it is mostly interested in translating its members' politics (mostly conservative) into constitutional doctrine; the much-criticized decision in *Bush v. Gore*, in which the Court split along ideological lines in favor of George W. Bush, reinforced this view. If this interpretation is correct, same-sex marriage would have virtually no chance of passing muster with the Court. But the justices ended their term in June 2003 with a flurry of liberal decisions in major cases involving affirmative action, the rights of criminal defendants, and, of course, sexual privacy.

I must note that the Court's overturning of *Bowers* meant that a few parts of this book were dated just before publication, an inevitability when the world changes quickly. Fortunately, only a very small part of this book deals with *Bowers*, and the rejection of that decision merely buttresses my arguments in those sections. I address *Bowers* mostly to show that the ruling did not contradict my arguments. Obviously, those sections that refer directly to *Bowers* should be read with *Lawrence* in mind. Most significantly, Chapter 2 discusses whether the government has a rational basis for banning same-sex marriage. It argues that most reasons given for the ban are ill considered, but that pursuant to *Bowers*, moral condemnation of homosexuality qualifies as a rational basis. After *Lawrence*, however, a ban on same-sex marriage is on even shakier ground and might not even pass the lowest standard of judicial review.

Indeed, one court has already come to that conclusion. *Bowers'* demise helped pave the way for the Supreme Judicial Court of Massachusetts' landmark ruling that the state's ban on same-sex marriage lacks a rational basis. In *Goodridge v. Department of Public Health* (November 2003), the Massachusetts court declared that "the marriage ban does not meet the rational basis test for either due process or equal protection." The *Goodridge* Court rejected all three of the State's reasons for the same-sex marriage ban: providing a "favorable setting for procreation"; ensuring an optimal setting for child rearing; and preserving state resources. Using reasoning nearly identical to the arguments in this book, the *Goodridge* Court concluded that the major impact of same-sex marriage on children would be to provide additional protections to children in same-sex-headed households, and would not adversely affect any other children.

In February 2004, the Supreme Judicial Court of Massachusetts issued a further ruling, clarifying that the *Goodridge* decision required same-sex marriage, not merely civil unions or any other marriage-like institution. The court reasoned that: "The history of our nation has demonstrated that separate is seldom, if ever, equal." The court ruled that same-sex couples must be allowed to marry by May 17, 2004. As this book goes into its second printing, the Massachusetts legislature was still debating whether to amend the state constitution. Passage of such an amendment, despite numerous premature predications that such action was imminent, remains uncertain. Also, because the Massachusetts constitution cannot be amended until the legislature votes to do so in two consecutive years, no amendment could take effect until Fall of 2006 at the earliest. Therefore, it appears inevitable that, as a result of *Goodridge*, there will be legally recognized same-sex marriages in the United States.

Much remains unclear about what the results of this will be. Legal experts sharply disagree about whether same-sex marriages will have to be recognized by other states and what the status of those marriages will be in Massachusetts, should that state choose to eventually amend its constitution. Nonetheless, the United States is about to pass a major milestone in the debate over same-sex marriage.

Another major event since the first printing of this book is the decision of city officials in San Francisco to allow same-sex marriages. Over 4100 couples got married in San Francisco between February 12, 2004, when the Mayor first implemented the new policy, and March 11, 2004 when the California Supreme Court ordered at least a temporary halt to them, until the court could rule on whether the Mayor of San Francisco exceeded his authority. Notably, the Court did not void these marriages, leaving the future of same-sex marriage in California very much up in the air.

After San Francisco officials began performing same-sex marriages, a number of other city and county officials across the nation followed suit, with officials in New Jersey, New Mexico, New York State and Oregon performing same-sex marriages or issuing marriage licenses to same-sex couples. In each case the officials argued that the equal protection language in their state constitutions, as well as the United States Constitution protected the rights of same-sex couples to marry.

Opponents of same-sex marriage reacted strongly to many of these events. Prosecutors charged the Mayor of New Paltz, New York with 19 criminal counts of violating state law by solemnizing weddings without a proper license. The Attorney General of New Jersey also threatened to bring criminal charges against local officials who conducted same-sec marriages. Prosecutors in New York brought criminal charges against two Unitarian Universalist ministers for performing same-sex marriage.

The response that gained the greatest national attention, however, was President Bush's call for an amendment to the Unites States Constitution that would ban same-sex marriage. This call for an amendment, although perhaps predictable in an election year, struck many legal and political experts as unnecessary and premature, even from the point of view that same-sex marriages are undesirable. For one thing, the President's call seemed to concede the central argument of this book, which is that, absent amendment, the Constitution does indeed protect same-sex marriage. The President's call was also surprising because it federalizes an issue that had always been left to the states. The President warned that courts might force all fifty states to recognize same-sex marriages performed in Massachusetts under the Constitution's "full faith and credit clause." But as many legal scholars have pointed out, the Court never used that clause to force Jim Crow states to recognize interracial marriages performed in other states.

Although the majority of the American public is opposed to same-sex marriage, both elite and popular attitudes toward a constitutional amendment are mixed. Of course, should such an amendment pass, which would require approval by two-thirds of both houses of Congress and ratification by the legislatures of three-quarters of the states, this would dramatically alter the landscape for same-sex marriage.

This is an exciting, sometimes confusing time to be studying same-sex marriage. From this author's point of view, the rapidity of the change in this area has been astonishing. This is an area in which law and politics are both moving swiftly, sometimes synergistically, sometimes in opposition. My hope is that this book will give the reader a solid grasp of the constitutional issues at the core of this debate and provide a foundation for understanding the quickly, sometime convulsively, changing terrain of the same-sex marriage debate.

Los Angeles,
2004

Acknowledgments

My first acknowledgment goes to Michael Gauger, who edited many of the chapters before I sent them to the publisher. A better friend or a more talented editor would be hard to find.

I am, as always, indebted to Donald A. Downs, who mentored me through graduate school and led me to Cambridge University Press and to Lewis Bateman, Cambridge's political science editor, who has supported this project from its inception.

Many thanks are due to my colleagues and the administration at Loyola Marymount University. Joseph Jabbra, Kenyon Chan, and Seth Thompson helped provide me with various types of support for this book. Thanks also to Ronald Kahn for his support and critique of this project and for introducing me to the wonderful subject of constitutional law when I was an undergraduate at Oberlin College. My undergraduate research assistants, Paula Angulo, Tanaz Mashafatemi, and especially Nick Stahl, did a great deal of hard work with diligence, intelligence, and good spirits. I was also helped by the library staff at Loyola Marymount, including Neil Bethke and Glenn Johnson-Grau, and my thanks go to them.

My love and thanks go to my wife Lauren, my father Kurt, my brother Elan, and my friends Robert Knopf and Matthew Bosworth, who have been my debate partners and sounding boards for many of the ideas in this book.

PART I

THE CHALLENGE OF SAME-SEX MARRIAGE

I

Introduction

This book is about same-sex marriage as a fundamental constitutional right. It is also about the role of law and courts in society and what our society's promise of equal protection of the law really means. Same-sex marriage is one of the most important constitutional issues facing America today. To some that might seem an overstatement in these days of concern over terrorism, civil liberties, and other pressing issues. But same-sex marriage is one of the issues that most directly challenge our commitment to genuine legal equality. Although people disagree about the specifics, there is broad agreement within the American legal and academic communities that all persons should have the same legal rights regardless of their race, ethnicity, national origin, gender, or religion. But when the subject turns to gays and lesbians, many people grow more confused and hesitant. Is being gay or lesbian really the same as being a racial or ethnic or religious minority? Are sexual orientation and gender really comparable? Are gays and lesbians seeking special rights rather than equal rights? Are they seeking more than toleration and demanding governmental endorsement of homosexuality? These questions trouble many people who are genuinely committed to legal equality for all persons.

Moving Past "Gay Rights"

This book argues that we must leave behind the debate over "gay rights" and move on to the far more productive and illuminating question of what legal rights all people in America share and what the contours of those rights should be. In truth, there is no such thing as gay rights. There are only legal and constitutional rights that must be applied and protected equally for all people.

This being so leads to many further questions. What are those rights and where do they come from? How are they defined and who defines them? If they are defined and protected by politically insulated courts, how do we reconcile this with a democratic society? Are courts really capable of, or inclined toward, the principled decision making that would truly protect these rights for the most marginalized Americans? Do legal rights actually make a difference in the real world?

The Importance of the Right to Marry

This book addresses each of those questions within the context of a particular right – the fundamental constitutional "right to marry," and the application of that right to gays and lesbians who want to wed the person they love. I have chosen this particular issue because of its great importance to law and society. Legally, same-sex marriage is a fast developing issue. As Richard Epstein none-too-happily concedes, "The question of the legality of same-sex marriages has bullied its way to the front of the Constitutional agenda."[1] Same sex couples have been litigating the issue since the early 1970s, but in 1993 the Hawaii Supreme Court stunned the nation, and perhaps the plaintiffs themselves, when it ruled that the ban on same-sex marriage most likely violated the equal protection guarantee of the state constitution. As a result of that decision, the issue of same-sex marriage "exploded onto the American political landscape,"[2] and "it now plays a central role in the public debate in America over the legal status of gays and lesbians."[3]

The voters in Hawaii were taken aback by that decision and voted to amend the state constitution to allow the legislature to keep marriage

---

[1] Epstein, Richard A., "Caste and the Civil Rights Laws: From Jim Crow to Same Sex Marriages." *Michigan Law Review* 92 (August 1994): 2456–2478, 2473.

[2] Koppelman, Andrew, "Forum: Sexuality and the Possibility of Same-Sex Marriage: Is Marriage Inherently Heterosexual?" *American Journal of Jurisprudence* 42 (1997) 51–95, 51.

[3] Koppelman, Andrew, "1997 Survey of Books Relating to the Law: II Sex, Law, and Equality: Three Arguments for Gay Rights." *Michigan Law Review* 95(1997): 1636–1667, 1639.

exclusively heterosexual. In 2000, the Supreme Court of Vermont added new complexity and momentum to the issue when it held that same-sex couples are entitled to all of the legal benefits of marriage if not access to the institution of marriage itself. The state legislature responded by creating the institution of "Civil Unions," which are open to both same and opposite sex couples and allow gays and lesbians to enter into a legal relationship that many believe is a marriage in all but name. The Civil Union includes the right to adopt children together, collect alimony upon severance of the relationship, become the legal guardian of their partner's children, qualify for family health insurance, and many other benefits.

Same-sex marriage has also become a global issue. On April 1, 2001, the Netherlands became the first country to legalize same-sex marriage, and the number of countries that allow quasimarital, same-sex unions is growing. The United States is becoming increasingly isolated among Western nations in its lack of any legal recognition for committed same-sex relationships. In recent years, Norway, Sweden, Iceland, and France "recogniz[ed] same-sex marriage by another name," in the form of registered partnerships.[4] Numerous other European countries have, or are seriously considering, some more limited forms of legal recognition for same-sex marriage.[5]

The United States has gone in the opposite direction. In 1996 Congress passed the Defense of Marriage Act, which prevents same-sex couples from receiving any of the federal rights or benefits of marriage even if a state eventually allows same-sex marriage. Barring repeal of the statute, the only institutions with the power to alter the status quo at the federal level are the federal courts. According to former Supreme Court nominee Robert Bork, "many court watchers believe that within five to ten years the U.S. Supreme Court will hold that there is a constitutional right to same-sex marriage."[6]

Regardless of what one thinks of the merits of same-sex marriage, this is too important an issue for the federal courts to ignore. No right is more important to basic human happiness than the right to marry

---

[4] Waaldijk at 80. France's civil solidarity pact is more limited than in the other countries mentioned.

[5] Ibid. See also Eskridge, "Comparative Law and the Same-Sex Marriage Debate: A Step-by-Step Approach Toward State Recognition," 641–670, 641.

[6] Bork, *The Wall Street Journal* editorial (9/21/01).

the person one loves. Ninety-three percent of Americans rate "having a happy marriage" either one of their two most important goals or as a very important goal – far above the percentage of people who similarly rated "being in good health."[7] In fact, the right to marry is intimately tied to a person's health and longevity. Mortality rates are 50 percent higher for unmarried women than for married women. For unmarried men, the mortality rates are an astounding 250 percent higher than for married men. Being unmarried chops about ten years off a man's life.[8] The elderly are particularly vulnerable if unmarried. Unmarried patients have longer and more expensive hospital stays than married patients, and are two and a half times more likely to be discharged into a nursing home even accounting for obvious alternative factors such as the severity of illness, age, race, and diagnosis.[9] Furthermore none of this can be explained as mere selection effects.[10] Nor is cohabitation a substitute for marriage. These health differences are between married and unmarried people, not between people who live alone and people who live together.

Gays and lesbians crave entry to this life-altering relationship that has meant so much to so many heterosexual couples. "The most ambitious poll on the topic, conducted by *The Advocate* in 1994, found that almost two-thirds of the gay men polled wanted to marry someone of the same sex, with 85 percent open to the idea and only 15 percent uninterested. *The Advocate*'s poll of lesbians, published in 1995, also revealed strong interest in getting married."[11] Not all gays and lesbians see marriage positively or wish to marry,[12] but that is hardly a reason to deny the right to marry to the great majority of gays and lesbians that do.

The Indispensability of "Rights Talk" to a Legally Equal Society

The Fourteenth Amendment grandly promises all persons in America the "equal protection of the laws." To enforce this promise, the Supreme Court asks two questions when someone alleges that a law

[7] Waite and Gallagher at 2.
[8] Ibid. at 47–48.
[9] Ibid.
[10] Ibid. at 51 et seq.
[11] Eskridge at 78–79.
[12] See, e.g., Polikoff at 1535.

is discriminatory. The first question is "who has been discriminated against?" If, for example, a state prison refuses to hire African Americans, women, and gay and lesbian prison guards, the Court will apply different levels of judicial scrutiny to each of these exclusions. In my book, *The Constitutional Underclass: Gays, Lesbians and the Failure of Class-Based Equal Protection*,[13] I criticize this approach for two reasons. One is that the Court has failed to give any rational justification for treating the rights of different groups differently, and the explanations it has put forward are incoherent. For these justifications to make sense, we would have to believe, for example, that gays and lesbians as a group are more politically powerful than women as a group, since gays and lesbians, but not women, have been told by the federal courts that they are too politically powerful to receive strong judicial protection from discrimination.[14]

The other reason I criticize the group-based approach to legal equality is that it is divisive. It requires groups that believe that their rights are being violated to argue that they need special protection from the Court because they are politically powerless victims of historical discrimination and modern prejudices. They must define themselves as a victim group. Many political theorists such as Jean Bethke Elshtain and Sheldon Wolin have warned of the dangers posed to democracy and civil society of "the politics of difference": defining oneself primarily as a member of a victimized group, rather than as a citizen who shares rights and responsibilities with other citizens.[15]

The Court also uses the equal protection clause to protect certain "fundamental rights," which are not explicitly mentioned in the Constitution but are deemed vital to a legally equal society. This approach is unitive rather than divisive. It requires us to ask what rights we all share, regardless of whether we are powerful or powerless, popular or despised. If we want Americans to think of themselves as citizens rather than members of aggrieved groups, then we need to take this question very seriously.

Gays and lesbians are often accused of seeking "special rights" or of trying to portray themselves as a persecuted minority analogous to

---

[13] See Gerstmann.
[14] This is explained in much greater detail in Chapter 4 of Gerstmann.
[15] See Elshtain, *Democracy on Trial*.

racial minorities.[16] But if we want gay and lesbian Americans to think of themselves as Americans first and as gays and lesbians second then we have an obligation to give serious, thoughtful consideration to the issue of what rights all American share regardless of sexual orientation. This book argues that we have not met this obligation. The reasons that courts have given for refusing to extend the right to marry – a Constitutional right that heterosexuals take for granted and do not lose even if they commit felonies or fail to support their children from previous marriages – are remarkably ill-considered. This will be discussed in Part I of this book.

Outside of liberal academic circles, the reaction of many to the issue of same-sex marriage is often one of weary dismissiveness. There is a sense that gays and lesbians are asking for yet more, or that the whole issue is rather silly because everyone knows that marriage is exclusively between two people of different genders. In fact, reasoned, genuinely attentive discussion on this issue is only just beginning as more courts are giving serious consideration to the scope of the right to marry and thereby requiring others to do so as well.

The question of who may marry whom is worthy of society's sustained attention, because marriage is absolutely fundamental to human freedom and happiness. Hannah Arendt believed that the right to marry whomever one wishes is even more fundamental than is the right to vote. As will be discussed in Chapter 4, the Supreme Court has long held that marriage is one of the fundamental rights of all people.

Consistent protection of the rights of all Americans is the only alternative to the politics of group rights and special grievance and is essential to a legally equal society. Unfortunately, the idea of legal rights is under attack from a multitude of sources. In her book *Rights Talk*, Mary Ann Glendon argues that the discourse of rights overemphasizes individual autonomy over the duties and responsibilities that make society worth living in.[17] But the right to marry is an excellent example of how rights protect not only individual autonomy but also the capacity for us to make meaningful commitments to others. Marriage is a unique and powerful institution for willingly taking on responsibility

[16] See Chapter 5 of Gerstmann.
[17] See, e.g., Glendon, *Rights Talk*.

for another human being. It is an indispensable means for making a meaningful long-term commitment to another person. People who merely live together are less sexually faithful to their partners than are married couples, are less committed to the idea of sexual fidelity, and are less willing to support or be financially responsible for their partners.[18]

Nonetheless, many influential scholars and lawyers are skeptical of rights-based equality. Court protection of individual rights is attacked by some as being antidemocratic. Others argue that judges decide cases based upon attitudes and strategic concerns rather than abstract legal rights. Still others argue that what courts say and do has little impact upon the outside world.

Unfortunately, there is a dearth of literature that addresses these various arguments in an organized fashion. "Originalists," who believe that the Court should not read modern values into the Constitution, rarely engage "attitudinalists," who believe that judges mostly read their own beliefs into the Constitution. Advocates of gay and lesbian rights rarely discuss the famed "Hollow Hope" thesis that Courts are usually ineffective at creating social change. Scholars of legal history and doctrine, mostly law professors, rarely engage scholars of judicial behavior, who are mostly social and political scientists.

This book attempts to bridge these several divides by taking a single important rights issue, same-sex marriage, through the gauntlet of objections and challenges posed by these various schools of rights skepticism. I have made an effort to address every substantial objection to judicial protection of same-sex marriage on its own terms. This book does not take for granted that the Court should protect rights that cannot be found in the text of the Constitution, or that the Court's past decisions protecting marriage were correctly decided, or that judges mechanically apply law to facts, or that Courts can change society with a bang of the gavel. Each of these important issues is specifically addressed in the following chapters. Thus, this book should be of interest to people who care about the issue of same-sex marriage, as well as to readers who are broadly interested in the role of courts and law in society.

---

[18] Waite and Gallagher at p. 39.

Advocacy and Objectivity

This is a work of advocacy, but it is not primarily advocacy for same-sex marriage, although I do support the right to marry a person of one's own gender. It is meant as advocacy for good faith engagement with an issue that people often react to in an angry or emotional manner. I make no claim to "objectivity," a term that is, to say the least, controversial. I do attempt fairness, by which I mean a willingness to take counter positions seriously and respond to them without ignoring or defining away their underlying merits. I believe that arguments speak for themselves and do not depend upon the identity of the person who makes them. It is worth noting, though, that when I began this project, I was planning on writing a book *against* courts requiring states to recognize same-sex marriage. I believed that the democratic process should resolve the issue rather than the courts. As I progressed in my research, I simply became won over by the strength of the arguments on the other side.

For a very long time, the Supreme Court has held that the Constitution protects our right to marry whomever we want and I was genuinely surprised at the lack of convincing reasons for denying this right to same-sex couples. Andrew Koppelman, who is actually a well-established advocate of same-sex marriage, has written, "This right [to marry] must, however, have implicit limits. It cannot mean that I have a right to marry my goldfish, or my sofa."[19] But marriage is a consensual relationship and animals and furniture are unable to consent to any contract, much less a marriage contract. Nor are children. The arguments for why two consenting adults cannot enter into a marriage are far murkier.[20]

The Book's Organization

The following two chapters explore and reject alternative theories as to why the Constitution might protect same-sex marriage. In Part I, Chapter 2 examines the argument that the heterosexual monopoly on

---

[19] Koppelman, Andrew, "Why Gay Legal History Matters." (book review). *Harvard Law Review* 113 (June 2000): 2035–2060, 2046.
[20] The analogies to incestuous and polygamous marriages require a lengthier treatment. See Chapter 4.

marriage is "irrational." Chapter 3 asks whether gays and lesbians as a group should receive heightened protection from the Court because they are a persecuted minority or because sexual orientation discrimination is really a disguised form of gender discrimination.

Part II of the book begins, in Chapter 4, the analysis of the fundamental right to marry. Chapter 4 lays out the history and development of that right. It demonstrates that the right to marry is one of the oldest recognized constitutional rights, far older than the better known, but more recent and amorphous "right to privacy." Chapter 5 examines whether there is any reason that the right to marry does not apply to same-sex couples.

Part III, in Chapters 6 and 7, engages in normative analysis of the Court's decisions on marriage. Just because the Court has held that there is a broad right to marry does not mean that the Court is right. Many scholars have argued that the Court should not be in the business of protecting rights that are neither mentioned in the Constitution nor in keeping with the intent of the people who framed or ratified the Constitution. These chapters address the question of why the Court enforces certain rights at all and what those reasons tell us about whether the Court should protect the right of same-sex couples to marry.

In Part IV, Chapters 8 and 9 discuss some of the broader issues. In a democratic society, should the Court take up this question at all? Does any of the doctrinal analysis even matter when many have argued that legal principles actually have little to do with how judges really act? Would judicial action make any difference as a practical matter? These chapters answer these questions in the affirmative. They use the Court's First Amendment jurisprudence as an example of an area in which judges have applied legal principles vigorously, even in the case of powerful public opposition and, in some cases, despite their own explicit distaste for the outcome. We will see that gays and lesbians have had their greatest and most consistent successes in First Amendment cases, because this is an area where the law is unusually well defined and therefore well situated to effectively protect unpopular litigants. This book argues that the best way for the courts to protect legal equality for all under the equal protection clause is to identify fundamental rights such as the right to marry and to define and protect those rights with the same rigor and consistency as in the area of freedom of speech.

One of the difficulties in addressing the issue of same-sex marriage is the common reaction that "of course" marriage is only between a man and a woman and that anything to the contrary is sophistry. Therefore the next chapter will examine the reasons most often given for this position. Although the chapter does not conclude that opposition to same-sex marriage is "irrational," as that term has been defined by the Court, we will see that the moral and policy arguments against same-sex marriage are far weaker than many suppose.

2

Reason and Prejudice

Is the Heterosexual Monopoly on Marriage Rational?

For same-sex couples who desire marriage, the Constitution's grand promise of "the equal protection of the laws" has been their greatest hope. Gays and lesbians have gone to court over and over again, pressing their claim that the heterosexual monopoly on marriage violates their right to legal equality[1]. But the promise of equal protection has proven to be complex terrain, especially as applied to the highly emotional issue of same-sex marriage. The public, the litigating attorneys, and especially the courts themselves have struggled to make sense of what legal equality really means for same-sex couples.

To understand this emotionally and intellectually challenging issue, one must begin by understanding how the Supreme Court has traditionally interpreted the equal protection clause of the Constitution. Over the decades, equal protection has come to mean not one standard of constitutional protection, but many standards. Although our intuitive understanding of equal protection might be that the same legal standards must apply to everybody, the reality is quite different; courts apply the equal protection clause differently, depending upon whose rights are allegedly being violated and which rights are at issue. Before

[1] Some courts and commentators have carefully avoided assuming that same-sex couples seeking marriage are gay. As I do not know of, nor have I ever heard of any, heterosexual same-sex couples, I will assume that the same-sex couples seeking to marry are gay, lesbian, bisexual, or transgendered. For the sake of brevity, I will sometimes use the terms "gay" or "gay rights" as shorthand for gays and lesbians or "gay and lesbian rights."

we discuss same-sex marriage, we begin with a brief overview of the framework of equal protection jurisprudence.

The Three-Tier Framework of Equal Protection

Under the equal protection clause, the Supreme Court subjects laws to three different "levels of scrutiny" that vary in their "strictness." The stricter the scrutiny the more likely the Court is to strike down the law on equal protection grounds.

Appropriately, the highest level of scrutiny is called "strict scrutiny,"[2] under which a law will be struck down unless it is "narrowly tailored to further a compelling interest." This standard has been referred to famously as "strict in theory, fatal in fact"[3] because it is virtually impossible for a law to survive strict scrutiny. Justices will apply strict scrutiny to a law if it pertains to a "suspect classification" – race, ethnicity, or national origin[4] – or interferes with a "fundamental" right. In an example of the former, the Court subjected laws that forbid interracial marriages to strict scrutiny and struck them down in 1967.[5] Many gay and lesbian plaintiffs have argued that sexual orientation should be added to the list of suspect classifications and that, accordingly, the Court should subject the ban on same-sex marriage to strict scrutiny. This argument will be addressed in Chapter 3. As for fundamental rights, these include the right to travel from state to state, the right to vote, and the right to "bear or beget children."[6] These rights are never explicitly mentioned in the Constitution and should not be confused with the Bill of Rights' guarantees of rights such as freedom of

[2] Unless otherwise noted, the terms, definitions, and standards described in this section are from the Supreme Court's majority opinion in *Cleburne v. Cleburne Living Center*, 473 U.S. 432 (1985).

[3] Gunther, Gerald, "Forward: In Search of Evolving Doctrine on a Changing Court: A Model for a Newer Equal Protection." *Harvard Law Review* 86 (1972): 1–48, 8.

[4] At one time the Court also included "alienage" (i.e., noncitizen status) as a suspect classification. *Graham v. Richardson*, 403 U.S. 365 (1971). But the Court has since backed away from this without formally announcing that it is overturning *Graham*. Lusky, Louis, "Footnote Redux: A *Caroline Products* Reminiscence." *Columbia Law Review* (1982): 1093–1105.

[5] *Loving v. Virginia*, 388 U.S. 1. The same decision also held that marriage is a fundamental right.

[6] Respectively, *Shapiro v. Thompson*, 394 U.S. 618 (1969); *Kramer v. Union Free School District No. 15*, 395 U.S. 621 (1969) and *Skinner v. Oklahoma*, 316 U.S. 535 (1942).

speech and religion. Fundamental rights are those that the Court has held are *implicitly* protected under the Fourteenth Amendment. This list of fundamental rights includes the "right to marry," and this book argues that the right is broad enough to guarantee the right of same-sex couples to marry one another.

The second tier of equal protection jurisprudence is "intermediate scrutiny." To withstand intermediate scrutiny, a law "must serve important governmental objectives and must be substantially related to the achievement of those objectives."[7] This is a difficult test, and most laws are struck down when measured against it. The question of why the Court gives lesser scrutiny to gender discrimination is complicated and has never really been answered;[8] nonetheless, there is a good chance that courts would strike down the same-sex marriage ban if they applied the intermediate standard. In fact, one of the theories that advocates of same-sex marriage advance most ardently is that the heterosexual marriage monopoly is a form of *gender discrimination* and, therefore, is subject to intermediate scrutiny. The argument is surprisingly straightforward: Mr. Y cannot marry Mr. Z, but Ms. X is free to marry Mr. Z; thus, Mr. Y is being discriminated against on the basis of his gender. This is the theory upon which the Hawaii Supreme Court relied in subjecting the state's same-sex marriage ban to strict scrutiny (under the Hawaiian state Constitution, gender discrimination is subject to strict scrutiny). This intriguing argument is discussed in Chapter 3.

The third and lowest tier of scrutiny under the equal protection clause is "rational basis" scrutiny, which courts apply to the vast majority of laws in this country. A very weak form of judicial review, rational basis scrutiny acknowledges that the legislative and executive branches and, ultimately, the people are supposed to decide the wisdom of laws and governmental policies; judges should not impose their political preferences on people in the guise of "interpreting" the equal protection clause. Under the rational basis test, a law "will be sustained if the classification drawn by the statute is rationally related to a legitimate state interest."[9] If the law is "rational" in this broad sense,

---

[7] *Craig v. Boren*, 429 U.S. 190 (1976).
[8] Gerstmann at Chapters 3 and 4.
[9] *Cleburne*, 473 U.S. at 439–440.

the courts will not strike it down just because it is foolish or narrow-minded. "The Constitution presumes that even improvident decisions will be rectified by the democratic process."[10]

The rational-basis standard is so weak that it has been called "minimal scrutiny in theory and virtually none in fact."[11] Courts will uphold laws that everybody agrees cause more harm than good, or laws that reflect outdated concerns, so long as they further, even slightly or tangentially, a legitimate goal of government. This is the level of scrutiny on which gays and lesbians have had to rely when challenging laws that discriminate against them.[12] Not surprisingly, their efforts have usually failed. Under rational-basis scrutiny, courts have upheld laws that prevent gays and lesbians from immigrating to the United States, serving in the military, receiving security clearance, or adopting children, among many restrictions. Also, courts have rebuffed a woman whose job offer from the Georgia Attorney General's office was withdrawn solely because she planned a same-sex "marriage" ceremony, and another who lost custody of her child primarily because she was a lesbian.[13]

But the Court has been willing to draw some lines. In 1996, in *Romer v. Evans*,[14] it struck down an amendment to the Colorado State Constitution that repealed all state and local laws banning discrimination on the basis of sexual orientation and prohibited any new versions of such laws. The broad scope of Amendment 2, passed by popular initiative, seemingly startled the Court, whose majority opinion, written by the Reagan-appointed Justice Anthony Kennedy, called the measure "unprecedented in our jurisprudence."[15] The Court cited an important precedent, *USDA v. Moreno*,[16] involving a United States Department of Agriculture regulation that defined food stamp eligibility in a way that

---

[10] Ibid.

[11] Gunther at 8.

[12] "Discriminate" is, of course, a rhetorically loaded term, and no doubt many would object to my description of the following laws as discriminatory. For now, it suffices to say that I use the term if the laws would generally be considered discriminatory if applied to racial minorities or to women. Whether such an equivalency among sexual orientation, race, and gender is appropriate will be discussed extensively later.

[13] See Gerstmann at 62–84 for discussion and citation of these cases.

[14] 517 U.S. 620.

[15] *Romer* 517 U.S. 633.

[16] 413 U.S. 528 (1973).

excluded members of "hippie communes" (a term that a legislator used during the debate on the bill). Employing language that has become crucial to current civil rights debates, the Court stated, "If... 'equal protection of the laws' means anything, it must at the very least mean that a bare congressional desire to harm a politically unpopular group cannot constitute a *legitimate* governmental interest."[17] In other words, bare desire to harm an unpopular group – *animus* toward that group by the government or by the majority population – is not a legitimate governmental interest. A law based upon hostility toward an unpopular group will be struck down even under the rational-basis standard.

But *Moreno* left many questions unanswered. How do we know whether a law is based upon animus? In *Moreno*, there was something of a smoking gun, in that a federal legislator publicly stated that the goal of the new law was to target "hippie communes," an unmistakably pejorative term in that context. Such smoking guns, however, are rarely available. Courts must be cautious about assuming that they can divine the "real" intent of a legislative body based upon the public pronouncements of one or more legislators.[18] Furthermore, the word "animus" is highly subjective. How can a court differentiate between impermissible animus towards hippies and communes and a legitimate policy determination that groups of unrelated individuals living together in a communal household should not receive food stamps? Such questions are particularly difficult in the area of gay rights, in which one person's moral objection to homosexuality is another person's example of intolerance and prejudice.[19] This is the difficult ground on which the *Romer* Court walked.

The Colorado Attorney General's office argued that Amendment 2 was rationally related to many legitimate governmental purposes, among them preserving people's freedom to not associate with gays and lesbians and avoiding the message that disapproval of homosexuality

---

[17] *Moreno*, 413 U.S. at 534 (emphasis in original).

[18] See Farber and Frickey on the difficulty of determining legislative intent and the question of whether there is any such thing as a unified legislative intent, as opposed to a collection of intentions of individual legislators.

[19] As Laurence Tribe has succinctly phrased the question, "How are we to distinguish... 'prejudice' from principled, if 'wrong' disapproval?" "The Puzzling Persistence of Process-Based Constitutional Theories." *Yale Law Journal* 89 (1980): 1063–1080, 1073.

is the moral equivalent of racism. Rejecting these arguments, the Court held that the broad negation of rights as a result of Amendment 2 was too sweeping to be rationally related to these purposes. The amendment's "sheer breadth is so discontinuous with the reasons offered for it that the amendment seems inexplicable by anything other than animus toward the class it affects; it [therefore] lacks a rational relationship with legitimate state interests."[20]

Some scholars, including myself, have argued that the *Romer* Court actually applied a level of scrutiny somewhat greater than rational basis review. The Court seemed unusually skeptical of Colorado's professed reasons for its sweeping ban on civil rights for gays and lesbians[21]; but perhaps such skepticism is justified in the case of laws regarding gays and lesbians. Public hostility toward gays and lesbians is still very great. "Homosexuals are more severely stigmatized than any other group in America."[22] Given the general social hostility toward homosexuality, it is probably appropriate for the Court to be particularly cautious about accepting benign explanations for laws that burden gays and lesbians. This is different from the Court's applying a higher form of scrutiny (that will be discussed in subsequent chapters). The suggestion is not that the Court require that the governmental interest be compelling, as in strict scrutiny, or even important, as in intermediate scrutiny. Rather, the suggestion is merely that courts be aware of the background hostility and not blindly accept whatever explanations are offered for the same-sex marriage ban. In any event, that seems to be the charge of the Court in *Romer*.

Romer, then, is the leading case for deciding whether the same-sex marriage ban has a rational relationship to legitimate governmental interests. In some ways, the same-sex marriage ban is more focused, less

---

[20] *Romer*, 517 U.S. at 632.
[21] We can only speculate on what might have motivated the Court to apply rational basis scrutiny in an unusually tough manner. Perhaps Court liberals were sympathetic toward gay rights, and perhaps some Court conservatives objected to the statewide intrusion on community power to pass local legislation in accordance with community values. For whatever reason, the Court appeared to apply a standard of review more strict than traditional rational basis. For a fuller discussion of this point, see Gerstmann at Chapter 6.
[22] Katz, Pamela S., "The Case for Legal Recognition of Same-Sex Marriage." *Journal of Law and Policy* 8 (1999): 61–106, 65, citing Wolfe, Alan, "The Homosexual Exception" *The New York Times*, p. 46 Feb. 8, 1998.

sweeping in its effects than was Amendment 2, which rescinded many laws. Confining marriage to heterosexuals involves just that one issue. Still, in its own way, the same-sex marriage ban is even more sweeping than the amendment. Preventing same-sex couples from marrying deprives them of hundreds, perhaps even thousands, of legal rights that heterosexual married couples enjoy. At the state level, these rights include hospital visitation, control over the funeral and burial arrangements for a partner, the privilege against testifying against one's spouse in court, automatic inheritance rights, and access to family health insurance benefits.[23] At the federal level, the General Accounting Office has identified over one thousand provisions in statutes that same-sex marriage would affect.[24]

The rational basis test is a particularly useful starting point for examining the constitutionality of the same-sex marriage ban, for although it is a legal test, it focuses on policy issues. Because it requires only that a law be rationally related to any legitimate governmental interest, it allows for a wide-ranging discussion of the reasons that state governments have proffered for banning same-sex marriage. No specialized debates over the meaning of technical terms such as "suspect class" or "intermediate scrutiny" are required. Why do we prevent gays and lesbians from marrying? Do any of these reasons, upon deeper reflection, really make sense? The rest of this chapter examines the reasons most often cited for the heterosexual monopoly on marriage, grouped into four general categories: 1) definition, tradition and religion; 2) natural law; 3) the equation of marriage with procreation and child-rearing; and 4) moral disapproval of homosexuality.

Definition, Tradition, and Religion

Arguments based on the definition of marriage, tradition, and religion fit in the same general category because each is basically self-contained: marriage should remain exclusively heterosexual because that simply is what marriage is, because that is what marriage has always been,

---

[23] See Chambers, David, "What if? The Legal Consequences of Marriage and the Legal Needs of Lesbian and Gay Male Couples." *Michigan Law Review* 95 (1996): 447–491, for a description of the many laws that same-sex marriage would affect.

[24] Leonard, Arthur, "*The Case for Same Sex Marriage.*" (book review) *Cornell Law Review* 82 (1997): 572–593, 572.

or because the major religious traditions have always understood marriage to be between a man and a woman. These are not consequentialist arguments about what will happen if gays and lesbians are allowed to marry; they are rooted in a particular understanding of how things have always been and how things are.

The argument from definition has been impregnable with the courts ever since same-sex marriage cases began reaching state high courts in the early 1970s. In 1971, the first to hear such a case, the Minnesota Supreme Court, relied upon dictionary definitions. Two years later, in *Jones v. Hallahan*, the Kentucky Supreme Court cited three different dictionary definitions of marriage to show that it has always been understood as a union of man and woman. In 1974, the Court of Appeals of Washington held that the one man/one woman nature of marriage is too obvious to even bother looking at the dictionary:

Although it appears that the appellate courts of this state until now have not been required to define specifically what constitutes a marriage, it is apparent from a review of cases dealing with legal questions arising out of the marital relationship that the definition of marriage as the legal union of one man and one woman who are otherwise qualified to enter into such a relationship not only is clearly implied from such cases, but also was deemed by the court in each case to be so obvious as not to require recitation.[25]

The court added, "We need not resort to the quotation of dictionary definitions to establish that 'marriage' in the usual and ordinary sense refers to the legal union of one man and one woman."[26] Legal commentators opposing gay marriage have also emphasized this argument. According to Richard F. Duncan, "homosexual marriage is an oxymoron. It simply does not exist, because the legal definition of marriage 'is that it is a union of a man and woman.'"[27]

In addition to the definitional argument, the belief that exclusively heterosexual marriage is firmly rooted in tradition and religion seems to resonate powerfully with the majority of the American public. Even the generally liberal, pro-gay rights Senator Hillary Rodham Clinton has publicly bowed to this sentiment. In January 2000, she said, "Marriage has got historic, religious, and moral content that goes back to the

[25] *Singer v. Hara*, 522 P.2d 1187, 1191–1192.
[26] 522 P.2d at 1192, n.6.
[27] Duncan at 589.

beginning of time, and I think a marriage is as a marriage has always been: between a man and a woman."[28]

All these arguments have intuitive appeal to many people, but none can fairly be said to be a rational reason for maintaining the heterosexual monopoly on marriage. The definitional argument fails by the very definition of "definition" – definitions are arbitrary. Suppose a mountain is defined as any hill whose peak is at least one thousand feet above sea level. If some geographers were to suggest that we start calling hills over nine hundred feet mountains because hills of this size have more in common geologically with mountains than with smaller hills, we would be surprised if a geographer responded, "But we can't do that; by definition, a mountain must be over one thousand feet." Such a response would obviously be seen as irrational. Regarding the argument that marriage is opposite-sex by definition, James Trosino nicely summarizes the problem: it "amounts to an intellectually unsatisfying response: marriage is the union of a man and a woman because marriage is the union between a man and a woman."[29]

This is not to say that all definitions are irrational or that the choice of one definition over another is purely a matter of fancy. Clearly, some definitions have greater utility than others for purposes such as ease and clarity of communication, facilitation of scientific research, or because we wish to convey certain values by the way we define words. The argument here, it should be stressed, is very narrow and simple. I am not arguing that it is irrational to define marriage as between a man and a woman only. I am merely arguing that it is irrational to continue to define marriage as exclusively heterosexual simply because marriage is *currently* defined as exclusively heterosexual. In Chapter 5, we will return to the issue of whether marriage, as a matter of legal policy, should be defined as exclusively heterosexual.

The reliance on tradition is similarly misplaced. Responding to Clinton's statement that "marriage has historic, moral and religious content that goes back to the beginning of time," Andrew Sullivan writes:

Even a cursory historical review reveals this to be fragile. The institution of civil marriage, like most human institutions, has undergone vast changes over

---

[28] Quoted in Sullivan, "State of the Union," at 20, 23.
[29] Trosino at 97.

the last two millennia. If marriage were the same today as it has been for 2,000 years, it would be possible to marry a twelve-year-old you had never met, to own a wife as property and dispose of her at will, or to imprison a person who married someone of a different race. And it would be impossible to get a divorce.[30]

Indeed, fundamental understandings of the definition of marriage have careened from one extreme to another and everywhere in between in Western culture. At one time, the dominant view of marriage vows in Catholic countries was that "any private promise (no witnesses needed) was an unbreakable sacrament."[31] Far from a Western consensus on the meaning of marriage, Protestants and Catholics battled throughout the millennia over the proper definition and status of marriage.[32] To make matters even more complicated, the United States was quite willing to split from its European roots and, in the nineteenth century, to create its own form of marriage, common-law marriage.[33]

Some traditions, of course, have remained remarkably stable, including the rejection of same-sex marriage throughout the Western world the past seven centuries. William Eskridge asserts that "same-sex marriages are commonplace in human history,"[34] but concedes that Western culture has been quite hostile toward same-sex unions since the thirteenth century;[35] and there is nothing irrational about respect for centuries-old tradition. There are dangers in defining families based upon individual associational rights, without regard to traditional understandings. Friedrich Nietzsche warned "that family will be slowly ground into a random collection of individuals [joined only] in the common pursuit of selfish ends and in the common rejection of structures and strictures of family, church, state and civil society."[36]

But respect for tradition is a reason for caution, not stasis. Even Edmund Burke, perhaps the most notable of the philosophers and historians who have warned of the dire consequences of ignoring traditions, granted that traditional institutions can and should change. As

---

30 Sullivan at 20.
31 Graff, E. J., "Marriage *a la mode*," *Boston Globe Magazine*, June 13, 1999, 11–32.
32 Ibid.
33 Ibid. at 25.
34 Eskridge at 16.
35 Ibid. at 35.
36 Letter of August 1886, cited in Blake, Jennie Holman, at 848.

Oliver Wendell Holmes declared in 1897, it is "revolting to have no better reason for a rule of law than that it was laid down in the time of Henry IV."[37] And as Sullivan points out, the institution of marriage has changed enormously over time, mostly in ways that we would consider for the better in terms of equality between the genders. Indeed, one reason the West has assumed that marriage is dual-gendered is that it has traditionally granted men and women such different, and unequal, legal rights within marriage. These differences have been entirely eliminated in almost all the Western world, as we will see in Chapter 3. If the sexist laws that required a woman to occupy the legally inferior role have been eliminated, perhaps the need for exclusively dual-gender marriage has evaporated with it. Western law has always recognized the edict *Cessante ratione legis, cessat et ipsa lex:* When the reason for a law disappears, so must the law itself.[38] When gays and lesbians plead that the marriage ban is harming them legally, economically and emotionally, society is obligated to explain why this particular aspect of marriage, compulsory heterosexuality, should remain unchanged when so much of marriage has changed drastically.

Nor can religion be a rational basis for the same-sex marriage ban. First of all, not all religions oppose same-sex marriage. Many religious groups support it,[39] including the Universal Fellowship of Metropolitan Community Churches, which performs over two thousand same-sex marriage ceremonies a year.[40] If the separation of church and state means anything, it surely means that the state cannot prefer the views of, say, Catholics and Baptists over those of Unitarians and Reform Jews because the former outnumber the latter. Moreover, as Sullivan points out: "No one is proposing that faith communities be required to change their definitions of marriage . . . The question at hand is civil marriage and civil marriage only. In a country where church and state are separate this is no small distinction. Many churches, for example, forbid divorce. But civil divorce is still legal."[41]

---

[37] Holmes, Oliver Wendell, in "The Path of the Law After One Hundred Years: The Path of the Law," *Harvard Law Review* 110 (1997): 991–1009, 1001. Justice Harry Blackmun quoted this passage in his dissent in *Bowers v. Hardwick* 478 U.S. 186, 199 (1986).

[38] Cited and translated in Katz at 30.

[39] Eskridge, *The Case for Same-Sex Marriage*, 46–47 and appendix.

[40] Ibid.

[41] Sullivan, "State of the Union," at 20.

Again, none of this is to say that current definitions of marriage are unreasonable, that respect for tradition is irrational, or that the opposition of some religions to same-sex marriage is illegitimate. But we can see that definition, tradition, and religion *by themselves* are not rational bases for the government to ban same-sex marriage.

Natural Law

Closely related, but at least formally distinct from the religious argument is the "natural law" argument. Natural law is rooted in both divinity and human nature:

Natural law has, from a historical perspective, an ephemeral basis, one derived from the Supreme Being, God, rather than humankind. In effect, natural law is reflective of God's will and therefore commands greater obedience given its more lofty genesis. These laws are of divine prescription and, therefore, remain embedded within the confines of human nature. They occur "naturally," making them an inexorable part of the world in which we live. Because humanity's existence is rooted in God, the Supreme Being, natural law becomes that which is a preservative of human nature itself.[42]

This theory has enjoyed something of a resurgence in law reviews the past few years. Among the most notable of the "new natural lawyers"[43] are John Finnis, Robert George, and Gerard Bradley, who argue that marriage is an intrinsic human good that homosexual union simply cannot achieve. Because this writing tends to be extremely dense, even turgid, and very difficult to paraphrase without loss of meaning, the following is quoted as length to best summarize the core argument of the new natural lawyers. Responding to the question of why "homosexual conduct (and indeed all extra-marital sexual gratification) is incapable of participating in, actualizing, the common good of friendship," Finnis writes:

Implicit in the philosophical and common-sense rejection of extra-marital sex is the answer: The union of the reproductive organs of husband and wife really unites them biologically (and their biological reality is part of, not merely an instrument of, their *personal* reality); reproduction is one function and so, in

---

[42] Morant at 76.
[43] This phrase comes from Steven Macedo, "The New Natural Lawyers," *The Harvard Crimson*, October 28, 1993.

respect of that function, the spouses are indeed one reality, and their sexual union therefore can actualize and allow them to experience their *real common good* – *their marriage* with the two goods, parenthood and friendship, which (leaving aside the order of grace) are the parts of its wholeness as an intelligible common good even if, independently of what the spouses will, their capacity for biological parenthood will not be fulfilled by that act of genital union. But the common good of friends who are not and cannot be married (for example man and man, man and boy, woman and woman) has nothing to do with their having children by each other, and their reproductive organs cannot make them a biological (and therefore personal) unit. So their sexual acts together cannot do what they hope and imagine. Because their activation of one or even each of their reproductive organs cannot be an actualizing and experiencing of the *marital* good – as marital intercourse (intercourse between spouses in a marital way) can, even between spouses who *happen* to be sterile – it can do no more than provide each partner with an individual gratification.[44]

The serpentine nature of this quotation hides fatal logical problems. Finnis emphasizes that gays and lesbians cannot have children by one another. Why, then, is intercourse between sterile heterosexuals unitive, but not intercourse between homosexuals? Clearly, neither is engaging in a reproductive act. Replying to natural law arguments, Steven Macedo writes, "All we can say is that conditions would have to be more radically different in the case of gay and lesbian couples than sterile married couples for new life to result from sex . . . but what is the moral consequence of that?"[45]

This is a difficult question for these natural lawyers, because nature has not equipped all heterosexuals with the capacity for reproductive acts. And the suggestion that those who lack the ability to have children should be barred from marriage seems so unspeakably cruel that no one is willing to own up to the idea. "The ancient philosophers . . . appear to take for granted what the subsequent Christian tradition certainly did, that such sterility does not render the conjugal sex acts of the spouses non-marital."[46] But why are sterile heterosexuals allowed to marry, whereas gays and lesbians are barred from marriage because their sexual acts are not reproductive? The great philosopher Immanuel Kant, apparently one of the few who at least admitted to confusion

---

[44] Finnis at 1066.
[45] Macedo at 2.
[46] Finnis at 1067.

on this point, and who opposed masturbation and homosexuality, still "was puzzled by the question why marital intercourse is right when the woman is pregnant or beyond the menopause."[47] But we do not forbid postmenopausal women from marriage, so to forbid gays and lesbians from marriage for this reason is the clearest possible example of a double standard.[48]

Finnis tries to answer this by calling genital intercourse between sterile heterosexuals "acts of the reproductive kind."[49] This is surely cheating. Acts that are not reproductive are not acts of the "reproductive kind." Such an act has the *visual appearance* of being of a reproductive kind, but between sterile people, it is obviously an act of an *unreproductive* kind. Such couples engage in sexual activity for many reasons – pleasure, intimacy, and so forth – exactly the reasons that gays and lesbians have sex. Certainly, some doubt that gays and lesbians can achieve the kind of deep intimacy we associate with romantic love. There is probably no way to measure this and convince skeptics. But this has nothing to do with reproductivity.

Two other prominent natural law advocates place similarly great reliance on "reproductive-type acts." George and Bradley argue that

Again, the intrinsic point of sex in any marriage, fertile or not, is, in our view, the basic good of marriage itself, considered as a two-in-one-flesh communion of persons that is consummated and actualized by acts of the reproductive type. Such acts alone among sexual acts can be truly unitive, and thus marital; and marital acts, thus understood, have their intelligibility and value intrinsically and not merely by virtue of their capacity to facilitate the realization of other goods.[50]

Like Finnis, George and Bradley never rigorously define what the term "reproductive type" act means, which is a major problem because so

[47] Ibid. at 1068 n.49.
[48] One court, in *Adams v. Howerton*, 486 F. Supp. 1119, 1125 (C.D. Cal. 1980) tackled the double standard issue by arguing that it is impossible to identify heterosexuals who cannot or will not have children. The court averred: "such tests and inquiries would themselves raise serious constitutional questions." But if natural reproduction is so central to marriage that we ban same-sex marriage because gay and lesbian couples cannot have children, then it is not clear why asking about sterility is any more intrusive than asking whether the couple are blood relatives or requiring blood tests, as some states do. This issue will be discussed extensively in Chapter 5.
[49] Finnis at 1067.
[50] George at 306.

much of their argument hinges upon it. For some, sterile penile-vaginal intercourse might seem more like a reproductive act than does sodomy, but why? It does not result in reproduction. Asserting that there is a deep distinction between sterile heterosexual sex and homosexual sex because the former is a "reproductive type act" is a remarkably conclusory, ill-supported assertion – hardly a sound basis upon which to base such a vital policy such as who may marry.

Recall that the Court in *Romer* rejected the arguments for Amendment 2 because the law was too broad to be justified under the rationales offered for it. Linking marriage to the unitive capacity of reproductive sex has the opposite problem: it would ban many marriages that we currently allow. If a political candidate suggested that older women should not marry (let alone not have the freedom to marry), the general reaction would be shock.[51] The fit between this rationale and the ban on same-sex marriage is far worse than the fit in *Romer*.

Promoting an Optimal Environment for Child Rearing

The argument about reproduction is distinct from the question of who should *raise* children. For some, the best reason to ban gays and lesbians from marriage stems from their objection to gays and lesbians raising children. Even those sympathetic to same-sex marriage must concede that "It would be silly to pretend otherwise: one of marriage's goals has always been to have children."[52] The connection between marriage and child rearing is crucial to the same-sex marriage debate. During the *Baehr* litigation, Hawaii argued that the state has an important interest in making sure that as many children as possible are raised in a home with their biological parents.[53] This argument cannot be dismissed lightly. Obviously, neither two men nor two women can have children in the traditional, reproductive manner, which has two important consequences: the child of a same-sex couple will not be the biological child of both parents, and the child will lack a mother

---

[51] One might be tempted to say that such a policy is wrong because it is gender discrimination, but a simple thought experiment rebuts this: Would such a law be any more acceptable if there were a male equivalent to menopause and postmenopausal adults of both genders were banned from marriage?

[52] Graff at 189.

[53] Marcosson.

or father in the household. "If Heather is being raised by two mom-
mies only, she is being deprived of the experience of being raised by a
daddy," Duncan says.[54]

If an important reason that the state sanctions marriage is to provide
an optimal environment for children, then perhaps the state should not
sanction same-sex marriages, as there appear to be inherent reasons
that same-sex couples might not provide that optimal environment.
There are several possible counterarguments. The first is that the whole
question represents a double standard; after all, the state does not
require heterosexuals to demonstrate that they are likely to provide an
optimal environment for children. Eskridge notes that the state grants
marriage licenses to a rogues' gallery of dual-gender couples, including
convicted felons, divorced parents who refuse to pay child support,
and even pedophiles.[55] Similarly, Marcosson argues that "states allow
people of opposite genders to marry without any inquiry into – without
showing the slightest interest in – whether they will provide an optimal
or even a decent environment for children."[56]

At first blush, this seems to be a powerful argument. How can we
consider concerns over the efficacy of same-sex parents to be legitimate
if society shows absolutely no concern for this issue when heterosexuals
apply for marriage licenses, even when there are obvious red flags such
as convictions for child abuse or pedophilia? Yet the argument that
same-sex couples provide a less-than-optimal environment for child
rearing is not so easily decimated. As Richard Posner points out, "there
is a difference between approving a particular form of union and approving particular individuals who are utilizing that form."[57] There
are many reasons the government does not make individualized determinations of whether applicants for marriage licenses would make
good parents. Depriving even a convicted child molester of the right to
marry could reasonably be viewed legally as a second punishment after
the prison sentence had been served. It violates the promise that even
convicted felons are entitled to move on with their lives eventually, that
even the most depraved among us can transform themselves.

---

[54] Duncan at 161.
[55] Eskridge, *The Case for Same-Sex Marriage*, 12.
[56] Marcosson at 737 n.49.
[57] Posner at 1583.

There is a difference between making individual determinations of which people are fit for marriage and deciding that certain social arrangements – two parents, one of each gender – provide the best arrangements for raising children. Remember, society does not tell *anybody*, gay or straight, whether he or she may have children; it is not illegal for gays or lesbians to father, bear, or raise children. The issue is whether society may decide that certain arrangements are, generally speaking, better than others for raising children and, therefore, limit the social approval of marriage to those relationships.

Indeed, despite the superficial appeal of the "double-standard" argument, further reflection shows that rights are often limited on a *general* basis for reasons that are not applied on an *individual* basis. We deny noncitizens the right to vote for reasons such as concern over their loyalty to the United States and whether they have sufficient knowledge about this country to vote wisely; yet we allow citizens to vote without any inquiry into their loyalty or political knowledge. This is not a double standard, but a reflection of our considered judgment that loyalty oaths and voter qualification tests have had and probably will continue to have drawbacks that outweigh their benefits. By the same token, society may decide that dual-gender marriages generally provide the optimal environment for child rearing, and decide that a case-by-case determination of who would make good parents would be bad public policy.

To choose an even more comparable example, states deny children the right to marry because of concerns about their maturity. Yet we make no effort to determine the maturity level of adults who apply for marriage licenses. While its true that children can marry after a few more years, that does not change the fact that we are denying licenses for child marriages based on a concern that we make no inquiry about when adults apply for marriage licenses. The fact is that society makes decisions about what kinds of arrangements should be called "marriage" based on considerations that probably should not be applied on an individual basis. In sum, there really is no double standard here.

Of course, this does not end the inquiry. We must also ask whether it is rational to assume that a same-sex family really offers a less-than-optimal environment for raising children. Testifying for Hawaii during the *Baehr* trial, Dr. Kyle Pruett of the Yale University School of Medicine and Yale Child Study Center, said biological parents have a natural bond that helps them effectively raise children, and that in a same-sex family, one parent must inherently lack such a biological bond. He also testified that same-sex parents provide an overabundance of information about one gender and little information about the other gender.[58] As Marcosson points out, however, the picture that Pruett painted was far from one-sided. He stated that "single parents, gay fathers, lesbian mothers and same-sex couples have the potential to, and often do, raise children that are happy, healthy and well-adjusted."[59] Further, numerous studies indicate little difference between the children of same-sex parents and those of dual-gender parents. "Studies have repeatedly shown that children raised in gay and (especially) lesbian households are as well socialized, as psychologically adjusted, and as capable of forming healthy peer relationships as children raised in different-sex or single parent house-holds," Eskridge notes.[60]

Based on these studies, perhaps we can reject the "optimal environment" argument as irrational prejudice – an expression of animus rather than reason. The situation is more complex, however. Lynn Wardle points out that serious methodological shortcomings in these studies prevent us from drawing firm conclusions about same-sex parenting. These studies suffer from problems such as small sample sizes; non-random samples that overrepresent educated, financially secure lesbians; overreliance upon single heterosexual parents rather than married heterosexual parents for control groups; a lack of longitudinal studies; and overreliance on self-reporting for data.[61] These are serious problems, and to the researchers' credit, in many cases they acknowledge these problems in the studies.[62] Carlos Ball and Janice Farrell Pea point out that many of these methodological problems are difficult to overcome when studying gay and lesbian parenting; there is still significant discrimination against gays and lesbians, and stigma is still attached to gay and lesbian parents, so finding large, representative

---

[58] Cited in Marcosson at 726–727.
[59] Marcosson at 753.
[60] Eskridge, *The Case for Same-Sex Marriage*, 112–113.
[61] Wardle at 844–50, citing Belcastro, Philip, et al., "A Review of Data Based Studies Addressing the Effects of Homosexual Parenting on Children's Sexual and Social Functioning." *Journal of Divorce and Remarriage* 20 (1993): 105–136.
[62] See discussion in Ball, Carlos and Janice Farrell Pea, "Warring with Wardle: Morality, Social Science, and Gay and Lesbian Parents." *University of Illinois Law Review* (1998): 253–339, 272.

samples of such parents is no easy task.[63] Ball and Pea also take Wardle to task for relying upon the same studies he criticizes to make his case that homosexual parenting is not in the best interests of the child.[64] They argue that "the literature, while in fact suffering from method-ical flaws, does support the (in our estimation) rather limited propo-sition that gay or lesbian parents (or prospective parents) are entitled to be evaluated individually on the basis of their ability to be good parents."[65]

These are reasonable points; and it is clear that the social science data certainly does not establish that same-sex households are *not* optimal environments for raising children. But this does not make it irrational for society to act on the assumption that it is best for a child to be raised by his or her biological mother and father. All we can say for now is that the social science data so far indicate that we should be cautious about assuming that traditional families are better environments than same-sex families for raising children. Still, we really cannot say that it is irrational to hypothesize that children benefit from being raised by both a mother and father. And that is what the rational basis test would require for the courts to strike down the heterosexual marriage monopoly on this basis.

There is one more point to consider, however: Is there a rational relationship between the ban on same-sex marriage and the goal of having children raised by their biological parents? There does not ap-pear to be one. In fact, it is difficult to imagine what such a connection might be. Nowhere in the literature is it suggested that people are indif-ferent to whether they marry a man or woman. It is not as though most gays and lesbians respond to the same-sex marriage ban by entering happy heterosexual marriages. No credible evidence would indicate this, as it would imply that people choose freely and consciously to be heterosexual or homosexual. Most literature indicates that sexual orientation is a matter of both genetic and environmental factors – a powerful combination. When states have attempted to convince courts that liberalized policies toward gays and lesbians might some-how affect marriage or divorce rates, those courts have soundly rejected

[63] Ibid. at 274.
[64] Ibid. at 258.
[65] Ibid.

these arguments for complete lack of evidence. In *Evans v. Romer*, the Colorado Supreme Court said, "we reject [the State's] suggestion that laws prohibiting discrimination against gay men, lesbians and bisexuals will undermine marriage and heterosexual families because married heterosexuals will 'choose' to 'become homosexual' if discrimination is prohibited. This assertion flies in the face of the empirical evidence presented at trial on marriage and divorce rates." The New York State high court was equally dismissive of this argument, stating, "Certainly there is no . . . empirical data submitted which demonstrates that marriage is nothing more than a refuge for persons deprived by legislative fiat of the option of consensual sodomy outside of the marital bond."[66]

So if the ban on same-sex marriage will not result in larger numbers of heterosexual marriages, then how does the ban cause more children to be raised by two-parent, dual-gender families? As many as eight million to ten million children are being raised in gay or lesbian households,[67] and it is difficult to see how they benefit from the same-sex marriage ban. It seems that the real question is whether children being raised by gay or lesbian parents and their significant others are better off if the legal privileges of marriage protect their families. Even Hawaii's own witness, Dr. David Eggebeen, testified that these children would benefit if their families had access to the legal benefits of marriage, such as state income tax advantages, public assistance, enforcement of child support and alimony, and the rights to pursue wrongful death actions and to inherit. Of course, it is possible that the same-sex marriage ban dissuades same-sex couples from having children together through sperm donors or other methods. But then the question is not whether these children would be better off with opposite-sex parents; the question is whether they would have been better off if they had not been born at all.

Indeed, the only situations in which the comparison of same-sex and dual-gender parents is at all relevant are adoption and custody

---

[66] 882 P.2d 1335, 1347 (Colo. 1994), aff'd 116 S. Ct. 1620 (1996) and *People v. Onofre*, 415 N.E. 936, 941 (N.Y. 1980), cert. denied 451 U.S. 987 (1981), respectively. Both cited in Strasser, *Legally Wed*, at n.138.

[67] Rubenstein, William B., ed. *Sexual Orientation and the Law* (2d ed.). Cambridge: Harvard University Press, 1996, at 801. Eskridge has noted that this figure might be too high, but nonetheless, "What can be said with confidence is that a lot of gay people . . . do have children and raise them in families," at 110.

cases. G. Sydney Buchanan forcefully argues that legalizing same-sex marriage would force the states to treat same-sex married couples as equivalent to dual-gender married couples for purposes of adoption and custody:

The principle of total equality would have particular relevance in proceedings concerning adoptions and child custody. For if the courts compel the states to recognize same-sex marriage, it becomes difficult indeed to justify any law that prohibits a married homosexual couple from doing what a married heterosexual couple might do, or more generally, any law that discriminates between the two kinds of married couples in defining their legal rights.[68]

Perhaps we have now found a rational link between the government's preference that children be raised by a mother and father and the same-sex marriage ban. If allowing same-sex marriage means that the state cannot prefer dual-gender couples as adoptive and custodial parents, then same-sex marriage could result in more children living in same-sex households who otherwise would have lived in dual-gender households.

But even this is a stretch. Adoption and custody decisions are made case by case, based upon the best interest of the child, and there is no reason that the benefits of having both a father and a mother cannot be taken into account. All we can say is that same-sex marriage would require decision-makers such as family court judges and adoption agencies to take into account all factors relevant to the child's well-being and not *automatically* disqualify same-sex parents. Presumably, though, society wants the people it has entrusted with these decisions to take all relevant factors into account, not just the single factor of the parents' genders. Also, Buchanan is obviously incorrect when he implies that no distinctions at all could be made between same-sex and dual-gender married couples. Elderly adults are allowed to marry, yet no one thinks it is illegal to prefer a couple in their thirties over a couple in their nineties as adoptive parents for an infant. It is also worth noting that in adoption and custody cases, decision-makers are no longer comparing same-sex parents to dual-gender parents when both parents are the biological parents of the child, which is the ideal against which same-sex

---

[68] Buchanan, G. Sydney, "Same-Sex Marriage: The Linchpin Issue." *University of Dayton Law Review* 10 (1985): 541–573, 568.

parents are so often measured. One could argue that the same-sex marriage ban is the strongest possible safeguard against decision-makers' granting custody of children to same-sex couples, which would lead to a double standard. After all, society does not prevent criminals or even pedophiles from marrying because of a fear that some misguided agency might let them adopt children.

Even assuming that it is rational to prefer dual-gender parents to same-sex parents (despite the lack of evidence), there is no rational connection between this preference and the same-sex marriage ban. The real effect of the ban is to prevent children *already being raised in same-sex households* from the protection afforded by the benefits of marriage, which has the irrational effect of punishing children for the 'sins' of their parents. Even if we assume that gays and lesbians are wrong to live with a same-sex partner, this is obviously not the moral responsibility of the child. Long ago, the U.S. Supreme Court struck down as irrational a law that prevented an illegitimate child from suing for wrongful death when his mother was killed;[69] the Justices held that it is irrational to punish a child for the perceived sins of the parent. Likewise, it is irrational to punish the children of same-sex couples by denying them the legal rights they would have if same-sex marriage were legal.

The "Endorsement" Question

There is one more issue to consider: Is it irrational to ban same-sex marriage out of fear that allowing it would go beyond tolerance and amount to government endorsement of same-sex relationships? This is really two separate questions. The first is whether allowing same-sex marriage could rationally be perceived as endorsement of gay and lesbian relationships. The second is whether denying this endorsement and endorsing heterosexuality is a legitimate government interest.

An interesting mixture of legal scholars has argued that legalizing same-sex marriage would not be an endorsement of gay or lesbian relationships. The very conservative Richard Epstein argues that, given the state monopoly on the legal benefits of marriage, limiting those

---

[69] *Levy v. Louisiana*, 391 U.S. 68 (1968).

benefits to certain kinds of personal associations (such as one man and one woman) violates the principles of a liberal state. Therefore, making these benefits available to couples regardless of gender is not endorsement, but simple respect for their freedom of association:

> This last set of demands [for the legal rights of marriage] cannot, I believe, be opposed on the ground that it is one thing for the state to suppress an arrangement and quite another to require the state to place its stamp of approval on the full arrangement, which is what legal recognition seems to demand. That question of conferring benefits means far less in the state context given the state monopoly power over the relevant set of licenses, so that the key question – at least for supporters of a liberal state – is whether the state skews private preferences among various forms of associational freedom, which it surely does when it gives one kind of sexual union a preferred position that is systematically denied to another.[70]

In other words, given the state monopoly on licensing, it is no more an endorsement of homosexuality to grant gays and lesbians marriage licenses than it is to grant them driver's licenses. In each case, the state is simply granting certain benefits to its citizens without respect to their sexual orientation. For Eskridge, who has pointed out that "it's harder to get a driver's license than a marriage license," the state approves of the *institution* of marriage, not particular couples marrying.

Important arguments cut the other way, however. First, this is an area in which reasonable people can differ. Richard Posner, one of the most thoughtful skeptics regarding same-sex marriage, argues that permitting such unions, unlike legalizing homosexual sodomy, sends the message that "homosexual marriage is a desirable, even a noble condition is which to live."[71] Posner has a point. Clearly, society broadcasts a message that the marital relationship should be respected, so if same-sex marriage is allowed, the message would be that those relationships are worthy of respect. Many support that message, but it is difficult to reconcile that with the message that homosexuality is morally wrong. Advocates for gay and lesbian rights often argue that civil rights laws protecting gays and lesbians from job and housing discrimination do

---

[70] Epstein, Richard, at 2474.
[71] Posner, Richard, "Relations between Consenting Adults: Sodomy Laws and Homosexual Marriage," from *Same-Sex Marriage* (Robert Baird and Stuart Rosenbaum, eds.) Amherst, MA: Prometheus Books, 1997, at 188.

not endorse homosexuality. This is true, but to make that argument credibly, such advocates have to concede that there are certain things that *do* amount to endorsement. The same-sex marriage issue has often been compared with interracial marriage, but who would dispute that one reason most people oppose a ban on the latter is to show that the love and commitment of interracial couples is as worthy of respect as those of same-race couples? Would the legalization of same-sex marriage send that same message about love between members of the same gender? Is it *irrational* to think that it would?

In other contexts, advocates of gay rights actually argue that such a societal imprimatur would be one of the benefits of same-sex marriage. "In time, moreover, same-sex marriage will likely contribute to the public acceptability of homosexual relationships," Eskridge says.[72] Another supporter of same-sex marriage, James Trosino, writes, "Perhaps most important to gays, legal marriage will provide a measure of social acceptance by legitimizing the relationship."[73] Perhaps a line can be drawn between contributing to the "public acceptability" of same-sex relationships or "legitimizing" and *endorsing* these relationships, but that would be a very blurry line.

Unfortunately, scholars on both sides of the same-sex debate have mostly been talking past one another rather than to each other, so there has been no real dialogue about what it *actually means* for the state to endorse a practice. One place to look for a constitutionally relevant definition of state endorsement is the Supreme Court's establishment-clause jurisprudence. When the Court needs to decide whether a government practice violates the separation of church and state, it asks whether the practice amounts to a government endorsement of religion.[74] Justice John Paul Stevens has articulated the test: "If a reasonable person *could* perceive a government endorsement of religion ... then the State may not allow its property to be used as a forum for that display."[75] This seems a fair way to pose the endorsement question. It should be noted

---

[72] Eskridge, William, *The Case for Same-Sex Marriage: From Liberty to Civilized Commitment*, at 9.

[73] Quoted in Strasser, Mark, "Domestic Relations Jurisprudence and the Great Slumbering Baehr: On Definitional Preclusion, Equal Protection and Fundamental Interests." *Fordham Law Review* 64 (December 1995): 921–986, 934.

[74] *Capitol Square Review and Advisory Board v. Pinette*, 515 U.S. 753, 799 (1995) (emphasis added).

[75] Ibid. at 799 (dissenting) (emphasis added).

that this is not a demanding standard – it requires only that *a* reasonable person *could* perceive something as a government endorsement of religion. And liberals who support the Court's prohibition of school prayer, religious symbols in public buildings, and so forth have been quick to point out that reasonable people can find a governmental policy to be an endorsement of religion, even if that policy could also reasonably be understood as not endorsing religion. By the same token, it seems hard to believe that *no* reasonable person *could* view government recognition of same-sex marriage as endorsement of same-sex relationships; and it is not irrational to reject a policy because it *might* have the effect of endorsing an undesired practice. For example, it would not be irrational for voters to reject a law legalizing heroin (despite the many serious policy arguments for doing so) because they fear that some people might view such a policy as governmental endorsement of drug use. Similarly, it is not irrational to continue to ban same-sex marriage because to do otherwise might be construed as endorsing same-sex relationships.

Even if we agree that allowing same-sex marriage could be seen as an endorsement of homosexuality, there is another question: is there a legitimate government interest in promoting heterosexuality over homosexuality? Some advocates of same-sex marriage argue that there is not. Citing a New York state court case, Pamela Katz says the Court's decision in *Romer* requires that a state have some reason other than the "political, cultural, religious and legal consensus" against same-sex marriage to ban it.[76] This is a very hard interpretation of *Romer* to defend. For one thing, in *Bowers v. Hardwick* the Supreme Court very explicitly stated that "majority sentiments about the morality of homosexuality" *is* a rational basis for law-making.[77] Cass Sunstein counters that moral disapproval is not always a legitimate basis for a law, citing miscegenation laws and discrimination against the mentally retarded as examples.[78] But these arguments are weak. Race is a very special area in the law; laws with racial classifications are subjected to a very high level of judicial scrutiny, and we cannot extrapolate from

---

[76] Katz, Pamela S., "The Case for Legal Recognition of Same-Sex Marriage." *Journal of Law and Policy* 8 (1999): 61–106, 96, citing *Storrs v. Holcomb*, 645 NYS 286, 287 (Sup. Ct. Tompkins County 1996).

[77] 478 U.S. 186 (1986).

[78] Sunstein at 6.

race-based laws to the issue of same-sex marriage. And laws affecting the mentally retarded are irrelevant; no one suggests that it is morally wrong to be mentally retarded.

The majority in *Romer* never suggests that moral disapproval of homosexuality is illegitimate. Instead, it holds that this moral disapproval cannot be the basis of a blunderbuss law that could prevent gays and lesbians from doing so much as checking a book out of a public library. One of the most prominent advocates of same-sex marriage, Andrew Koppelman, describes *Romer*'s holding thusly: "If the law targets a narrowly defined group, and then imposes upon it disabilities that are so broad as to bear no discernable relationship to any legitimate governmental interest, then the Court will infer that the law's purpose is simply to harm that group, and so will invalidate that law."[79] So there is a difference between discouraging homosexuality and seeking to harm gays and lesbians out of sheer animus, and *Romer* and Bowers are compatible in law, if not in spirit. Society can oppose homosexuality as a moral matter without engaging in unconstitutional animus. As it is not irrational for society to fear that *some* reasonable people *might* view the allowance of same-sex marriage as creating a moral equivalence between same-sex and dual-gender marriage, then the ban is not irrational.

Strasser has also argued that public morality is an insufficient basis for banning same-sex marriage, but the constitutional cases he cites actually show the opposite.[80] He quotes the Court decision in *Coates v. Cincinnati* as saying that "mere public intolerance or animosity cannot be the basis for abridgement of . . . constitutional freedoms." Yet that case involved the very special area of freedom of speech and expression, in the form of a law that prohibited people from assembling in public places to "conduct themselves in a manner annoying to persons passing by." One of the most basic of all constitutional distinctions is the difference between government regulation of *speech* and of *action*. Although the line between speech and action can sometimes be blurry,[81] courts

---

[79] Koppelman, Andrew, "*Romer v. Evans* and Invidious Intent." at 94.

[80] To be fair, Strasser makes this argument in the context of an argument that promotion of morality is not a *compelling* governmental interest.

[81] See Ely, John Hart, "Flag Desecration: a Case Study in the Roles of Categorization and Balancing in First Amendment Analysis." *Harvard Law Review* 88 (1975): 1482–1508.

have long emphasized that freedom of speech is uniquely immune from moral regulation.[82] Outside of speech, the government regulates many areas of human activity on moral grounds: gambling, prostitution and so forth. Non-moral harms are associated with all these activities, but the Court has never once held that the government has the burden of establishing this before regulating them. In fact, the Court has unequivocally stated that "a state may, *for the purpose of guarding the morals of its own people*, forbid all sales of lottery tickets within its limits."[83] Therefore, there is a valid debate over whether it is *wise* to ban practices based upon majoritarian morality, but there is nothing to indicate that it is unconstitutional. Unless we truly believe that no reasonable person could interpret the legalization of same-sex marriage as a positive endorsement of same-sex relationships, there is indeed a rational basis for the same-sex marriage ban.

Conclusion

We have seen that it is not irrational for society to ban same-sex marriage, but also that most of the reasons the government gives for banning same-sex marriage do not make sense. They are tautologies such as "marriage is between man and woman because marriage is defined as being between man and woman," or are based upon an impermissible elevation of one set of religious beliefs over another, or premised upon demonstrably illogical connections between who can marry and who will raise children. All we have established is that it is not irrational to fear that some reasonable people might view legalizing same-sex marriage as endorsement of same-sex relationships.

This is probably enough to pass the weakest form of judicial scrutiny, even after *Romer*, but certainly it is not saying very much. As a policy matter, society would do well to rethink a ban that destroys the marital aspirations of so many people and deprives their children of the legal protections that come from having married parents, especially when most of the reasons for the ban are so poorly considered. Further,

---

[82] Indeed, even pornographic speech cannot be censored solely on the basis of objectionable moral content alone. See *Miller v. California*, 413 US 15 (1973).

[83] *Champion v. Ames*, 188 U.S. 321, 357 (1903) (emphasis added).

these preliminary arguments make clear that the same-sex marriage ban would be unlikely to survive stricter judicial scrutiny. From a legal perspective, the next question is whether there is any reason for applying strict or intermediate review to the ban. Several arguments have been made for why the courts should apply a higher level of review. The next chapter will examine two of these arguments.

3

Looking for Stricter Scrutiny

Sexism, Heterosexism, and Class-Based Equal Protection

We have seen that the same-sex marriage ban can most likely survive a 'rational basis' challenge. The courts have certainly believed so, and, for the reasons set out in the last section of Chapter 2, they are arguably right. We will see shortly that the Court has been unwilling to apply heightened scrutiny to laws that discriminate against gays and lesbians. Because they cannot qualify for heightened scrutiny and cannot win the right to marry without it, advocates of same-sex marriage appear to be caught between the proverbial rock and hard place.

Yet this is not the end of the debate. In the early 1990s a new idea emerged.[1] Like alchemists turning lead into gold, these advocates have, with some success, metamorphosed claims of discrimination against gays and lesbians into gender discrimination claims. Because the courts subject gender discrimination to a higher level of judicial scrutiny, the legal case against the same-sex marriage ban has the potential to grow much stronger under this approach.

The most prominent exponent of this approach is Andrew Koppelman. Although Koppelman would not agree that there is a rational basis for banning gay marriage, he recognizes the difficulty of proving the negative proposition that there is no rational basis for the ban.

---

[1] Although the idea had been circulating before this, it gained prominence in 1994 when it was the centerpiece of Andrew Koppelman's "Why Discrimination Against Lesbians and Gay Men is Sex Discrimination." *New York University Law Review* 69 (1994): 197–287.

Therefore a new strategy is required to pursue gay and lesbian rights claims. "If an argument were available that shifted the burden of proof to the state to justify discrimination against lesbians and gays, this might be a more strategically promising alternative for gay rights advocates. The sex discrimination argument, I argue, has this strength."[2]

His argument is surprisingly straightforward. "If a business fires Ricky, or if the state prosecutes him, because of his sexual activities with Fred, while these actions would not be taken against Lucy if she did exactly the same things with Fred, then Ricky is being discriminated against [on the basis] of his sex."[3] In a later piece, Koppelman spelled out the argument less humorously, but just as effectively. "When one focuses on the sex of the choosing person, rather than the sex of the chosen partner, one realizes that it is the choosing person's sex [that] makes both their choice of direction of emotional-sexual attraction . . . objectionable, and which therefore constitutes the grounds of distinction."[4]

This approach has proved extremely popular among academics. Many law review articles argue that discrimination on the basis of sexual orientation is actually a form of sex discrimination.[5] Not only has there been widespread support for this theory in the nation's law reviews, but, within academia, the debate has been remarkably one-sided. The view that the courts should treat sexual orientation discrimination as a form of sex discrimination "has gone relatively unchallenged in the academy."[6]

One of the few dissenting voices has been that of Lynn Wardle, who dismisses the theory as mere word play. "[U]pon careful analysis, the argument that discrimination on the basis of type of sexual relations is sex discrimination for Fourteenth Amendment purposes is based on a

[2] Ibid. at 199.
[3] Ibid. at 208.
[4] Koppelman at 1661.
[5] Among the most prominent of these, in addition to the Koppelman articles are Fajer, Mark, "Can Two Real Men Eat Quiche Together? Storytelling, Gender Stereotypes and Legal Protection for Gays and Lesbians," *University of Miami Law Review* 46 (1992): 511–615; Law, Sylvia A., "Homosexuality and the Social Meaning of Gender," *Wisconsin Law Review* 1998 (1988): 187–235; Schroeder, Theodore A., "Fables of the Reconstruction: The Practical Failures of Gay and Lesbian Theory in the Realm of Employment Discrimination." *Journal of Gender in the Law* 6 (Spring 1998): 333–367.
[6] Schroeder, supra, at 356.

pun – the double meaning in colloquial language of sex, referring both to gender and to sexual relations."[7]

But Wardle is wrong on this point. The argument is far more sophisticated than this. Indeed, there are multiple arguments equating sexual orientation discrimination with sex discrimination, none of which could accurately be referred to as "puns" or mere wordplay. Theodore Schroeder helpfully divides the arguments into three basic categories: 1) the 'formal' argument; 2) the 'feminist approach,' and 3) 'sex stereotyping' theories.[8]

The 'formal argument' is the one set out by Koppelman above. Mr. X cannot marry Mr. Y, but Ms. Z can, so Mr. X is being discriminated against on the basis of his gender. But for his gender, Mr. X would have no legal problem marrying the person whom he loves. The other two arguments, the feminist and stereotyping arguments, are closely related and argue that the structures and stereotypes that repress homosexuality have the effect, and perhaps the intent, of oppressing women as well and rigidifying sexual roles in society.[9]

These latter two arguments will be discussed later in this chapter. But the most well known and influential of the arguments is the formal argument. This is due in part to academic enthusiasm for it, but, even more significantly, this was the theory that the Supreme Court of Hawaii relied upon when it held that the same-sex marriage ban is a form of sex discrimination.

The Breakthrough Case: *Baehr v. Lewin*

As discussed earlier, in 1993, the Supreme Court of Hawaii became the first state supreme court ever to hold that the same-sex marriage ban violates constitutional guarantees of equal protection. Technically, the Court did not hold that there is a right to same-sex marriage. It merely held that the ban is subject to strict scrutiny. But, as strict scrutiny is widely perceived as "strict in theory and fatal

---

[7] Wardle, Lynn, "A Critical Analysis of Constitutional Claims for Same-Sex Marriage." *Brigham Young University Law Review* 1996 (1996): 1–101, 86.

[8] Schroeder, supra, 342–355.

[9] In fact, the feminist argument and stereotyping arguments are sufficiently close that I discuss them under a single subheading.

in fact,"[10] this holding appeared to sound the death knell for the ban on same-sex marriage. The Hawaii court was later, in essence, overruled by a voter-approved amendment to the Hawaiian Constitution, but the case attracted massive publicity and was the cutting edge case on the constitutionality of the ban until the *Baker* decision in Vermont.

The fact that the Hawaii case, *Baehr v. Lewin*[11], became the leading case for the gender discrimination approach is actually a bit ironic. When the plaintiffs, a group that included both men and women, filed their case in May 1991, they did not even bother to allege that they were being discriminated against on the basis of their gender. When the trial court dismissed their complaint and they appealed, they once again declined to even allege that they were victims of gender discrimination. The lead attorney for the plaintiffs, Dan Foley, did not argue the gender discrimination claim because, he says, "I didn't think it would win – I thought that other arguments were better."[12] In fact, the only way that the gender discrimination came up at all was that, for whatever reason, the State of Hawaii brought it up in its answering brief, denying that any such claim would have merit.

Foley and the *Baehr* plaintiffs argued that the same-sex marriage ban violated their right to privacy and was discriminatory against gays and lesbians. But the State Supreme Court rejected the plaintiffs' argument that the Hawaiian constitution's guarantee of due process and privacy protected their right to marry someone of their own gender.[13] The Court also rejected the argument that the same-sex marriage ban discriminates against gays and lesbians. In fact, the Court repeatedly insisted that homosexuality was completely irrelevant to the case.

But the Court, unprompted by Foley or the plaintiffs, declared that the ban was a form of gender discrimination and therefore probably ran afoul of the Equal Protection Clause of the Hawaiian Constitution. The Court also held that because the Hawaiian Equal Protection Clause, unlike its counterpart in the United States Constitution, explicitly protects against 'sex' discrimination, that the same-sex

---

[10] Gunther at 8.
[11] 852 P.2d 44 (1993).
[12] Interview with Evan Gerstmann (July 26, 1999).
[13] This will be discussed at length in the next chapter.

marriage ban is subject to the highest level of judicial scrutiny: strict scrutiny.[14]

Although the Court did not cite Koppelman or the other scholars mentioned above, it relied completely upon the formal approach. The Court held that: "It is the state's regulation of access to the status of married persons, *on the basis of the applicant's sex*, that gives rise to the question of whether the applicant couples have been denied the equal protection of the laws in violation of . . . the Hawaii Constitution."[15]

The Court was, to say the least, unimpressed by the state's argument that marriage was restricted by definition to opposite-sex couples. The Court dismissed that argument as "circular and unpersuasive."[16] Later in its opinion, the Court was even more contemptuous, dismissing the argument as an "exercise in tortured and conclusory sophistry."[17]

With the *Baehr* decision, the formal approach became the leading theory in favor of the argument that the same-sex marriage ban is a form of unconstitutional gender discrimination. If Nina Baehr were a man, she could have married the woman she loves. Thus, she is a victim of gender discrimination. According to the Supreme Court of Hawaii and numerous distinguished academics, the question is really quite simple and the answer is quite obvious: the ban is a form of gender discrimination since "but for" Ms. Baehr's gender, she would have no legal problem.

But controversial legal and social issues are rarely so straightforward and simple. As will be argued below, there are serious, indeed fatal, problems with these arguments. The most obvious weakness with the formal argument is that the same-sex marriage ban actually treats both genders exactly alike. Neither men nor women may marry someone of their own gender.[18] If the formal argument were taken seriously, numerous perfectly legal institutional arrangements would have to be struck down as unconstitutional. One example is men's and women's sports

---

[14] Article I, Section 5 of the Hawaiian Constitution provides that "No person shall be . . . denied the enjoyments of the person's civil rights or be discriminated against in the exercise thereof because of race, religion, sex or ancestry."

[15] 852 P.2d at 56 (emphasis added).

[16] Ibid. at 57.

[17] Ibid. at 63.

[18] Upon reading this sentence, many knowledgeable readers are probably thinking (perhaps shouting) "but what about *Loving v. Virginia?*" This very important issue will be discussed at length in the final section.

teams at public universities. Mr. Smith may not play on the women's volleyball team and Ms. Jones may not play on the men's volleyball team. Both athletes are being treated alike – they can only compete with and against athletes of their own gender. So long as there are teams for both men and women and neither team is being subjected to inferior treatment, the arrangement of men and women playing separately is perfectly constitutional. But according to the formal argument, virtually every public university (not to mention public high school) is engaging in gender discrimination. When Mr. Smith is forbidden from taking his showers in the women's locker room he is being restrained solely upon the basis of his gender.[19] Yet few people would seriously argue that Mr. Smith is a victim of gender discrimination. So something is wrong with the formal argument.

Proponents of the formal argument are highly aware of this criticism. Their response is almost always as follows: the above argument was exactly the same argument that was made by the Jim Crow states in defending their antimiscegenation laws. These states argued that since members of each race could marry members of their own race, every person was being treated equally. This argument was soundly and emphatically rejected in the great civil rights case *Loving v. Virginia*,[20] which struck down Virginia's laws banning interracial marriage. The next section analyzes this crucial analogy to *Loving* in detail.

The Problems with the *Loving* Analogy

The analogy to *Loving* is absolutely crucial to the formal argument that the same-sex marriage ban is a form of gender discrimination. As a logical matter, it provides a possible answer to the objection that the ban applies equally to both genders. Further, it enhances the moral gravity of the argument for same-sex marriage. If opponents of same-sex marriage are resorting to the same arguments as Jim Crow legislators, perhaps that speaks for itself. Even some opponents of same-sex marriage concede the power of the *Loving* analogy. As David Ogden

---

[19] I do not mean to equate "Mr. Smith's" rather trivial interest in showering with the women's sports teams with Nina Baehr's very significant interest in marrying the person she loves. But this goes to the nature of the interest, not with formal arguments of 'but for' gender discrimination. This will be taken up in the next chapter.

[20] 388 US 1 (1967).

Coolidge puts it, the argument "with the greatest rhetorical punch is the *Loving* analogy."[21]

In fact, the battle over same-sex marriage could reasonably be described as a war of analogies. Proponents see the situation in *Loving* as the best analogy to same-sex marriage. Superficially equal treatment of the races and genders masks deeper structures of oppression. On the other hand, opponents of same-sex marriage often rely upon analogies to bigamy and incestuous marriage. They argue that society has the right to define marriage in specific ways and that it is no more unreasonable to keep marriage dual-gendered than it is to keep it limited to two people or to persons who are not blood relatives.

So how strong is the analogy to *Loving*? As will be shown below, it is not a good analogy at all. It is true that there are some important similarities between *Baehr* and *Loving*. Ms. Loving could not marry the person she loved because of her race and Ms. Baehr could not marry the person she loves because of her gender. In both cases the state argued that it was treating all persons equally even though state barriers to marriage turned upon people's race or gender, respectively. These are not trivial similarities, but they are not enough to make the cases legally analogous. The analogy to *Loving* ignores the vital question of *context*. The most crucial context is the central place of antimiscegenation laws to the South's systems of racial segregation. As Gunnar Myrdal observed in 1944, antimiscegenation laws had "the highest place in the white man's rank order of social segregation and discrimination."[22]

In other words, the anti-miscegenation laws were not stand-alone laws. They were central pillars of a pervasive system of racial segregation and oppression. Further, even apart from its Jim Crow context, the law itself contained provisions that made it obvious that it was treating whites as the favored race. The Court correctly argued that: "The fact that Virginia prohibits only interracial marriages involving white persons demonstrates that the racial classifications must stand on their own justification, *as measures designed to maintain White Supremacy*."[23]

---

[21] Coolidge at 201.

[22] Myrdal Gunnar, *An American Dilemma: The Negro Problem and Modern Democracy*. New York: Harper, 1944 at p. 606, cited in Eskridge, *The Case for Same-Sex Marriage*, at 157.

[23] 388 U.S. at 11. (emphasis added).

The situation of Ms. Baehr cannot be responsibly analogized to that of Ms. Loving. There is no legal system of gender oppression remotely comparable to the system of racial discrimination faced by Ms. Loving in the American South under the Jim Crow regime. Although there are serious issues regarding whether women are paid equally, face glass ceilings, or receive adequate protection from sexual harassment and violence, among many other important issues, these issues are fundamentally different from the Jim Crow laws that had been directed at African Americans. While the South was forbidding interracial marriage, its states and cities were also segregating its parks and even forbidding African Americans and whites from visiting the zoo at the same time.[24] The paranoia over racial mixing was so great that, although it formally ended only a few decades ago, it is difficult for most people to recall a regime of segregation so intense that it reminds one more of Nazi Germany than of America. The images of separate bathrooms and water fountains are well known, but southern segregation was so intense that Alabama actually forbade Whites and African Americans from playing checkers together. Taxicabs, telephone booths, and even prostitutes were segregated.[25]

Further, the relationship between antimiscegenation laws and Jim Crow segregation was very different from the relationship between the same-sex marriage ban and obstacles to equality faced by women today. As noted, antimiscegenation laws were at the very center of a larger system of legal segregation. It would be very difficult to seriously argue that the same-sex marriage ban is the central pillar of an apartheidlike system of gender discrimination.[26] As Cass Sunstein, a strong supporter of same-sex marriage, concedes: "For Participants in the current legal system, it is much harder to say that bans on same-sex relations are connected to a similarly unacceptable social institution [as Jim Crow segregation]."[27]

This is a crucial point. The *Loving* Court rightly rejected Virginia's argument because it was obvious, *in context*, that the antimiscegenation

---

[24] Sitkoff, Harvard. *The Struggle for Black Equality 1954–1992.* New York: Hill and Wang, 1993, at 5.

[25] Ibid.

[26] There are more subtle arguments being made about the relationship between heterosexual marriage and gender hierarchy. These will be addressed in the next section.

[27] Sunstein at 19.

law's intent and effect was anything but neutral: it was a central pillar of a vicious system of racial oppression. As for the same-sex marriage ban, it is actually true that the genders are being treated equally by this particular law. Neither men nor women may marry a member of their own gender. A simple pair of questions drives this point home. Under the antismiscegenation laws it was obvious which race was receiving unequal treatment. Under the same-sex marriage ban, is it men or women who are the oppressed gender? Are lesbians more burdened or targeted by the ban than are gay men?[28] As will be discussed below, the obvious fact is that the oppressed group is neither men nor women – it is gays and lesbians. Unfortunately, as will be discussed shortly, this does not get one very far under equal protection analysis.

A further problem with the *Loving* analogy is that anti-miscegenation laws and the same-sex marriage ban are fundamentally different laws. The latter is not merely a gendered version of the former. The principal purpose of the anti-miscegenation laws was to *segregate* the races. The requirement that marriage be gender neutral has the opposite purpose: it is meant to bring men and women together. As the State of Hawaii argued in its post-trial brief to the court: "The evil of the marriage prohibition in Loving was that the law sought to continue artificially segregating races. Whereas, in this case the sexes are not separated, neither sex is burdened relative to the other, and in fact the law only bans marriage where one sex is excluded."[29]

Another problem with the Loving analogy is that the purpose of antimiscegenation laws actually went far past 'mere' segregation. They were part of a eugenics movement, analogous to Hitler's program of maintaining the 'purity' of the so-called Aryan race. While Virginia's antimiscegenation laws pre-date the eugenics movement, eugenic concerns were an important part of the rationale for maintaining these laws. Virginia was a strong supporter of eugenics in the 1920s and codified eugenic principles in state legislation. In response to calls to protect whites from 'defective germ plasm,' Virginia passed the "Eugenical Sterilization Act" and the "Virginia Racial Integrity Act,"

---

[28] One possible answer to this question is to say that it is a false choice. *Both* genders are oppressed by the rigid enforcement of gender-based boundaries. This argument will be addressed later in this chapter.

[29] Defendant State of Hawaii's Post Trial Brief at 6, Baehr (No. 91–1394–05), cited in Coolidge at 210 n.35.

both in 1924.[30] The eugenic implications of Virginia's legal scheme of segregation were an important part of the Court's reasoning in *Loving*. The Court noted that the law allowed nonwhites to marry members of other nonwhite races and took this as evidence that Virginia was seeking to maintain the purity of the white race.

The analogy between the same-sex marriage ban and antimiscegenation laws completely breaks down at this point. Dual-gender marriage is clearly not an attempt to keep either gender genetically pure – this racist concept simply doe not apply here. Nor is it based upon either gender's presumed genetic superiority the way Virginia's laws were based upon white genetic superiority.

In sum, the context of Virginia's law at the center of the twin evils of Jim Crow segregation and the eugenics movement made it absolutely appropriate for the Court to reject Virginia's pallid claim that all races were being treated equally. Although issues of gender equality are complex and significant, it would demonstrate a disturbing lack of perspective to analogize the intent or effect of the same-sex marriage ban on women (or men) to the intent or effect of antimiscegenation laws on African Americans.

Finally, it should be noted that Koppelman has argued that the most relevant case is not *Loving*, but *McLaughlin v. Florida*,[31] which struck down a state law banning interracial cohabitation. He avers that, unlike *Loving*, *McLaughlin* struck down the law simply on the grounds that it drew racial lines, and that the case did not turn upon the fact that the law was part of a vicious system of racial oppression of African Americans. For Koppelman, the "move, of ignoring *McLaughlin* and only talking about *Loving*, has become depressingly typical of those who wish to deny the formal power of the sex discrimination argument."[32] While Koppelman is correct that the *McLaughlin* Court did not discuss the Jim Crow or eugenic context of the Florida law, this hardly means that these considerations were not crucial. If the Court believed that the context was irrelevant, then it would not have needed to make that context central to its decision in *Loving* three years later.

---

[30] Destro at 1220.

[31] 379 U.S. 184 (1964).

[32] "Defending the Sex Discrimination Argument."*UCLA Law Review* 49 (2001): 519–538, 522, n.19.

The *Loving* Court would have simply cited *McLaughlin* as controlling precedent and struck down the Virginia law. Instead, *Loving* explained why the *McLaughlin* holding was correct, i.e., the broader racist context made the formal neutrality of Jim Crow laws irrelevant.

Heterosexism and Patriarchy

We have seen that it is far too simplistic to equate *Baehr* and *Loving*. Despite the superficial appeal of calling the same-sex marriage ban a form of gender discrimination, the ban is not actually gender discrimination as the courts have defined that term. Men and women are subject to exactly the same law – they can only enter into dual gendered marriage. The retort that *Loving* rejected such reasoning is far too decontextualized to be persuasive. The ban on same-sex marriage, whatever its problems, is not a pillar of segregation or eugenics as were Virginia's laws and the argument that both genders are being treated equally is not a transparent falsehood as were Virginia's claims.

But this is not the end of the debate. The formal argument is not the only argument that the same-sex marriage ban is a form of gender discrimination. There are other, more subtle versions of the argument. One version is what Theodore Schroeder calls the feminist approach. Pioneered by Sylvia A. Law, this approach "begins with the premise that homosexual conduct is despised because it challenges our culture's traditional gender roles, roles with a hierarchical bias against women."[33] Law calls this phenomenon "heterosexism." According to this theory, "sexual orientation discrimination furthers the ultimate goal of sex discrimination: maintenance of the traditional model [of gender roles.]"[34]

For radical feminists such as Catherine MacKinnon, these traditional roles, which are furthered by heterosexism, are at the core of the oppression of women. "[W]e have had enough of the glorification of this heterosexuality, this erotization of dominance and submission, while woman-centered sexual expression is denied and stigmatized."[35]

---

[33] Schroeder at 343–344, citing Sylvia A. Law, "Homosexuality and the Social Meaning of Gender" *University of Wisconsin Law Review* 1998 (1998): 187–235, 196.

[34] Ibid. at 345.

[35] MacKinnon. *Feminism Unmodified: Discourses on Life and Law*. Cambridge: Harvard University Press, 1987, at 29, cited in Schroeder at 344, n.61.

One of the best elucidations of this view is by William Eskridge, who describes homophobia as a "weapon of sexism."[36] According to Eskridge, "Homophobia became one way modern urban culture responded to women's political and social equality."[37] Homosexuality is despised because it is a threat to a gender-dichotomized world in which men are active and powerful and women are weak and passive. In the homosexual world, men can be passive and penetrated while women can be dominant and take on the traditionally male sexual role. By demonizing gays and lesbians, heterosexual men keep women in their place.[38] "Numerous studies by social psychologists have shown that support for traditional sex roles correlates strongly with disapproval of homosexuality."[39]

But this demonization of homosexuality does not only oppress gays and lesbians. "This is the argument that in contemporary American society, discrimination against lesbians and gay men reinforces the hierarchy of males over females and thus is wrong because it oppresses women."[40]

This argument has also been applied to the same-sex marriage debate. The requirement that marriage be dual gendered railroads men and women into roles of husbands and wives and into a heterosexual institution that is historically and perhaps inherently oppressive toward women. Cass Sunstein argues:

It is possible to think that the prohibition on same-sex marriages, as part of a social and legal insistence on "two kinds" [of gender], is as deeply connected with male supremacy as the prohibition of racial intermarriage is connected with White Supremacy. Perhaps same-sex marriages are banned because of what they do to – because of how they unsettle – gender categories. Perhaps same-sex marriages are banned because they complicate traditional gender thinking, showing that the division of human beings into two simple kinds is part of sex-role stereotyping, however true it is that men and women are 'different.'[41]

[36] Eskridge, *The Case for Same-Sex Marriage*, at 167.
[37] Ibid. at 168.
[38] Ibid. at 167–172.
[39] Koppelman, Andrew, "1997 Survey of Books Relating to the Law: Sex, Law, Equality: Three Arguments for Gay Rights," 1636–1667, 1662.
[40] Koppelman, Andrew, "Why Discrimination Against Lesbians and Gay Men is Sex Discrimination," 197–287, 199.
[41] Sunstein at 20–21.

Traditional marriage is often described as 'complimentary.' It draws on the complementary strengths of men and women to create a balanced whole. The feminist approach takes strong issue with this idea. According to David Ogden Coolidge, "American family law has reflected the traditional view that marriage is a unique community based on sexual complementarity."[42] For feminist critics, this belief that the genders are inherently different and that dual gendered marriage requires their complimentary characteristics is an oppressive stereotype. As characterized by Coolidge: "The . . . criticism is that the Complimentary model's emphasis on 'sexual difference' presents a false picture of human persons. The model confuses sex and gender, it is said, and mistakes socially-'constructed' differences for real ones. As long as it conceptualizes marriage as based on 'difference,' so the argument goes, it will remain a sociolegal order that fosters domination."[43]

This is certainly an intriguing argument. If successful, it could cast doubt that upon all sorts of laws that restrict the rights of gays and lesbians. If discrimination against gays and lesbians is actually an indirect form of gender discrimination, then laws that punish homosexual sodomy, ban gays and lesbians from the military and many other laws would be constitutionally suspect.

But there are strong reasons to reject this argument. Most importantly, it relies upon far-reaching, sociological speculation that courts are poorly suited to engage in. It is probably true that homophobia and sexism are inextricably linked. The problem is that many different forms of prejudice are inextricably linked. Just as a court could reasonable find a link between homophobia and sexism, it could easily find equally strong links between, say, sexism and racism, sexism and ageism, or sexism and prejudices regarding weight and body type. It certainly would not be surprising to find that people respond more negatively to overweight women than they do to overweight men. And it can be seriously argued that prevailing prejudices against people who are overweight or otherwise do not conform to standard notions of physical attractiveness are a powerful mechanism for the oppression

---

[42] Coolidge, "Same-Sex Marriage? *Baehr v. Miike* and the Meaning of Marriage," *Southern Texas Law Review* 38 (March 1997): 1–119, 33.

[43] Ibid. at 34, citing Catherine A. MacKinnon, "Difference and Dominance: On Sex Discrimination." In *Feminist Legal Theory: Foundations*, D. Kelly Weinberg, ed. Philadelphia: Temple University Press, 1993, 276–287.

of women.[44] But relatedness is not sameness. To go from a recognition that various forms of prejudice are related to a judicial decree that discrimination based upon weight *is* gender discrimination would completely collapse the system of constitutional categories that the Court has created over the past fifty years. The Court would have to apply heightened scrutiny to a virtually endless sequence of categories as each one is demonstrated to be, in part, based upon or furthering conscious or unconscious gender stereotypes.

Prejudice is an extremely complex phenomenon and strong links exist between many, perhaps all, types of prejudices. As Gordon Allport explained in his classic work *The Nature of Prejudice*, prejudice is not so much a conviction that a particular group is inferior or vile as it is a fervent emotion that attaches itself to multiple, unrelated target groups:

> Prejudice...exists whenever there is irrational hostility toward a group of people whose evil attributes are exaggerated and overgeneralized...vigor of conviction is not the same as prejudice.... Conviction is by no means devoid of emotion but it is a disciplined and differentiated emotion, point at the removal of a realistic obstacle. By contrast, the emotion behind prejudice is diffuse and overgeneralized, saturating unrelated objects.[45]

So the difficulty with linking homophobia to sexism is not that the link is false. The problem is that so many other such links exist. Advocates of the "homophobia as sexism" approach might argue that these other links are not as strong or direct as this particular pair of linked prejudices. But that would be a hard argument to make. Is it really stronger than, for example, the link between racism and sexism?[46] Are the courts in any position to make such a judgment?

The fact that two forms of prejudice are linked does not *convert* one form of discrimination into the other. Such an approach would turn

---

[44] See, e.g., Wolfe, Naomi, *The Beauty Myth*. New York: William Morrow and Co., 1990) at p. 10. "We are in the midst of a violent backlash against feminism that uses images of female beauty as a political weapon against women's advancement: the beauty myth."

[45] Allport, Gordon. *The Nature of Prejudice*, Reading, MA: Addison Wesley, 1979 at 430.

[46] For an excellent introductory discussion of the complex relationship between racism and sexism, see Harris, Angela, "Race and Essentialism in Feminist Legal Theory." *Stanford Law Review* 42 (1990) 581–616.

the Supreme Court into our sociologists-in-chief, deciding which prejudices are sufficiently linked to other prejudices against constitutionally protected classes to merit closer constitutional scrutiny. The fact that various prejudices are linked may call into doubt the Court's approach of subjecting discrimination against different groups to different levels of judicial scrutiny. But for the Court to engage in the sociological freelancing called for by the advocates of this approach would only compound the problem.

Asking the courts to engage in this sort of freewheeling sociological expedition would be particularly inappropriate in such a speculative context. Even Eskridge, who strongly advocates the position that "Homophobia became one way that modern urban culture responded to women's political and social equality," concedes that "[t]his account is not so much a demonstrated thesis as much as a coherent hypothesis."[47]

But not everyone would agree that it is even a coherent hypothesis. Even some advocates of gay rights such as Toni Massaro and Janet Halley believe that the argument is far too reductionist. Homophobia is a complex phenomenon that cannot simply be equated with another form of prejudice. As Massaro argues: "If gender role deviance were the total explanation for homophobia, then there would be noticeably less discrimination against the gay men and lesbians who do not deviate from traditional gender roles in their appearance or other visible respects."[48] Thus, while homophobia and sexism are not entirely separate phenomena, it goes too far to say, as Koppelman does in the title of his widely cited article, that discrimination against lesbians and gay men *is* sex discrimination.[49] Homosexuality is a multifaceted identity. To Massaro, "The homosexual is not merely a gender outlaw, but also a religious heretic and a political seditionist. Gender theory captures but one part of this complex construction of the sexual 'deviant'."[50] The complexity of the social construction of, and fear of, homosexuality

---

[47] Eskridge, *The Case for Same-Sex Marriage*, at 168–169.

[48] "Gay Rights, Thick and Thin." *Stanford Law Review* 49 (November 1996): 45–110, 82.

[49] Koppelman, Andrew. "Why Discrimination against Lesbians and Gay Men is Sex Discrimination," (emphasis added).

[50] Massaro, Toni M., "Gay Rights, Thick and Thin." *Stanford Law Review* 49 (November 1996): 45–110, 83.

means that it cannot be reduced to a disguised form of gender discrimination or even a variation of sexism. "[T]he more convincing interpretation is that heterosexism is not a mere additive to, or by product of,
gender discrimination. Rather, it is an independent concept that inter-
sects in a complex, dynamic and contextual manner with other social
forces."[51]

Furthermore, even if one accepts the argument that homophobia
is a form of gender prejudice, that does not mean that opposition to
same-sex marriage is a form of gender discrimination. Feminist scholars link homophobia to heterosexual fear and revulsion at the male
being the passive, penetrated partner. Perhaps this is so. But it fails
to account for the widespread opposition to same-sex marriage. After all, while every state remains ardently opposed same-sex marriage,
most states have rapidly been legalizing homosexual sodomy. At the
beginning of the 1960s, "all fifty states in the United States had some
sort sodomy laws on their books."[52] But the legislatures of twenty-
five states plus the District of Columbia repealed those laws between
1971 and 1993 and the state courts of seven other states struck down
their sodomy laws between 1980 and 1998.[53] Keeping marriage heterosexual and dual gendered clearly has more widespread support than
other homophobic policies. If revulsion to male sexual passivity were
at the core of homophobia, we would expect that banning homosexual
sodomy would be at the top, rather than the bottom of the anti – gay
rights agenda. It would be rightfully difficult to convince the courts,
which are already cool to gay and lesbian rights claims, that the ban on
same-sex marriage is primarily an attempt to enforce male dominance
and female passivity.

A related but distinct argument is that dual gendered marriage is
inherently sexist because it forces women into the (subservient) role
of the wife. Eskridge writes: "The idea that everyone must be heterosexual is closely associated with the idea that every wife must have a
husband, which is in turn correlated (though not absolutely) with a
belief that the wife rules the home while the husband supports the

[51] Ibid.
[52] Rubenstein, William (ed.) *Lesbians, Gay Men and the Law.* New York: New Press,
1993, at 87–88.
[53] ACLU Web site: www.aclu.org/issues/gay/sodomy.hmtl.

family. At the level of common sense as well as theory, there is connection between compulsory different-sex marriage and sexist assumptions."[54]

But it is quite a stretch to say that dual-gendered marriage is inherently a sexist institution, or that disallowing same-sex marriage relegates women to inferior status within marriage. As even Eskridge concedes, "There is no inevitable connection between the prohibition of same-sex marriage and sexism, as the history outlined in Chapter 2 [of Eskridge's book] illustrates."[55]

Of course, marriage has been in some societies a savagely sexist institution, with women usually the inferior partners. But this inferiority was the result of sexist laws; it is not an inherent aspect of dual-gendered marriage. Upon the founding of the United States, men declared themselves independent of the king, but kept in place laws that made them, so to speak, the kings of their own castle. Most notably, they kept the doctrine of 'coverture,' popularly known as "The Law of Baron et femme [Lord and woman]."[56] These laws deprived a married woman of the power to own property under her own name and effectively put her under the power of her husband. These laws have long since been repealed. If a major purpose of the same-sex marriage ban is to force women into inferior marital roles, then it is difficult to explain why women have become legally equal partners in dual-gendered marriage while opposition to same-sex marriage stands firm.

The far more straightforward explanation for the same-sex marriage ban is that it has more to do with prevailing attitudes toward gay men and lesbians than it does with prevailing attitudes toward women. Not only have sexist marriage laws been taken off the books, but there has also been a sea change in how the law treats women. During the past thirty-five years a legal regime has taken shape that prohibits unequal pay for women, gender discrimination, and sexual harassment. Women are now permitted, indeed recruited, into the military, police forces, and fire departments. All of these entail women taking on traditionally masculine roles. Yet every state continues to ban same-sex marriage. Is

---

[54] Eskridge, *The Case for Same-Sex Marriage*, at 171.
[55] Ibid. at 167.
[56] Kerber, Linda, "A Constitutional Right to be Treated Like American Ladies," in *U.S. History as Women's History*, Linda Kerber, Alice Kessler-Harris, and Kathryn Kish Sklar, eds. Chapel Hill: University of North Carolina Press, 1995, at 20–21.

it really plausible to argue that the same-sex marriage ban is primarily about keeping women, rather than gays and lesbians, in their place?

This is not to say that sexism plays no part whatsoever in this debate. But sexism, in some form or another, no doubt affects legislators in a great many decisions ranging from restrictions on welfare benefits to which diseases deserve the most funding for research. If the courts applied heightened scrutiny to every legislative decision for which sexism might be an unconscious factor, then the distinction between different levels of judicial scrutiny would collapse and the courts would replace legislatures as the chief architects of public policy.[57]

The analogy to *Loving v. Virginia* breaks down even further here, because in that case, the Supreme Court emphasized that Virginia's antimiscegenation policy rested *solely* upon racially discriminatory distinctions. As Craig M. Bradley points out, a similar argument regarding gender discrimination cannot credibly be made regarding the same-sex marriage ban:

> By contrast, the Georgia legislators responsible for the sodomy statute in *Bowers*, and authors of statutes that forbid same-sex marriages would deny truthfully and adamantly, that they had any purpose to discriminate against women. They would, in fact, be astonished at such a suggestion. While such a subconscious motivation may have been one of a number of reasons behind the legislators' action, it likely was neither their conscious nor their primary purpose. In any event, it is highly unlikely that it could be *proven* to be such a purpose.[58]

To his credit, Eskridge acknowledges this point to a degree. He concedes that: "A gap in the analogy to *Loving* is that the connection between the discriminatory classification (sex) and the harm (reinforcing gender stereotypes) is ... hard to connect with legislative motivations. Judges may find it difficult to understand how denying two gay men the right to marry is driven by an ideology that oppresses straight women."[59]

---

[57] Some might argue that collapsing the rigid categories of modern equal protection analysis would be a good thing, as I have done in previous writings. But that would truly be a radical legal project, with consequences far beyond that of legalizing same-sex marriage.

[58] Bradley, Craig M.,"The Right Not to Endorse Gay Rights: A Reply to Sunstein." *Indiana Law Journal* 70 (1994): 29–38, 32–33.

[59] Eskridge, "A History of Same-Sex Marriage," at 1509–1510, cited in Bradley, supra, at 33 n.27.

Beyond all of this, there is an even greater problem with the "ban as gender discrimination" argument. It is deeply, indeed fundamentally, dishonest. It is based upon the dubious assertion that the same-sex marriage ban is best understood as a policy that discriminates against women. It would be difficult to say this to gay men with a straight face.

It is obvious that the group that is being discriminated against is homosexuals, be they male and female. They are the ones being told that their love and commitment is not worthy of being solemnized by marriage; that their relationships are not worth the legal protection that marriage would bring; that their life partners cannot be stepparents to their children, and so forth. To say that this is about discrimination against women rather than gays and lesbians is blatantly misleading. It is the use of the law to manipulate categories and to mislead rather than to cast light, as *Loving* did, upon the true nature of state-sponsored discrimination.

The law serves its highest purpose best when it serves the side of truth and strips away the obfuscations of prejudice. This purpose was served when the Court declared that Virginia's antimiscegenation laws were a pillar of "White Supremacy" rather than a neutral system of laws that treated the races equally. Could even the most enthusiastic supporters of the gender discrimination theory say that the same-sex marriage ban is primarily about keeping women in their place as Virginia's laws were primarily about keeping African Americans and other racial minorities in their place? Is the insistence of the legislatures of all fifty states that they believe that they are treating men and women equally really just a façade?

While *Loving* is most notable for its candid exposure and denunciation of racism, *Baehr* is most notable for its Alice in Wonderland insistence that rights and status of gays and lesbians were completely irrelevant to the case.[60] The court averred that "'Homosexual' and 'same-sex' marriage are not synonymous . . . a 'heterosexual' same-sex marriage is, in theory, not oxymoronic."[61] The court continued, "Parties to a same-sex marriage could theoretically be either homosexuals or

---

[60] "One of the striking features of the decision is its repeated insistence that the issue of homosexuality is irrelevant to the case." Coolidge, David A., "Same-Sex Marriage? *Baehr v. Miike* and the Meaning of Marriage." *Southwest Texas Law Review* 38 (March 1997): 1–97, 24.

[61] 74 Haw. 530 at 543, n.11.

heterosexuals."[62] Later in its opinion, the court stated that "it is immaterial whether the plaintiffs, or any of them, are homosexuals."[63] Later, the court repeated, yet again, "it is immaterial whether the plaintiffs, or any of them, are homosexuals."[64] The court was so adamant about this point that when it quoted the state's brief it followed that brief's use of the term "homosexual marriage" with the demarcation "sic," which notes that the error is that of the person being quoted rather than that of the author. This insistence is particularly odd in light of the fact that all of the plaintiffs in this case had identified themselves as gay and lesbian.[65]

If one believes that the role of courts is to find and reveal the truth rather than to obscure it, then *Baehr* is strange animal indeed. Gays and lesbians across the nation would surely be very surprised if they found out that the issue of whether they can marry the person they love was not really an issue of their rights but, rather, of the rights of unidentified heterosexuals to enter into "theoretically possible" marriages with persons of their own gender.[66]

So *Baehr* is really the exact opposite of *Loving*. The latter stripped away pretense and willful blindness to reveal the true nature of a racist law. In contrast, Baehr hides the true nature of the discrimination being challenged. The court attempts to hide the gay and lesbian plaintiffs in that case. Where *Loving* enlightened, *Baehr* obfuscated.

Indeed, the enthusiasm of so many gay rights advocates for the *Baehr* approach is a victory of expedience over principle. The gender discrimination theory is actually a deeply conservative, capitulating argument. As Megan E. Farrell has noted, "The court's questionable determination that the statute classifies on the basis of sex is a way for it to

---

[62] Ibid.

[63] Ibid. at n.14.

[64] Ibid. at n.17.

[65] Baehr, 852 P.2d at 52.

[66] The one empirical example of heterosexual same-sex marriage cited in the literature is that of transsexual marriage, some of which have been invalidated by the courts. See Damslet, Otis R., "Note: Same-Sex Marriage." *New York Law School Journal of Human Rights* 10 (1993): 555, 563–565, n.37. But even this is an exception that proves the rule. It is hardly obvious that a marriage between two people who were once of the same gender is better described as a heterosexual marriage than as a homosexual marriage. In any event, it is very difficult to see how the existence of transsexual marriages converts the issue of same-sex marriage to a gender discrimination issue.

apply a strict scrutiny analysis without dealing with such controversial issues as whether there is a fundamental right to same-sex marriage or whether homosexuals constitute a suspect class."[67]

The gender discrimination argument has the unfortunate effect of putting gays and lesbians back in the legal closet. Despite the fact that all six plaintiffs were gay and lesbian, as are virtually all of the people seeking to marry someone of their own gender, the *Baehr* court insisted over and over again that it was not acknowledging that gays and lesbians had any rights under the constitution. To rule in favor of the gay and lesbian plaintiffs, the *Baehr* court first had to render their homosexuality invisible.

Some might argue that all of this dishonesty and disassembling is nonetheless worthwhile as practical matter. One could view the argument in *Baehr* as an admirable sort of judicial jiujitsu, using whatever maneuvers are necessary to pin down the right to same-sex marriage. Perhaps, if just one state would legalize same-sex marriage and make it stick, over time the rest of the nation would see that the sky is not falling and the political climate would change dramatically.

This argument should be rejected. If we are to elevate expedience over principle, then, at a minimum, we need to take a hard look at practical consequences of that approach. As we will see in Chapter 9, the *Baehr* decision was in many ways disastrous for advocates of same-sex marriage – a population that had been regarded as tolerant or accepting prior to this controversy soundly rejected it. Indeed, public opposition to same-sex marriage actually *hardened* after *Baehr*.[68]

For all of these reasons, the sex-discrimination argument deserves to be rejected. But this is not the end of the argument. If the ban on same-sex marriage is best understood as discrimination against gays and lesbians, perhaps that discrimination is itself a reason for heightened judicial scrutiny. This argument will be taken up in the next section.

Gays and Lesbians as a "Suspect Class"

If we should not confuse gender discrimination with sexual orientation discrimination, then perhaps there is a more straightforward argument.

---

[67] Farrell at 591–92.
[68] This will be discussed in Chapter 9.

Can the courts subject the laws that discriminate on the basis of sexual orientation to heightened scrutiny based upon the minority status of gays and lesbians? The Court protects certain minorities by subjecting laws that discriminate against them to heightened scrutiny.[69] In order to qualify for this heightened protection, gays and lesbians would have to establish that they meet each of the following three criteria: (1) they have suffered from a history of discrimination; (2) they are defined by an immutable characteristic; and (3) they are "politically powerless," and therefore need extra judicial protection.[70]

A strong argument can be made that gays and lesbians satisfy all three of these criteria, and I have made that argument in previous writings. However, there are several enormous practical problems with this approach. I have discussed these problems extensively elsewhere[71] and therefore will address them only briefly here. The first problem is that these criteria have proven to be completely impossible to work with. The Court has utterly failed to define any of the critical terms such as "history of discrimination," "immutability," and "political powerlessness." It has continually applied these terms so inconsistently as to make them virtually useless in framing a legal argument. Gays and lesbians are told that they are too politically powerful to qualify for heightened protection, yet white men challenging affirmative action programs are not too powerful. Gays and lesbians are told that they are not a suspect class, because sexual orientation is not immutable, yet the Court has held that noncitizens qualify as a suspect class even when they are eligible to apply for citizenship but choose not to.[72]

For all practical purposes the constitutional doctrine regarding suspect classes is a dead letter. The Court has not found any group to be a suspect class since the mid-1970s and both the conference notes and memos of the justices, as well as the Court's pattern of decisions, amply demonstrate that the Court has no intention of creating any new

---

[69] In fact, the Court is quite inconsistent about whether it is actually protecting minorities or, rather, protecting both the majority and minority from discrimination on the basis of certain characteristics. For an extensive discussion of this point, see Gerstmann, *The Constitutional Underclass* at chapter 4.

[70] See Gerstmann, *The Constitutional Underclass* at pp. 61–62.

[71] Ibid. at chapters 4 and 5.

[72] See Gerstmann, *The Constitutional Underclass*, at chapter 4, for extensive discussion of all of these points.

suspect classes. The only time the Court uses the three criteria outlined above is to justify *denying* groups suspect class status.[73]

The suspect class approach also creates enormous political problems for gays and lesbians. It exacerbates the public perception that they are seeking *special rights* rather equal rights. This perception is one of the greatest political liabilities that gays and lesbians face in seeking equal protection of the laws, and the Court's class-based approach to equal protection forces them to frame their arguments in terms of special pleading rather than legal equality. Further, gays and lesbians get little in return from the courts, as those courts have consistently rebuffed the argument that gays and lesbians are a suspect class.[74]

Conclusion

Fundamental differences between interracial and same-sex marriage mean that the same-sex marriage ban cannot honestly be viewed as gender discrimination. The ban may well be a form of discrimination on the basis of sexual orientation, but gays and lesbians do not qualify for heightened judicial protection. There is, however, another, far more straightforward, road to constitutional protection for same-sex marriage. Indeed, it will be argued that this argument has largely been avoided because it is so powerful that liberals and conservatives alike fear that it could be effectively used by polygamous Mormons and other groups toward whom the academy is unsympathetic. This approach will be taken up in the next section.

[73] Ibid.
[74] See Gerstmann, *The Constitutional Underclass*, at chapter 5, for extensive discussion of all of these points.

PART II

MARRIAGE AS A FUNDAMENTAL CONSTITUTIONAL RIGHT

4

The Fundamental Right to Marry

Having reviewed and rejected several of the leading arguments for finding a constitutional right to same-sex marriage, we turn to what this book argues is by far the most powerful argument in favor of such a right: *The Constitution guarantees every person the right to marry the person of his or her choice.* This is not to say that the right is limitless; nobody has the right to marry a nine-year-old, to mention just one example. No constitutional right is absolute, as all are balanced against other societal interests. Few rights are more intensely protected in this country than is freedom of speech, but the Constitution[1] allows limitations on obscene speech, libel, perjury, shouting "Fire!" in a crowed theater, and many other forms of speech in which the harm outweighs the First Amendment interest of the speaker.[2]

---

[1] By "the Constitution," I mean the Constitution as interpreted by the United States Supreme Court, or sometimes lower federal courts or state courts. For the proposition that lawyers and academics too often fail to distinguish between constitutional law and the Constitution itself, see Whittington, Keith E., *Constitutional Interpretation: Textual Meaning, Original Intent, and Judicial Review.* Lawrence: University of Kansas Press, 1999.

[2] "There are certain well defined and narrowly limited classes of speech the prevention and punishment of which have never been thought to raise any Constitutional problem. These include the lewd and obscene, the profane, the libelous ... such utterances are no essential part of any exposition of ideas and are of such slight social value as a step to truth that any benefit that may be derived from them is clearly outweighed by the social interest in order and morality." *Chaplinsky v. New Hampshire*, 315 U.S. 568, 571–572 (1942).

Recognizing the constitutional right to marry, then, does not send us plunging down a slippery slope to a purely libertarian, "anything goes" view in which society loses all control over the definition of marriage.[3] Marriage is not an exclusively personal decision, for the government has an interest in what is called "marriage" and is not prevented from preferring some forms of it over others. The First Amendment right of association may protect one's right to join the Ku Klux Klan, but the government has not lost its power to endorse, fund, and promote organizations that fight racism, or to teach schoolchildren that certain associations are worthier than others, and that the Klan is not a worthy organization. Similarly, legalizing same-sex marriage will not end the social debate over issues such as what to teach children about unconventional families, how adoption agencies should treat same-sex couples, or whether civil rights laws should protect such couples from discrimination when they buy or lease property. The fundamental right to marry, however, means that legislatures will have to articulate the necessity for placing certain restrictions on marriage. If same-sex marriage truly represents a threat to society or cannot really be considered a form of marriage, the government may ban it, just as government may ban libelous and obscene speech. As with speech, though, mere unpopularity or disdain cannot justify a ban. Gays and lesbians will be entitled to demand that the government justify the same-sex marriage ban by reference to social interests other than pure majoritarian moral preference.

In contemporary constitutional parlance, there is a "fundamental right" to marry that is protected under the Constitution. Nothing is radical or shocking about this position, which is in keeping with the broad range of protections of personal and family life that the Supreme Court has been enforcing for some time. The government has long been held to a heightened level of judicial scrutiny with regard to its treatment of many aspects of family life. Courts have not permitted the government free rein in treatment of unconventional family structures, illegitimacy, or divorce;[4] and freedom of personal association is a cherished constitutional value.[5] Indeed, it is the position denying

---

[3] Polygamous and incestuous marriages will be discussed in the next chapter.
[4] See, respectively, *Moore v. City of East Cleveland*, 431 U.S. 494 (1977), *Glona v. American Guarantee*, 391 U.S. 73 (1968) and *Boddie v. Connecticut*, 401 U.S. 371 (1971).
[5] *Roberts v. United States Jaycees*, 468 U.S. 609 (1984).

the existence of the fundamental marriage right that is extreme. Does anyone believe that the government could simply ban divorce, forbid remarriage by divorced people, or prevent people with genetic disorders from marrying one another? Most people would undoubtedly be alarmed over the idea of this sort of unchecked power.

Although the Supreme Court has repeatedly held that there is a constitutionally protected right to marry, it has been extraordinarily sloppy in explaining where this right comes from and in delineating its contours. The following two sections attempt to flesh out this crucial right; the first explains the concept of fundamental rights, the second traces the development of the right to marry. The next chapter discusses its applicability to same-sex marriage.

Fundamental Rights

The Court has long held that the Constitution protects numerous "fundamental" rights that are not explicitly mentioned therein; sometimes they are called "unenumerated" rights. These rights have been elevated to a par with those rights enumerated in the Bill of Rights, including freedom of speech, assembly, and religion. Fundamental rights, many people know, include the right to abortion and contraception and the right to vote. These rights also include such lesser-known rights as the right to receive welfare payments immediately upon moving to a new state, and the right of genetically related people to live in a neighborhood zoned for single-family housing, even if the people living in the house do not meet the law's definition of a single family. In addition, the Court has implied, if not firmly held, that fundamental rights might include access to public education (although not to an equal public education).[6] Understanding this system of unenumerated rights is difficult because the Court has left so many questions unanswered or only partly answered. It is extremely unclear what part of the Constitution the Court believes is the basis for these rights. On this point, the

---

[6] See, respectively, *Roe v. Wade*, 410 U.S. 113 (1973), *Griswold v. Connecticut*, 381 U.S. 479 (1965), *Shapiro v. Thompson*, 394 U.S. 618 (1969), *Harper v. Virginia Bd. of Election*, 383 U.S. 663 (1966), *Moore v. East Cleveland*, 431 U.S. 494 (1977), *Plyler v. Doe*, 457 U.S. 202 (1982), and *San Antonio Independent School District v. Rodriguez*, 411 U.S. 1 (1973).

justices have been free ranging, sometimes holding that fundamental rights come from the due process clause,[7] while at other times holding that these rights come from the equal protection clause,[8] and have recently said that at least one fundamental right, the right to travel, comes from the privileges and immunities clause.[9] As will be explained in more detail later, the Court has also held that these rights do not come from any single part of the Constitution, but "emanate" from the Bill of Rights as a whole.[10]

John Hart Ely, in his famous book *Democracy and Distrust*,[11] argues that these rights come from broad principles of democratic process and equality and from the Ninth Amendment, which states, "The enumeration in the Constitution, of certain rights, shall not be construed to deny or disparage others retained by the people." Still, if these rights are unenumerated, how can the Court discern what they are or what they should be? Should the Court even be in the business of discerning unenumerated rights, or should this be left to the democratic process? Each of these questions will be addressed in subsequent chapters. For now, it suffices to point out that despite these questions, the doctrine of fundamental rights has important attributes. In fact, I shall argue throughout this book that the recognition of fundamental rights is an imperative of constitutional law.

The Supreme Court cannot apply the same level of judicial scrutiny to all laws. As discussed in Chapter 2, when the Court applies strict scrutiny to a law, it will strike the law down unless the statute is narrowly tailored to advance a compelling governmental interest. If the Court applied such a standard to all laws, it would become a "super-legislature," constantly substituting its judgment for that of the democratically elected branches of the government. But if it always applied only the deferential "rational basis" scrutiny discussed in Chapter 2, judicial review would not mean very much. Therefore, the Court must have a means by which it varies its level of judicial review, deferring to the legislature on some matters and applying stricter scrutiny to others.

---

[7] *Roe v. Wade*, 410 U.S. 113 (1973).
[8] *Skinner v. Oklahoma*, 391 U.S. 535 (1942).
[9] *Saenz v. Roe*, 526 U.S. 489 (1999).
[10] *Griswold v. Connecticut*, 381 U.S. 479 (1965).
[11] Ely, *Democracy and Distrust*.

Some have suggested that the Court should defer to the democratic process except when the text of the Constitution or the clear intent of the Constitution's drafters compels the justices to do otherwise.[12] This approach has advantages, but the Court has never adopted it, for it would drastically change the constitutional world (the Court would probably not apply heightened scrutiny to gender discrimination by the government, for example). Consequently, the Court has adopted other approaches. As discussed in Chapter 3, the Court has applied strict scrutiny to laws that discriminate against "suspect classifications" such as race. The disadvantages of this approach have been discussed. Presumably as a result of these problems, the Court has backed away from this approach as well and has frozen the list of suspect classes to where it stood in the 1970s: racial and ethnic minorities, women, and illegitimate children.[13] This has left the Court with lines that are arbitrary and incapable of responding coherently to the claims of groups such as senior citizens, the poor, the mentally retarded, or gays and lesbians when they assert that their rights are entitled to constitutional protection.[14]

To deal with the rigid boxes of suspect classes that it has created, the Court has turned to another method of varying the level of judicial scrutiny. Sometimes the Court simply cheats, purporting to apply mere rational-basis scrutiny yet applying a much stricter level of scrutiny, to protect such groups as the mentally retarded, "hippies," and, arguably, gays and lesbians.[15] This silent application of strict scrutiny, or something close to it, is sometimes called a "second-order rational basis" test.[16] It is the worst possible way to vary the level of judicial scrutiny because it is utterly without standards or accountability. Justice Thurgood Marshall has eloquently explained the problems of silently applying stricter scrutiny in selected cases:

The suggestion that the traditional rational-basis test allows this sort of searching inquiry creates precedent for this Court and lower courts to subject economic and commercial classifications to similar and searching "ordinary" rational-basis review – a small and regrettable step back toward the days

---

[12] See Whittington for an excellent account of this view.
[13] See Gerstmann for a more thorough explanation. At one point, citizenship status was a suspect classification, but the Court has backed away from this position.
[14] For much more on this, see Gerstmann.
[15] Ibid. at 129–139.
[16] Ibid.

of [judicial nullification of laws meant to protect worker health and safety].
Moreover, by failing to articulate the factors that justify today's 'second order'
rational-basis review, the Court provides no principled foundation for determining when more searching inquiry is to be invoked. Lower courts are thus
left in the dark on this important question, and this Court remains unaccountable for its decisions employing, or refusing to employ, particularly searching
scrutiny.[17]

The other approach the Court has used is the fundamental rights
approach. Although the Court has applied it sporadically and has explained it poorly, this approach has advantages that the others lack.
Focusing on the question of *what* liberty is at stake, rather than *whose*
liberty is at stake, it is unitive rather than divisive. With those rights
explicitly mentioned in the Constitution, fundamental rights are those
that we all share as citizens and as persons in a free society. Under
the fundamental rights approach, gays and lesbians are not forced to
claim that they are an oppressed minority that requires special protection from a prejudiced majority; nor do they have to transmogrify
their claims into gender-discrimination claims, as if it were women
rather than gays and lesbians who are being denied the right to marry.
Gays and lesbians can come forward as equal citizens, claiming nothing more than the right that the great majority of people currently take
for granted: the right to marry the person they love.

One of the strengths of the fundamental rights approach to same-
sex marriage is its accessibility to the average thoughtful person. (By
contrast, the idea that the same-sex marriage ban is a form of gender
discrimination is highly counter-intuitive, as discussed in Chapter 3;
neither men nor women see the ban as oppressing them.) Casting the
debate this way moves us directly to the questions that are genuinely
at the heart of the debate over same-sex marriage. Is marriage inherently dual-gendered? Is it essentially an individual freedom or is it
just a socially created institution for procreation and raising children?
If it is both, what happens when there is friction between these two
understandings? Would same-sex marriage cause some demonstrable
harm to society? Does the same-sex marriage ban violate the fundamental right to marry? To answer these questions, we must address three

---

[17] *City of Cleburne v. Cleburne Living Center*, 473 U.S. 432, 459–60 (1985) (Marshall, J.
concurring).

issues: is there a fundamental right to marry in the Constitution? Does that right include the right to marry someone of one's own gender? If the other two questions are answered in the affirmative, is there some compelling reason for society to ban same-sex marriage anyway? I shall turn to the first question in the next section and take up the second and third in the next chapter.

Marriage as a Fundamental Right

This section will trace the evolution of the Court's understanding of marriage from that of an institution completely under the regulatory power of the government to that of an individual right akin to the other fundamental rights outlined above. Bruce C. Haffen has asserted that "The constitutional freedom to marry as a substantive fundamental right sprang full-blown from the pen of Justice Marshall...in 1978."[18] But as will be seen, the truth is quite different. The right to marry was among the very first fundamental rights the Court recognized. Indeed, what is most striking in the Court's development of fundamental rights is the preeminent place of the right to marry in that jurisprudence.

"During the first 130 years of its existence, the Supreme Court did not refer to the right to marry as a basic or fundamental or presumed right in any constitutional sense," Lynn D. Wardle writes.[19] Although the Court sometimes referred to a "right to marry," these references meant simply that a person had a right to marry under state law because they were of sufficient age, not already married, and so forth.[20] Throughout the nineteenth century, marriage was considered to be a common law right, not a constitutional right.[21] Common law rights are derived from a combination of judicial pronouncements and custom and are subject to legislative revision or revocation. Marriage therefore was subject to state regulation so long as the state was sufficiently clear that it was intending to alter the common law.[22]

[18] Hafen at 509.
[19] Wardle, Lynn D., "Loving v. Virginia and the Constitutional Right to Marry, 1790–1990." *Howard Law Journal* 41 (winter 1998): 289–347, 291.
[20] Ibid.
[21] *Meister v. Moore*, 96 U.S. 76 (1877).
[22] Ibid.

In 1877, in *Pennoyer v. Neff*, the Court explicitly stated that "The State...has an absolute right to prescribe the condition upon which the marriage relation between its own citizens shall be created, and the cause for which it may be dissolved."[23] The next year, in *Reynolds v. U.S.*,[24] the Court held that the government had the power to outlaw polygamy and that the marriage contract was subject to state power, as were the terms of any other civil contract. "Marriage, while from its very nature a sacred obligation, is nevertheless, in most civilized nations, a civil contract, and usually regulated by law."[25] Finally, ten years later, in *Maynard v. Hill*, the Court stated, "Marriage, as creating the most important relation in life, as having more to do with the morals and civilization of a people than any other institution, has always been subject to the control of the legislature."[26]

These early decisions, however, must be read in their historical context. It is not surprising that throughout much of the nineteenth century, the Court declined to call marriage a fundamental right because the concept of unenumerated fundamental rights did not exist at all until the very end of that century. Indeed, the Court did not really enforce even many of the rights explicitly guaranteed in the Bill of Rights, such as freedom of speech, until the middle of the twentieth century. The history of constitutional law is riddled with Court cases upholding prison terms for peacefully expressing opposition to war and the draft or for joining the Communist Labor Party.[27] It would be surprising indeed for the nineteenth century Court to declare marriage, or anything else, a fundamental right.

But in the late 1890s, the Court began seriously to consider the idea that the due process clause of the Fourteenth Amendment of the Constitution protected certain unenumerated rights from unreasonable interference by state legislatures. The Fourteenth Amendment forbids states from "depriv[ing] any person of life, liberty or property without due process of law." In the 1890s, as the "laissez-faire" philosophy of unrestricted capitalism reached its zenith, numerous federal and state

---

[23] 95 U.S. 714, 734–35 (1877).
[24] 98 U.S. 145 (1878).
[25] 98 U.S. at 165.
[26] 125 U.S. 190, 205 (1888).
[27] See, respectively, *Schenck v. United States*, 249 U.S. 47 (1919), *Whitney v. California*, 274 U.S. 357 (1927).

judges, attorneys, and even some dissenting justices began arguing that the due process clause guaranteed certain substantive individual rights against the states.[28] This theory, known as "substantive due process," began to command a majority of justices late in the decade. In *Allgeyer v. Louisiana*,[29] the Court held that the state could not prevent an out-of-state insurance policy from being effectuated without state approval. Although the issue was narrow, the Court's language indicated that it was prepared to protect certain individual rights regardless of whether they were listed in the Constitution. In sweeping language, the Court heralded a constitutional age of substantive due process in which the justices stood ready to challenge state interference with certain fundamental, if unenumerated, constitutional rights:

The 'liberty' mentioned in the [due process clause of the Fourteenth Amendment is] deemed to embrace the right of the citizen to be free in the enjoyment of all of his faculties, to be free to use them in all lawful ways; to live and work where he will; to earn his livelihood by any lawful calling; to pursue any livelihood or avocation; and for that purpose to enter into all contracts which may be proper, necessary and essential to his carrying out to a successful conclusion the purposes above mentioned.

In 1905, in the famous (perhaps notorious) case of *Lochner v. New York*,[30] the Court made it clear that the era of substantive due process had arrived. Striking down a maximum-hours law for bakers, the Court held that the "general right to make a contract in relation to his business is part of the liberty of the individual protected by the Fourteenth Amendment."[31] Because of the historical significance of this case, this era of the emergence of substantive due process is often referred to as "the Lochner era." But it was also during this period that the Court began its defense of noneconomic unenumerated liberties. In 1923, in the first noneconomic substantive due process case, *Meyer v. Nebraska*,[32] the Court struck down a state law prohibiting teachers

---

[28] See Twiss, Benjamin R., *Lawyers and the Constitution: How Laissez-Faire Came to the Supreme Court*. Princeton: Princeton University Press, 1942 at pp. 18–173; Corwin, Edward S., *Liberty Against Government: The Rise, Flowering and Decline of a Famous Juridical Concept*. Baton Rouge: Louisiana State University Press, 1948 at pp. 129–152.
[29] 165 U.S. 578 (1897).
[30] 198 U.S. 45 (1905).
[31] *Lochner v. New York*, 198 U.S. 45, 53 (1905).
[32] 262 U.S. 390 (1923).

from instructing children in any language other than English. Although *Meyer* had nothing to do with marriage, the Court went out of its way to include marriage, home, and children along with the aforementioned economic rights and freedom of religion as among the essential rights of free people:

> While this Court has not attempted to define with exactness the liberty thus guaranteed, the term has received much consideration and some of the included things have been definitely stated. Without doubt, it denotes not merely freedom from bodily restraint, but also the right of the individual to contract, to engage in any of the common occupations of life, to acquire useful knowledge, *to marry*, establish a home and bring up children, to worship God according to the dictates of his own conscience, as generally to enjoy those privileges long recognized at common law as essential to the ordered pursuit of happiness by free men.[33]

The constitutional right to marry was present at the very birth of noneconomic substantive due process rights.

Although the noneconomic substantive due process cases such as *Meyer* have often been cited favorably, the dominant, laissez-faire aspect of substantive due process eventually proved disastrous for the Court. In the 1930s it led the justices into a battle with President Franklin D. Roosevelt, as they attempted to dismantle his famed New Deal programs, repeatedly holding that the creation of an expansive regulatory state violated these laissez-faire liberties. The sweeping victory of Roosevelt and the Democratic party at the polls in 1936, combined with FDR's threats to pack the Court with additional Democratic appointments, effectively cowed the Court into submission from 1937 onward.[34] This battle so undermined the Court's authority that it was forced into an almost complete retreat on substantive due process. "Indeed, the Court had been so politically discredited by its constitutional defense of laissez-faire capitalism, that it was hardly obvious whether *any* firm ground remained upon which to rebuild the institution of judicial review," Bruce Ackerman says.[35]

---

[33] Ibid. at 399 (emphasis added).

[34] For elaboration on Roosevelt, the Court, and the impact of the threatened "Court-packing" plan, see Courrie, David P., *The Constitution and the Supreme Court*. University of Chicago Press, 1985.

[35] Ackerman, Bruce, "Beyond Carolene Products." *Harvard Law Review* 98 (1985): 713–746, 713–714.

From 1937 until the emergence of the powerful and active Warren Court in the 1950s, the Court was extremely reluctant to rule that there are any unenumerated rights in the Constitution. It made an exception in 1942, striking down the Habitual Criminal Sterilization Act in *Skinner v. Oklahoma*.[36] That law called for the sterilization of criminals who had in engaged in two or more crimes of "moral turpitude," exempting white-collar crimes such as embezzlement, tax evasion, and "political offenses." Although the Court was not particularly adventurous, it was clearly disturbed by the eugenic implication of the law and by the ascendance of Nazism and fascism in Europe, opining that in "evil or reckless hands [the power to sterilize] can cause races or types that are inimical to the dominant group to whither and disappear."[37]

The Oklahoma law had nothing to do with marriage, yet the Court felt compelled to state that: "We are dealing with legislation that involves one of the basic civil rights of man. Marriage and procreation are fundamental to the very existence and survival of the race."[38] Interestingly, the Court chose not to rely on the theory of substantive due process. Rather, it held that the law violated the equal protection clause of the Fourteenth Amendment, which commands that "[no State shall] deny to any person within its jurisdiction the equal protection of the laws." Because the law exempted white-collar crimes without good reason, it violated the basic principle of treating like cases alike. "When the law lays an unequal hand on those who have committed intrinsically the same quality of offense and sterilizes one and not the other, it has made as invidious a discrimination, as if it had selected a particular race or nationality for oppressive treatment."[39] The significance of the justices' reliance on equal protection rather than substantive due process and their linkage of marriage and procreation will be discussed in Chapter 6. For now, it is enough to note that even at a time of extreme caution for the Court, the justices went out of their way to assert that marriage is one of the fundamental rights of humankind.

The next case involving the right to marry was *Griswold v. Connecticut* in 1965.[40] Considering a statute that prohibited the use of

[36] 316 U.S. 535 (1942).
[37] 316 U.S. at 541.
[38] Ibid.
[39] Ibid.
[40] 381 U.S. 479 (1965).

"any drug, medicinal article or instrument for the purpose of preventing conception,"[41] the Court struck down the law, emphasizing that
it covered even married people and that it violated their right of marital privacy. This time, the Court avoided basing its decision on the
due process clause or the equal protection clause. Justice William O.
Douglas found that a right to privacy was implicit in the "penumbras"
of the Constitution. By this, he meant that every explicit constitutional
right implies that the Constitution protects related rights. For example, the First Amendment protects the rights of free speech, but does
not mention freedom of association[42]; nonetheless, the Court has held
that as part of their freedom of speech, people have the broader right to
freedom of association, including the right to join groups without their
membership being reported to the government.[43]

Douglas concluded that the First Amendment, coupled with other
amendments that protect the home and the person in various ways,
forms a penumbra of protected privacy. Although the Connecticut
statute did not specifically target married couples, Douglas emphasized
the sacredness of marital privacy: "Would we allow the police to search
the sacred precincts of marital bedrooms? The very idea is repulsive
to the notions of privacy surrounding the marriage relationship.... We
deal with a right of privacy older than the Bill of Rights... Marriage
is a coming together for better or for worse, hopefully enduring and
intimate to the degree of being sacred."[44]

Two years later, the Court decided perhaps the most famous case
ever to deal with the right to marry, *Loving v. Virginia*.[45] As discussed
in Chapter 3, *Loving* was the great civil rights case that struck down
the ban on interracial marriage in Virginia and in fifteen other states.
Because of its historical importance, *Loving* has taken on a central
role in the debate over same-sex marriage.[46] Unfortunately, for all the

---

[41] Connecticut General Statutes Sec. 53-32 (1958 Rev.).
[42] The First Amendment protects "the right of the people peaceably to assemble," but
does not mention association.
[43] *NAACP v. Alabama*, 357 U.S. 449 (1958).
[44] *Griswold*, 381 U.S. at 486.
[45] 388 U.S. 1 (1967).
[46] As discussed in Chapter 3, the analogy between the same-sex marriage ban and the
interracial marriage ban that the *Loving* Court rejected has been one of the prime
rhetorical approaches of same-sex marriage advocates. Also, the decision has received
a great deal of attention from both sides of the debate.

attention paid to this case, assessing *Loving*'s meaning for the right to marry is a bit like reading tea leaves. As Robert A. Destro puts it, "Depending on who is reading it – and for what purpose – the case can be characterized as a 'race' case, a 'eugenics' case, a 'marriage' case, or a 'substantive due process' case."[47] *Loving* is difficult to interpret for two reasons, one of which is Virginia's slippery argument in defending its racist statute. Virginia argued that the law was not racially discriminatory because blacks and whites were subject to the same set of rules (i.e., people of all races could marry only within their own race). The other reason has to do with internal Court politics. Chief Justice Earl Warren considered the case so important that he decided to write the opinion himself and desired a unanimous opinion. Initially, he emphasized that Virginia was violating the Lovings' right to marry. But Justice Hugo Black strongly objected to relying on an unenumerated right,[48] which was not surprising, because he was an appointee of Roosevelt's in 1937, the apex of the clash between FDR and the Court over substantive due process. To satisfy Black, Warren deemphasized the right-to-marry argument.[49]

As a result, the decision in *Loving* follows an odd trajectory. The Court briefly discusses the right to marry near the beginning and again at the very end. The middle of the decision is devoted to countering Virginia's arguments that the drafters of the Fourteenth Amendment did not intend to make antimiscegenation laws unconstitutional and that the law treated all races equally. As noted earlier, the Court dismissed the latter argument as a rather transparent attempt to hide the fact that the ban on interracial marriage was part of a system of white supremacy and perhaps eugenics that supported a deeply racist social structure.[50] Justices therefore held that the statute violated the equal protection clause, but at the end of the decision added the famous Part II:

These statutes also deprive the Lovings of liberty without due process of law in violation of the Due Process Clause of the Fourteenth Amendment. The freedom to marry has long been recognized as one of the vital personal rights

[47] Destro at 1209.
[48] Schwartz at 293.
[49] Ibid.
[50] See chapter 3, supra.

essential to the orderly pursuit of happiness by free men. Marriage is 'one of the basic civil rights of man,' fundamental to our very existence and survival. [Skinner]. See also [Maynard v. Hill]. To deny this fundamental freedom on so unsupportable a basis as the racial classifications embodied in these statutes, classifications so subversive of the principle of equality at the heart of the Fourteenth Amendment is surely to deprive all of the States of liberty without due process of law. The Fourteenth Amendment requires that the freedom of choice to marry not be restricted by invidious racial discriminations. Under our Constitution, the freedom to marry, or not marry, a person of another race resides within the individual and cannot be infringed by the state.[51]

Because of the brevity of this part of *Loving*, some scholars have suggested that it should not be construed to endorse an independent "right to marry" that would apply outside of the context of race. Destro argues that the "first and most obvious way to characterize *Loving* is as a 'race' case."[52] If *Loving* is best understood as a race case, though, it has little to say about same-sex marriage or anything else outside the important but narrow topic of antimiscegenation laws:

If Loving is a race case and the discussion of 'the freedom to marry or not marry' merely adds weight to the equal protection holding, the Court's remarks about marriage are not so significant. Like a generalized discussion of the community's in assuring non-discriminatory access to safe and affordable housing in a housing discrimination case, the discussion of marriage in Loving can be understood as underscoring the intensely personal nature of the damage inflicted on Mr. and Mrs. Loving.[53]

In other words, it is possible that the Court, in the context of a race discrimination case, was merely pointing out that the racial discrimination was of a very serious nature. Under this interpretation, the Court was not holding that the Constitution limits state power to restrict access to marriage except in the unique context of race discrimination. According to Destro: "The Court has indicated on many occasions that marriage is an important relationship, but generalized statements concerning the importance of marriage would not necessarily provide the

---

[51] 388 U.S. at 17–19.
[52] Destro at 1219. To be clear, Destro does not commit to the opinion that *Loving* is in fact best understood as a race case.
[53] Ibid. at 1217.

basis for federal oversight of State laws governing marriage, divorce and child custody."[54]

Although race was obviously crucial to *Loving*, it is far too cramped of a reading to assume that the decision turned on race alone. Near the beginning of the decision, the Court addressed the claim of the Supreme Court of Appeals of Virginia (which had upheld the Virginia law) that the regulation of marriage "should be left to exclusive state control." The Virginia court had relied upon the 1888 case, *Maynard v. Hill*. As discussed earlier, that case was decided before the development of modern doctrines of fundamental rights and described marriage as a common-law right that was entirely subject to state regulation. The Court rejected the state court's argument, citing the more recent cases on the right to marry, *Meyer* and *Skinner*:

> While the state court is no doubt correct in asserting that marriage is a social relation subject to the State's police power, *Maynard v. Hill*, the State does not contend in its argument before this Court that its powers to regulate marriage are unlimited notwithstanding the commands of the Fourteenth Amendment. Nor could it do so in light of *Meyer v. Nebraska* and *Skinner v. Oklahoma*.[55]

Because neither *Meyer* nor *Skinner* involved race, it is difficult to see how the Court could be saying only that the state may not ban interracial unions. In fact, the Court has since made it clear that the right to marry extends far beyond protection from racial discrimination. In 1978, in *Zablocki v. Redhail*,[56] the Court stuck down a Wisconsin statute that prohibited a person under a court order to support minor children from marrying without judicial permission. To obtain such permission, the person would have to demonstrate that he or she was in compliance with the support order, and that the children were not public charges or likely to become so. Zablocki was thousands of dollars in arrears in child support payments and was in no financial position to come into compliance soon.

The Court accepted that Wisconsin had "legitimate and substantial interests" at stake – "The permission-to-marry proceeding furnishes an opportunity to counsel the applicant as to the necessity of fulfilling his prior support obligations; and the welfare of the out-of-custody

---

[54] Ibid.
[55] 388 U.S. at 7 (citations omitted).
[56] 434 U.S. 374 (1978).

children is protected."[57] Nonetheless, the justices struck down the statute because "the means selected by the State for achieving these interests unnecessarily impinge on the right to marry."[58] Writing for the Court, Marshall made it as clear as possible that *Loving* was based on two rationales: racial equality and an *independent* constitutional right to marry:

The Court's opinion could have rested solely on the grounds that the statute discriminated on the basis of race in violation of the Equal Protection Clause. But the Court went on to hold that the laws arbitrarily deprived the couple of a fundamental liberty protected by the Due Process Clause, the freedom to marry ... *Although* Loving *arose in the context of racial discrimination, prior and subsequent decisions of this Court confirm that the right to marry is of fundamental importance to all individuals.*[59]

Marshall and the Court majority were certain that the Constitution limits the state's ability to restrict who may marry. The Court did not hold that all state regulation of marriage had to be subject to strict scrutiny. "To the contrary, reasonable regulations that do not significantly interfere with decisions to enter into the marital relationship may legitimately be imposed."[60] Thus, the Court drew a line between regulating marriage and excluding people from entering into marriage. "Under *Zablocki*, the state's power to define the legal relationship of marriage does not encompass the power to exclude persons from it," William M. Hohengarten says.[61]

The next 'right to marry' case to reach the Court was *Turner v. Safley* in 1987,[62] centering on a Missouri state prison regulation that forbade inmates from marrying under almost all circumstances. "The challenged marriage regulation ... permits the inmate to marry only with the permission of the superintendent of the prison, and provides that such approval should be given only 'when there are compelling reasons to do so.'"[63] Missouri argued that prisoner marriages could jeopardize prison security. The situation facing the justices was difficult

[57] 434 U.S. at 388.
[58] Ibid.
[59] 434 U.S. 383–84 (citations omitted, emphasis added).
[60] 434 U.S. at 386.
[61] Hohengarten at 1507.
[62] 482 U.S. 78 (1987).
[63] 482 U.S. at 82.

because prison security and administration, like military affairs, is a sphere in which the Court traditionally defers to the executive and legislative branches of government.[64] If the Court had any doubt at all about whether the right to marry is a fundamental constitutional right, *Turner* presented it with abundant opportunity to express that doubt. Yet neither the Court nor the government expressed such doubt. "In support of the marriage regulation, petitioners first suggest that the rule does not deprive prisoners of a constitutionally protected right. *They concede that the decision to marry is a fundamental right under* Zablocki v. Redhail *and* Loving v. Virginia, but they imply that a different rule should obtain 'in . . . a prison forum.'"[65] Unanimously, the Court[66] rejected even the limited proposition that the fundamental right to marry did not apply in prison, holding, "We disagree with petitioners that *Zablocki* does not apply to prison inmates."[67] The prison had "legitimate security concerns [that] may require placing reasonable restrictions upon an inmates' right to marry . . . [t]he Missouri regulation, however, represents an exaggerated response to such security objectives."[68]

If there had been even a scintilla of doubt about whether there is a fundamental right to marry, *Turner* and *Zablocki* settled the question. As even Wardle, one of the most ardent opponents of same-sex marriage, concedes: "The [Turner] Court did not so hold; the parties merely conceded the point [that there is a fundamental right to marry]. Nevertheless, the Court consistently, easily, unquestioningly and unanimously accepted that concession. After Turner it will be of little value to try to contest that 'the decision to marry is a fundamental right.'"[69]

Conclusion

We have seen that the Court has repeatedly and unequivocally held that there is a constitutionally protected fundamental right to marry.

---

[64] 482 U.S. at 84–85.
[65] 482 U.S. at 94.
[66] The Court was divided over a restriction on prisoner correspondence, but all justices joined the part of the opinion overturning the marriage restrictions.
[67] 482 U.S. at 94.
[68] 482 U.S. at 97–98.
[69] Wardle, Lynn D., "*Loving v. Virginia* and the Constitutional Right to Marry, 1790–1990." *Howard Law Journal* 41 (winter 1998): 289–347, 332.

Also, we have seen that it was among the first fundamental rights the Court recognized, included in opinions at the very dawn of the era of unenumerated constitutional rights, and recognized by liberal and conservative courts alike. Finally, we have seen that the right to marry is broad indeed. Far from being limited to a racial context, it has been applied to individuals whom society has every reason to punish, individuals whose fitness for marriage and parenthood could be doubted. Mr. Zablocki was a "deadbeat dad" who was seriously behind in his child support payments; the plaintiffs in *Turner* were convicted criminals.

But this is merely the beginning of the inquiry. Many important questions remain. Is there is some good reason to believe that same-sex marriage is an exception to this fundamental right to marry? If the right to marry is not limited to traditional marriages, what is the logical stopping point? Does it protect polygamy or incestuous marriages? What harm would it cause society if it does? The next chapter will address these questions.

5

Same-Sex Marriage and the Fundamental Right to Marry

As we have seen, the right to marry is well established. Kenneth Karst enthusiastically proclaims, "*of course* there is a right to marry."[1] Also, Mark Strasser observes, "The question then is not whether the right to marry is fundamental – it clearly is – but whether the fundamental right to marry includes the right to marry one's same-sex partner."[2] The more appropriate question, however, is "Why would same-sex marriage *not* be included under the fundamental right to marry?" In a nation in which the right to marry is constitutionally protected for convicted criminals and parents who fail to make court-ordered child support payments, the right to marry must mean, at a minimum, that the state bears the burden of explaining why gays and lesbians cannot exercise this right.

Three related explanations have been proffered for the exclusion of same-sex marriage from the right to marry:

1. The right to marry is a predicate of the right to procreate and raise children in a traditional family setting.
2. The ability to have children is at the core of marriage.
3. Marriage is by definition dual-gendered.

[1] Karst at 667.
[2] Strasser at 51.

This chapter will argue that these arguments quickly collapse in the face of analytic scrutiny. The next three sections examine each argument in turn.

The Right to Marry as a Primary Right

It has been suggested that the right to marry is a predicate to other rights, rather than a right in and of itself. The idea that the right to marry is simply the logical predicate to procreation and childbearing has been an important and influential part of the debate on same-sex marriage. In this view, marriage is not a free-standing constitutional right, but a right that results from society's interest in the bearing and raising of children in a traditional family setting. Lynn D. Wardle has often emphasized this point. "[In *Meyer*] the constitutional right to marry was directly linked to the traditional family, and it was seen as closely connected to the traditional home into which children were born and in which they would be reared."[3] Each case that elaborates upon the right to marry links it to traditional families or to procreation, Wardle says.

Regarding *Skinner v. Oklahoma*, Wardle argues that its "most important contribution to the evolution of the constitutional 'right-to-marry' doctrine was the direct linkage of procreation with the 'right to marry.' The conjoined rights of marriage and procreation embodied fundamental concerns of society."[4] As for *Griswold v. Connecticut*, "the case underscored that marriage is linked with, and the basis for, the traditional family and child-rearing."[5] Wardle notes that even Justice Marshall ties marriage to children and the traditional family, explicitly mentioning the "decision to marry and raise children in a traditional family setting."[6] Wardle concludes: "Marriage provides the most secure environment in which to bring children into the world, and in which to raise children. For this reason, it has been deemed essential to the survival of the human race. Marriage may sometimes best be understood as a legal relationship created for

[3] Wardle at 299.
[4] Ibid. at 300.
[5] Ibid. at 301.
[6] 434 U.S. at 386.

the benefit of children who grow and flourish best in marriage-based families."[7]

It is not only academic commentators who subscribe to this view of the right to marry. Even the Supreme Court of Hawaii, which held that the same-sex marriage ban is a form of gender discrimination,[8] saw the marriage right as the "logical predicate" to the right to procreate and raise children. It therefore held that the right to marry does not apply to same-sex marriages. As Megan E. Farrell explains, "The *Baehr* court interpreted *Zablocki* to provide an implicit link 'between the right to marry, on the one hand, and the fundamental rights of procreation, childbirth, abortion, and child rearing' because the right to marry 'is simply the logical predicate of the others.'"[9]

Procreation and children, of course, are part of the reason that many people want to marry, and part of the reason that society has an interest in the institution of marriage. But that is very different from the idea that the marriage right is *solely* concerned with children, and that the right does not protect couples who cannot conceive children or raise them in a "traditional family setting." A reference to the right of free speech can help illustrate this point. Courts and scholars have often linked the right of free speech to democratic debate and deliberation,[10] yet it is well settled that freedom of speech covers a great deal of speech that is completely unrelated to democratic debate and deliberation. The sexual images of the Playboy Channel are protected speech, despite their lack of political content[11]; so is advertising the price of liquor.[12] Speech is related to democracy, but "related to" does not mean "the same as." Similarly, marriage might be related to child rearing, but it is far more than a mere child-rearing arrangment. As is obvious to any childless, married couple, there are powerful reasons for being married that are completely unrelated to children. Unsurprisingly, the Supreme Court has never held that the fundamental right to marry is dependant upon or ancillary to a couple's intention or ability to have children.

---

[7] Wardle at 338–339.
[8] Chapter 3, supra, for a critical analysis of this claim.
[9] Farrell at 603, citing *Baehr v. Lewin*, 852 P.2d at 56.
[10] See, e.g., *New York Times Co. v. Sullivan*, 376 U.S. 254 (1964).
[11] *United States v. Playboy Entertainment Group, Inc.*, 120 S. Ct. 1878 (2000).
[12] *44 Liquormart, Inc. v. Rhode Island*, 517 U.S. 484 (1996).

Furthermore, the argument that the right to marry is merely a derivative of reproductive rights ignores the development of both sets of rights. The Court took the position that marriage was a fundamental right long before it ever considered reproductive issues. In *Meyer* in 1923, the justices averred that marriage was "without doubt" among the liberties protected by the Fourteenth Amendment.[13] Not until nineteen years later in *Skinner* did the Court explicitly discuss reproduction, stating that "Marriage and procreation are fundamental to the very existence and survival of the race." The modern doctrine of reproductive freedom began in 1965 with *Griswold*. Justice Douglas's effort to locate a right to contraceptives in the Constitution required him to reach far for support, because there is little in the text or history of that document to point to such a right.[14] He found that support in the marital bedroom. Although the ban on contraceptives applied to married and unmarried couples, Douglas used the understood sacredness of marital privacy to establish the right of sexual privacy, as we have seen.

The Court thus connected marriage and children in a way very different from what many opponents of same-sex marriage suggest. The right to marry preceded *Griswold* by many years; and what Douglas actually said in that case was that marriage includes the right *not* to have children at all. Indeed, in his homage to marriage, Douglas describes it "as an association that promotes a way of life, not causes; a harmony in living not political faiths; a bilateral loyalty, not commercial or social projects."[15] Nothing in phrases such as "a harmony in living" or "a bilateral loyalty" implies that marriage is reserved only for those capable of reproduction or planning to raise children. In fact, the emphasis on harmony in living and bilateral loyalty points to the primacy of the couple's autonomy, instead of their willingness to bear children.

There is really no good reason to believe that the right to marry is derivative of the right to reproductive freedom or the right to raise children in a traditional setting. The Court has never held that it is; such

[13] *Meyer v. Nebraska*, 262 U.S. 390, 399 (1923).
[14] Tushnet, Mark, V., "Two Notes on the Jurisprudence of Privacy," reporting that Justice Douglas' opinion in *Griswold* "is widely regarded among law professors as fatally flawed." *Constitutional Commentary* 8 (1991): 75–86, 75.
[15] Ironically, the only instance in a Supreme Court case that actually involved Douglas' frightening imagery of a police officer in the bedroom involves the arrest of a gay man for committing sodomy in the privacy of his own bedroom, *Bowers v. Hardwick*, 478 U.S. 106 (1986).

a holding would be quite out of step with its jurisprudence on the family. Indeed, although the health and well-being of children is certainly a state concern, the Court has repeatedly held that the Constitution forbids the state from mandating conformity in family structure or child rearing. In *Pierce v. Society of Sisters* in 1925, the Court eloquently explained that the duty to impart values to a child, as well as decisions about the ideas to which a child should be exposed, properly belongs to the parents, not the state. "The child is not the mere creature of the State; those who nurture him and direct his destiny have the right, coupled with the high duty, to recognize and prepare him for additional obligations."[16]

Over and over again, the Court has rejected efforts to create a standardized, governmentally approved family life. In *Moore v. East Cleveland*,[17] it connected the freedom to marry to the freedom to choose one's family structure. Invalidating a single-family zoning ordinance that excluded a grandmother and her two grandsons (who were cousins rather than brothers) from living together as a family, the Court stated:

A host of cases, tracing their lineage to *Meyer v. Nebraska*, and *Pierce v. Society of Sisters*, have consistently acknowledged a 'private realm of family life which the state cannot enter.' Of course, the family is not beyond regulation. But when the government intrudes on choices concerning family living arrangements, this Court must examine carefully the importance of the governmental interests advanced and the extent to which they are served by the challenged regulation.[18]

As noted, the Hawaii Supreme Court interpreted *Zablocki* to mean that the right to marry applies only to dual-gendered couples because the *Zablocki* Court linked marriage to "procreation, childbirth, abortion, and child rearing."[19] The *Baehr* Court cited the following passage from *Zablocki*:

The woman whom appellee desired to marry had a fundamental right to seek an abortion of their expected child or to bring the child into life to suffer the myriad social, if not economic, disabilities that the status of illegitimacy brings. . . . Surely, a decision to marry and raise the child in a traditional family

---

[16] *Pierce v. Society of Sisters*, 268 U.S. 510, 535 (1925).
[17] 431 U.S. 494 (1977).
[18] 431 U.S. at 499 (citations omitted).
[19] 852 P.2d at 56.

setting must receive equivalent protection, and, if appellee's right to procreate means anything at all, it must imply some right to enter the only relationship in which the State of Wisconsin allows sexual relations legally to take place.[20]

This passage clearly does not limit the marriage right to people who can or wish to have children. Justice Marshall was merely noting that it would be ironic if Mr. Zablocki's intended wife were to become pregnant and the Constitution protected her right to have the child out of wedlock, or even to abort the child, but not her right to marry and raise the child in a traditional family setting. This is an excellent point, yet it shows merely that raising a child in a traditional family should not receive *less* protection than aborting the child or having the baby out of wedlock.

Further, Marshall makes this argument in the middle of a long passage in which he outlines the many reasons that the Court considers marriage a fundamental right. In that passage he includes much language about the importance of marriage that is unrelated to having or raising children. Much of this language should now be familiar to the reader: Marriage is "essential to the orderly pursuit of happiness by free men," "the most important relationship in life," an association that promotes "a bilateral loyalty," and "among the personal decisions protected by the right to privacy."[21] All these points are just as applicable to childless couples as to anyone else. To interpret Marshall as saying that marriage is a fundamental right only because it is a precursor to having and raising children is to ignore much of what he wrote.

If there were any doubt about whether the right to marry is merely derivative of the right to bear children or to raise them in a traditional family, it was answered in *Turner*. Recall that *Turner* involved the right of a state prisoner to marry, even though he was still serving his sentence and was obviously in no position to father children at that time, much less to bring them up in a traditional family setting. Although the Court assumed there would be no conjugal visits even if Mr. Safley did get married, it held that many of the purposes of marriage could be fulfilled while he remained incarcerated:

First, inmate marriages, like others, are expressions of emotional support and public commitment.... In addition, many religions recognize marriage as

[20] Ibid., quoting *Zablocki*, 434 U.S. at 386.
[21] 434 U.S. at 383–386.

having spiritual significance; for some inmates and their spouses, therefore, the commitment of marriage may be an exercise of religious faith. . . . Third, most inmates eventually will be released by parole or commutation, and therefore most inmate marriages are formed in the expectation that they ultimately will be fully consummated. Finally, marital status often is a pre-condition to the receipt of government benefits (e.g., Social Security benefits), property rights (e.g., tenancy by the entirety, inheritance rights), and other, less tangible benefits (e.g., legitimation of children born out of wedlock).[22]

The Court's list of these important attributes of marriage makes it crystal clear that the right to marry is not merely a precursor of the right to have children or raise them in a traditional setting. In fact, like Marshall's points about marriage in *Zablocki*, most of these attributes are as applicable to same-sex couples as to heterosexual couples. "Expressions of emotional support and public commitment" apply to all couples. As for marriage as an "exercise of religious faith," recall that in Chapter 2, we saw that many religions recognize same-sex marriages and that even without state sanction, many same-sex couples have sought spiritual or religious fulfillment by participating in religious commitment ceremonies.[23] Regarding the numerous governmental benefits to which spouses are entitled, most would be available to same-sex couples as well as "traditional" couples: Social Security benefits, tenancy in the entirety, and inheritance rights. In fact, the only attribute of marriage that could remotely be construed as inherently heterosexual is that most prisoners would eventually be released and could then "consummate" their marriage. But the Court speaks only about the couple's eventual consummation of the relationship, *not* about the couple's eventually having children or raising them in a traditional family setting. The Court's most thorough discussion of the attributes of marriage barely mentions the issue of having or raising children.

It is also worth noting that the right to marry includes the right to divorce – hardly a hallmark of "traditional" family life or child rearing. In *Boddie v. Connecticut*,[24] the Court held that court fees for indigent persons seeking a divorce violate the Constitution. Opponents of

---

[22] *Turner v. Safley*, 482 U.S. 78 (1987) at 95–96.
[23] Ironically, some have been fired or have had job offers revoked for participating in such ceremonies. See *Shahar v. Bowers*, 120 F. 3d 211 (11th Cir. 1997), *McConnell v. Anderson*, 451 F. 2d 193 (8th Cir. 1971).
[24] 401 U.S. 371 (1971).

same-sex marriage argue that *Boddie* is concerned only with procedure, not a substantive right to divorce,[25] but substance and procedure cannot be so neatly separated. The Court did not create a general right to free access to the courts for indigent parties; for instance, there is no constitutional right to have court fees waived for bankruptcy filings, no matter how poor the person.[26] The justices were quite clear that the Constitution protects access to divorce courts because of the fundamental nature of the right to marriage, which is broad enough to include the right to divorce. "We do not decide that access for all individuals to the courts is a right that is, in all circumstances, guaranteed . . . for, as we have already noted, in the case before us this right is the exclusive precondition to the adjustment of a fundamental human relationship," they said.

Finally, the position that marriage is a fundamental right only as a precursor to having children is illogical. Although the Constitution protects the right to bear children, it also protects the right to avoid having them by using contraceptives, to abort them, to bear them out of wedlock, and to raise them in nontraditional settings. "Implicit in the *Zablocki* court's link between the right to marry, on the one hand, and the fundamental rights of procreation, childbirth, abortion, and child rearing, on the other, is the assumption that the one is simply the logical predicate of the others," the *Baehr* Court said. One can see the link between marriage and child rearing, yet it is difficult to imagine how marriage is the logical predicate of abortion. And the Court has expressly held that the constitutional right to contraception is not limited to married couples,[27] so it certainly has not held that marriage is the necessary prerequisite to sexual relations.

We have seen that the Court has protected the right to contraceptives for married and unmarried couples alike; the right to abortion on demand; the right to free access to divorce courts; the right to marry even if one is failing to support his or her children; the right of felons to marry while still serving their sentences; the right of grandmothers, grandsons and cousins to live together as a legally recognized family; and so on. If the right to marry were solely for the benefit of traditional,

---

[25] Wardle at 311–313.
[26] *U.S. v. Kras*, 409 U.S. 434 (1973).
[27] *Eisenstadt v. Baird*, 405 U.S. 438 (1972).

childbearing families, this would cut against the grain of the great majority of the Court's jurisprudence concerning the Constitution and the family.

Children as the Sine Qua Non of Marriage

Related to the argument that the marriage right is reserved only for dual-gendered, childraising couples is the notion that regardless of what the Court has said, having children is so central to marriage that it makes no sense to protect the right for couples who obviously cannot have them. The state of Vermont, for example, argued that procreation is the defining feature of marriage when it defended its same-sex marriage ban to the state Supreme Court.[28] This argument has been accepted in federal court as well; in *Adams v. Howerton*, the judge held that "the main justification in this age for societal recognition and protection of the institution of marriage is procreation, perpetuation of the race."[29] As we will see, this is perhaps the least supportable of the reasons proffered for denying same-sex couples the right to marry.

The idea that marriage inherently requires the ability to reproduce is utterly foreign to Western traditions. Even John Finnis, who strongly opposes same-sex marriage, concedes that:

The ancient philosophers do not much discuss the case of sterile marriages, or the fact (well known to them) that for long periods of time (e.g. throughout pregnancy) the sexual acts of a married couple are naturally incapable of resulting in reproduction. They appear to take for granted what the subsequent Christian tradition certainly did, that such sterility does not render the conjugal sexual acts of the spouses non-marital. (Plutarch indicates that intercourse with a sterile spouse is a desirable mark of marital esteem and affection.)[30]

Even the Christian moralist St. Augustine stated that companionship is an important goal of marriage and never indicated that sterility voided a marriage.[31]

The idea that marriage requires reproductive ability has no support in contemporary law either. "Opposite-sex couples may marry without

---

[28] Bonauto, et al.
[29] *Adams v. Howerton*, 486 F. Supp. 1119, 1124 (Central District of California 1980).
[30] Finnis at 1067–1068.
[31] Eskridge at 96–97.

showing that they possess either the ability or the intention to have children,"[32] William Hohengarten observes. Why, then, does the issue of fertility prevent same-sex marriages but not infertile dual-gendered marriages? In *Adams*, the Court answered that in the case of dual-gendered couples, sterility tests or inquiries about plans for having children would be too intrusive:

> The state has chosen to allow legal marriage as between all couples of opposite sex. The alternative would be to inquire of each couple, before issuing a marriage license, as to their plans for children and to give sterility tests to all applicants, refusing licenses to those found sterile or unwilling to raise a family. Such tests and inquiries would themselves raise serious constitutional questions.[33]

This reasoning cannot withstand even brief analysis. Some people, such as post-menopausal women, obviously cannot have children; no intrusive inquiries would have to be made to establish the inability of a eighty-year-old woman to bear children. But it is inconceivable that a court or legislature would bar such a woman from marrying for this reason.

In addition, states are perfectly willing to force would-be married couples to take other kinds of intrusive tests. "Most states still require examination for venereal disease and other appropriate clinical testing before marriage," Frank B. Grad notes.[34] If potency and fertility are truly the sine qua non of marriage, then they could be tested for, just as the state tests for venereal disease and other medical conditions. The *Adams* court does not explain why one form of testing is more intrusive than the other. If the primary purpose of marriage were reproduction, surely the state would want to inform a person if his or her intended spouse were infertile, just as it would notify the person about the presence of venereal disease.

The position of the *Adams* court is not only illogical, but also without empirical support. The court makes no effort to discover or demonstrate that concern for undue intrusiveness is the actual reason that states refrain from fertility testing. It is simply unsupported speculation on the court's part – a thin reed upon which to rest a decision of

[32] Hohengarten at 1513–1514.
[33] *Adams*, supra, 486 F. Supp. at 1124–1125.
[34] Grad at 383.

such importance.[35] Unfortunately, this has been the *sole* explanation the courts have given, when they have given one at all, for why the inability to reproduce bars same-sex, but not dual-gendered, couples from marriage.

Further, as Hohengarten has pointed out, divorce and annulment laws make it abundantly clear that potency and fertility are *not* essential components of marriage. He notes that:

If...the primary function of legal marriage is the facilitation of a committed intimate relationship between two adults, then the grounds for divorce and annulment should center on their relationship inter se, without reference to their procreative capacities or accomplishments. An examination of the law of divorce, both before and after the "no-fault" revolution, bears out [this thesis].... Similarly, although the law of annulment does refer to gender-specific sexual roles, it carefully avoids referring to the procreative potential of these roles.[36]

As far back as 1898, moreover, the law was clear that infertile women are eligible to marry: "[I]t cannot be held, as a matter of law, that the possession of the organs necessary to conception are essential to entrance to the marriage state, so long as there is no impediment to the indulgence of the passions incident to that state."[37] It is not logically possible that procreational ability is a vital component of marriage, but the lack of it is not a ground for dissolving that marriage. Because the courts, in the context of divorce proceedings, do not shy away from inquiries about the ability to perform sexually or about other embarrassing and private matters, the *Adams* explanation for why the courts do not inquire about fertility is an extremely poor one.

In sum, nothing in the law indicates that the ability to have children is a vital component of marriage. The courts, frankly, have made up this standard out of thin air, and have applied it only to same-sex couples. Additionally, it is not true that same-sex couples cannot have children; they simply cannot have them via conventional means. Like

---

[35] As discussed in Gerstmann, *The Constitutional Underclass*, the courts have developed an unfortunate habit of denying the constitutional claims of gays and lesbians based upon unsupported pseudosociological speculation such as the repeated assertion that gays and lesbians are too "politically powerful" to require judicial protection from government discrimination. See *The Constitutional Underclass* at 80–90.

[36] Hohengarten, supra, at 1514.

[37] *Wendel v. Wendel*, 52 N.Y.S. 72, 74 (App. Div. 1898) (cited in Hohengarten at n. 84).

many heterosexual couples, lesbians can have children through means such as third-party artificial insemination. Courts have scrupulously protected the parental rights of heterosexual fathers whose wives conceived children via third-party insemination.[38] The heterosexual couples are allowed to marry so the nongenetic parent receives full legal recognition as the child's parent. This legal provision cannot justify allowing only dual-gendered couples to marry, as it is the *result* of the fact that only dual-gendered couples are allowed to marry. The argument that only dual-gendered couples can marry because only they can have children is a tautology.

Marriage as Dual-Gendered by Definition

Chapter 2 examined whether it is rational to ban same-sex marriage simply because marriage has traditionally been defined as dual-gendered. This section examines a similar but distinct question: Does the fundamental right to marry apply only to marriages that fit that relatively narrow dictionary definition of marriage?

As noted, numerous courts and commentators have relied upon traditional and dictionary definitions of marriage to show that same-sex couples cannot be married.[39] There are several fatal problems with their arguments. First, definitions themselves are not beyond the reach of judicial review. As Strasser argues, "The argument is fallacious insofar as it implies that the legislature is not itself responsible for the legal definition of marriage or insofar as it implies that definitions (as opposed to other types of classifications) can escape judicial scrutiny."[40] Even if dictionaries in the 1950s and 1960s had defined marriage as a union between persons of the same race, they would not have saved the Virginia statute at issue in *Loving*.

Courts have consistently ignored the dictionary in defining constitutional rights. Constitutional law would be very different if the courts used dictionary definitions to shape the contours of our rights. The First Amendment protection for freedom of speech is an illuminating example. *Webster's New Collegiate Dictionary* defines "speech" as "the

38 Yaworsky at 295–302.
39 See Chapter 2, supra.
40 Strasser at 922.

communication or expression of thoughts in *spoken words*," "something that is *spoken*," "public *discourse*," an individual manner or style of *speaking*," or "the power of expressing or communicating thoughts through *speaking*." All these definitions make clear that speech is something that is spoken, yet freedom of speech protects much more than the spoken word. For constitutional purposes, speech includes wearing black armbands to school, silent picketing, donating money to political candidates, burning the American flag, and printing pornographic cartoons.[41] If the Court relied upon the dictionary to define the right to free speech, that right would be drastically narrower.

The Court has also explicitly rejected the dictionary definition of "search" in interpreting the Fourth Amendment. In a recent case involving a thermal-imaging device that measured heat radiating from a private home,[42] the majority opinion rejected *Webster's American Dictionary of the English Language*.[43] Citing *Webster's*, Justice Antonin Scalia observed that "When the Fourth Amendment was adopted, as now, to 'search' meant 'to look over or through for the purpose of finding something; to explore; to examine by inspection; as to search the house for a book; to search the wood for a thief.'" Scalia noted that the Court pays this definition no heed: "One might think that the new validating rationale would be that examining the portion of a house that is in plain public view, while it is a 'search' [according to the dictionary] despite the absence of trespass, is not an 'unreasonable' one under the Fourth Amendment. But in fact we have held that visual observation is no 'search' at all."[44]

With the argument about fertility, however, the dictionary definition argument is used to reject same-sex marriage and then tucked away again in other contexts. Even if we were to refer sometimes to dictionaries to define constitutional rights, it would be particularly inappropriate in the case of marriage. As we saw in Chapter 2, the law

---

[41] See, respectively, *Tinker v. Des Moines School District*, 393 U.S. 503 (1969); *Chicago Police Department v. Mosley*, 408 U.S. 92 (1972); *Buckley v. Valeo*, 424 U.S. 1 (1976); *Texas v. Johnson*, 491 U.S. 397 (1989); and *Hustler Magazine v. Falwell*, 485 U.S. 46 (1988).

[42] *Kyllo v. U.S.* 533 U.S. 27 (2001).

[43] Webster, Noah. *An American Dictionary of the English Language* 66 (1828) (6th ed. 1989).

[44] *Kyllo v. U.S.* 533 U.S. 27, 32 (2001).

of marriage was once deeply sexist, with the husband as master of the wife.[45] Of course, marriage was defined as dual-gendered; without a woman, who would occupy the legally subordinate role? Rigid reliance on longstanding dictionary definitions makes even less sense in the case of marriage than it does in the other examples discussed above.

The Court consistently defines rights according to their underlying purposes. Speech is defined as that which has a specific expressive intent and which is likely to be so understood;[46] a search is defined by reference to a person's expectation of privacy.[47] As discussed, there is nothing about same-sex couples that precludes them from enjoying many of what the Court has defined as the purposes of marriage, even if one regards homosexuality as immoral. Unless the Court drastically alters its method of constitutional interpretation, dictionary definitions do not justify the disqualification of same-sex couples from the fundamental right to marriage.

Of Nature and Intuition

If the arguments against same-sex marriage discussed in this chapter are so weak, why have the courts been so reluctant to hold that the long-established fundamental right to marry applies to same-sex marriage? Judges are reluctant to speak publicly about cases that might again come before them, so the answer here is necessarily speculative.

One probable answer is the overwhelming intuition that marriage is *naturally* heterosexual. Intuitions about what God or nature intended can be very powerful for us, although they can also be disastrously misleading, and we should be skeptical of them, even when they are our own. The Virginia judge who upheld that state's antimiscegenation laws in *Loving* opined: "Almighty God created the races white, black, yellow, malay and red, and he placed them on separate continents. . . . The fact that he separated the races shows that he did not intend for the races to mix."[48] The idea that interracial marriage is

---

[45] See Chapter 2, supra.
[46] *Texas v. Johnson*, 491 U.S. 397 (1989).
[47] *Kyllo*, supra.
[48] 388 U.S. 1, 3 (1967).

unnatural or against God's will because God put the races on different continents had an internal logic for its proponents – just as the idea that same-sex marriage is unnatural has logic for the heterosexual majority. "Was there ever any domination which did not appear natural to those who possessed it?" asked the great political thinker John Stuart Mill.[49]

But intuitions about nature are not the only reasons cited for opposition to same-sex marriage. Judges, political leaders, and commentators have expressed more substantive concerns, among them the specters of polygamy and incest, which have haunted the debate over same-sex marriage even before it really started. If there is a fundamental right to marry that is not confined by tradition, nature, and so forth, what is the logical stopping point? Will society go down the slippery slope to marital anarchy, in which the public will be forced to accept marriages to many spouses or to one's brother or sister? Much more challenging than the issues discussed above, these questions represent legitimate concerns, and advocates of same-sex marriage have not always addressed them honestly. These issues will be addressed in the following sections.

Polygamy and the Fundamental Right to Marry

The argument that there is a fundamental right to marriage that applies to same-sex marriage threatens conventional morality in ways that extend beyond the issue of homosexuality. Polygamists and practitioners of incest could argue that such a right protects them as well, a possibility very much on Justice Potter Stewart's mind when he declined to join the majority in *Zablocki*. He warned that the Court's support for a fundamental right to marry could open the door to all three forms of prohibited marriage, writing that "A 'compelling state purpose' inquiry would cast doubt on the network of restrictions that the States have fashioned to govern marriage and divorce."[50]

Stewart was not alone in these fears. Many opponents of same-sex marriage have expressed concerns that if society allows same-sex

---

[49] Mill, John Stuart. "The Subjection of Women," in *Essays on Sex Equality*, Alice S. Rossi, ed. Chicago: University of Chicago Press, 1970, at 137.

[50] 434 U.S. 374, 399.

marriage, it would have to allow polygamy. Numerous Republican congressmen, in addition to noted political commentators William Bennett, George Will, Robert Bork, and William Safire, have made similar arguments.[51] Also, during congressional hearings on the Defense of Marriage Act, the analogy between polygamy and same-sex marriage was a dominant theme.[52] Many prominent liberal academics have been circumspect on this point, perhaps because polygamists, mostly associated with Mormons in the public mind, are not as popular in the academy or with the political left as are gays and lesbians.[53] Among the many law review articles on same-sex marriage, the vast majority of which support it,[54] apparently not one has argued that polygamists are also entitled to enter into unconventional marriages.[55] When academics have addressed polygamy, they treated it with the sort of contempt or indifference that they decry when directed at other marginalized people.

The otherwise careful William Eskridge attempts to dismiss polygamy as patriarchal, arguing that "allowing a man to take two wives might create or exacerbate hierarchical structures within the marriage. As the center of competition, the husband would be able to play one wife against the other."[56] This vague, speculative generalizing about the potential evils of nontraditional families is exactly the

---

[51] Sullivan, Andrew, "Three's a Crowd," *The New Republic* (June 17, 1996) at p. 10; Chambers, David, "Polygamy and Same Sex Marriage." *Hofstra Law Review* 26 (1997): 51–61, 53.

[52] Ibid.

[53] See Chambers, 54. "In the United States, polygamy has been regarded with hostility by the right, the middle and the left – today and in the past."

[54] Wardle at 837. "Only one of the seventy-two pieces published in the nineties unequivocally supports the rule of exclusive heterosexual marriage, while sixty-seven pieces advocate or support same-sex marriage. Thus, the ratio of recent law review literature that favors same-sex marriage to that opposing it is roughly 67:1 – hardly a record of a fair exchange or serious examination."

[55] A partial exception is Chambers, David, "Polygamy and Same Sex Marriage," 81, which discusses the claims and history of polygamists sympathetically, although Chambers demurs, "at a time when no group in the United States is seriously lobbying for plural marriage, I have no desire to become its champion." Mark Strasser, in *Legally Wed: Same-Sex Marriage and the Constitution*, at p. 65, also discusses this point very briefly, stating if courts were to strike down bigamy and incest laws under strict scrutiny, "then the state restrictions on bigamy and incest, for example, must not be serving important state interests and arguably should be invalidated."

[56] Eskridge, *The Case for Same-Sex Marriage*, at 149.

sort of attack that has so often been used against same-sex couples. Richard F. Duncan points out that "Eskridge cites no data supporting these conclusory assertions."[57] A second problem with Eskridge's analysis is that it is inapplicable to polyandry, the practice of a wife taking more than one husband. There might be some justification for this because the practice is less common than that of a man taking multiple wives. But if patriarchy is the primary evil of polygamy, this suggests there is no problem with polyandry. The focus on multiple wives suffers from the same problem as the gender discrimination argument critiqued in Chapter 3: It is an attempt to shoehorn a complex social issue into the more familiar (and less threatening) category of gender discrimination.

Furthermore, the argument equating polygamy with patriarchy is oddly indifferent to the views of the very women whom the polygamy ban purportedly protects. David Chambers, one of the very few academics who have given genuine consideration to the perspective of polygamists, writes of the oft-repeated assertion that polygamy oppresses women:

> At many points in the political attack on the Church, large numbers of Mormon women joined together to speak publicly in support of plural marriage and to affirm that polygamous husbands were living up to the highest callings of their religions.... there is no reason to doubt the sincerity of these women's beliefs in the sacred meaning of plural marriage.... These women and their children seem to have lived lives that were as satisfying as the lives of most of their contemporaries.[58]

In fact, there is substantial empirical evidence that the stereotype of women in polygamous marriages competing with one another for the husband's attention, bearing huge numbers of children with distant relationships from the one father, is a myth. Chambers points to Jessie Embry's study of Mormon plural-marriage families in the late nineteenth century, which concludes that "plural wives established harmonious relationships with each other and tolerable relations with their

---

57 Duncan, Robert F., "Symposium: *Romer v. Evans*: The Narrow and Shallow Bite of Romer and the Eminent Rationality of Dual-Gender Marriage: A (Partial) Response to Professor Koppelman." *William and Mary Bill of Rights Journal* 6 (1994): 147–166, 164, n.98.

58 Chambers, David, "Polygamy and Same Sex Marriage." *Hofstra Law Review* 26 (fall 1997): 66–67 (citations omitted).

husbands. Many children, perhaps most, had relationships with their fathers typical of other children of their era. Commonly, the children formed close relationships with both their mothers and their fathers' other wives. Women in plural marriages were motivated by the sacred function of plural marriage to strive to make the complex and awkward familial relationships succeed."[59] Mormon women in Utah in that century also had greater economic independence than their counterparts back east, despite polygamy. Historian Julie Roy Jeffrey says: "The goals of self-sufficiency and productivity led the Church to encourage and praise those women who became producers.... As one female traveler observed, 'They close no career on a woman in Utah by which she can earn a living.'"[60]

Eskridge argues that multiple spouses could undermine the "companionate" aspect of marriage and diminish "the intensity of the emotional bond" between spouses. Again, however, there is no empirical support for this claim. As with the patriarchy argument, this is the sort of seat-of-the-pants sociology that some have used to paint same-sex relationships as shallow, perverse, and so forth.[61] Chambers says that "To my reading, the actual experience of American men and women in plural marriages seems more complex and less sinister than [Maura] Strassberg portrays them and than Eskridge imagines them. Many people in plural marriages find temporal and religious satisfactions that greatly outweigh their disadvantages."[62]

Other critics of polygamous marriage argue that polygamy "has been rife with abuses – including forced marriages, sexual exploitation of minors, and welfare dependency."[63] This is the sort of fallacious argument that all social scientists should avoid. When a lifestyle is illegal and driven underground, that can lead its practitioners toward antisocial behavior. We should not blithely conclude that such antisocial behavior is inherent in the lifestyle itself. This is the fallacy so often directed at gays and lesbians who are banned from marrying and then

---

[59] Ibid.
[60] Jeffrey, Julie Roy. *Frontier Women: Civilizing the West? 1840–1880*, rev. ed. New York: Hill and Wang, 1998.
[61] See Gerstmann, at chapter 4, for examples of how the Supreme Court's willingness to rely upon unsupported pseudosociological assertions about gays and lesbians harms legal equality.
[62] See Chambers, David, "Polygamy and Same Sex Marriage," at 81.
[63] See Chapman, Steve.

chided for promiscuity. Steve Chapman writes:

Such unsavory conduct stems partly from the fact that when polygamy is illegal, the only people likely to practice it are nut cases and people with a deep-seated contempt for authority. Plural marriage, in this group, may be just one of many expressions of aggressive nonconformity. If the practice were legally permitted, on the other hand, it would be more likely to attract people with a strong law-abiding disposition. The need to stay under the radar of law enforcement agencies also breeds abuse by discouraging its victims from going to the authorities. Legalizing the practice would bring polygamists out from underground, making it easier to combat the real evils found in some plural marriages. Those who persist in such abuses can be prosecuted along with all the other pedophiles and welfare frauds – the vast majority of whom, it will surprise you to learn, are non-polygamous.[64]

Indeed, it is surprisingly difficult to articulate why it is perfectly legal for a man to sleep with many women and have children by all of them, even though it is illegal for that man to marry those women. "If consenting adults who prefer polygamy can do everything else a husband and wife can do – have sex, live together, buy property, and bring up children jointly – why should they be prohibited from legally committing themselves to the solemn duties that attach to marriage?" Chapman asks. "How is society worse off if these informal relationships are formalized and pushed toward permanence?"[65]

The history of American treatment of polygamists hardly supports the notion that the practice is banned out of concern for women's rights or for any of the more palatable reasons offered today. Our treatment of polygamy is rife with racism, sexism, intolerance, and extremism. Attempts to destroy the Mormon Church and polygamy led Congress to violate such basic civil rights such as jury service, property ownership, and even the vote for women, Chambers writes:

[Congress] began in 1862 by banning polygamy in the territories. Several years later, it enacted additional legislation declaring that in order to be eligible to vote in the territories, men had to take an oath that they were not cohabiting with more than one woman. It also barred polygynists from jury service and political office. Finally, in 1887, in an astonishing gesture, Congress invalidated the corporation of the Mormon Church itself, authorizing the escheat to the

[64] Ibid.
[65] Ibid.

United States of all Church property not used exclusively for religious purposes. In the same Act, unhappy that Mormon women continued to vote for Mormon candidates, it took away from women the right to vote.[66]

When the Supreme Court was asked to rule upon polygamy, its holding was steeped in racism and nativism. "Polygamy has always been odious among the northern and western nations of Europe, and, until the establishment of the Mormon Church, was almost exclusively a feature of the life of Asiatic and of African people," justices wrote.[67] The Court apparently assumed that a practice's association with non-whites was convincing evidence of its degraded nature.

It must be emphasized that my argument here is *not* that polygamy is a positive institution or that it should be legalized. My argument, first, is that the position that gays and lesbians have the fundamental right to marry someone of their own gender leads many people to worry that polygamists would be protected as well, which may better account for judicial hostility to same-sex marriage than do the very weak explanations offered by the courts themselves. Second, liberal and left-leaning academics and lawyers have responded by avoiding the fundamental rights argument, preferring the analytically weaker gender discrimination argument because it helps gays and lesbians but not polygamists or other groups to which they may be unsympathetic. Third, advocates of same-sex marriage should take the same hard look at the reasons for banning polygamy that they are asking heterosexuals to do with same-sex marriage. In evaluating ways of living, we must not rely upon mere speculation or intuitions that support our prejudices; we should hold ourselves to stringent standards of evidence. Gays, lesbians, and their allies should not compromise these high standards when critiquing nontraditional families that are vilified even more than are same-sex couples.

Nonetheless, it is quite possible to distinguish same-sex marriage from polygamy without resorting to unsupported, stereotype-based attacks. There certainly seems to be a difference between a right to marry *who* you want and marrying *however many* people you want. Multiple marriages raise several legitimate state concerns that same-sex marriage does not. Eskridge has made a credible argument that

---

[66] See Chambers, David, at 63–64.
[67] *Reynolds v. United States*, 98 U.S. 145, 164 (1879).

polygamy threatens the social safety net by diluting social insurance;[68] if a polygamist dies, presumably several spouses would have to divide his or her Social Security survivor's benefits, for instance. Polygamy could create confusion over issues of custody, who has final say over medical decisions in the case of an incapacitated spouse, and so forth. Multiple wives might increase incidence of incest (a topic to be discussed shortly) between half-siblings. Finally and most importantly, a right to multiple spouses has no logical stopping point. If a person can have two wives, then why not twenty, fifty, or a thousand? What would stop a whole town or religious cult from marrying and gaining the legal privileges of marriage?

So, there can be a strong case made for the ban on polygamy. Still, polygamists have the same right as same-sex couples to go to court and demand that the state give real reasons – not just stereotypes and unsupported generalizations – for banning their marriage. Because the polygamy issue clearly shadows same-sex marriage, advocates of the latter need to address the differences and similarities between these two forms of nontraditional marriage more honestly.

Incest and the Fundamental Right to Marry

The issue of incestuous marriage has also shadowed same-sex marriage. If one may marry another of the same gender, the argument goes, then why not a close relative? This is a viscerally powerful argument because incest is such a strong taboo. "The mere word 'incest' triggers strong feelings of revulsion in most people," Carolyn S. Bratt notes.[69]

It is far easier to distinguish incestuous marriage from same-sex marriage because of the strong genetic concerns that incest raises.[70] But even in this case, society has been quick to judge and slow to analyze the quality of its own argument. Contrary to popular myth, consanguineous mating (mating among genetically related people) does not increase the number of defective genes in offspring. "Rather, such matings increase the probability that the spouses both carry an identical

---

[68] See Eskridge at 148–149.
[69] See Bratt at 257–297.
[70] Jaber, L, G. Halpern, and M. Shohot, "The Impact of Consanguinity Worldwide." *Community Genetics* 1 (1998): 12–17.

recessive gene which will be passed to the offspring in the double dose necessary for the expression of the trait associated with that recessive gene," Bratt says.[71] This danger is quite small, especially for first cousins.[72] In fact, there is a credible argument that incest statutes "may actually increase the likelihood of deleterious recessive gene traits appearing in future generations," she writes.[73]

More important, the incest ban stands alone among laws in its protection of the gene pool. Society does not prohibit the marriage of people with grave genetic disorders that they will pass on to their children; nor does it prevent such people from marrying others with similar conditions that make the genetic risks even higher. If the law prevented two unrelated people from marrying because of their undesirable genetic combination, the public would no doubt consider that cruel. Furthermore, nothing requires incestuous couples to have children in an age of consistently effective birth control. Ironically, should birth control fail, the Constitution protects the woman's right to abort the child, although not her right to marry the father should she decide to bring the child to term. Also, incestuous couples have the option of adopting or of using third-party donors to have children, as do thousands of "mainstream" married couples.

The best policy argument against incest has nothing to do with genetics and everything to do with the protection of minor children. The protection of children from sexual exploitation is among the most compelling of state interests and overrides any constitutional rights.[74] Many incidents of sexual abuse of children, especially girls, are incestuous, occur at a shockingly high rate,[75] and result in trauma that is

---

[71] See Bratt at 271.

[72] Ibid. at 272–273.

[73] Ibid. at 274. "If incest statutes prevent the coming together of two recessive genes in the present generation, the gene will be disbursed throughout the population in general."

[74] See *New York v. Ferber*, 458 U.S. 747, 757 (1982). The "prevention of sexual exploitation and abuse of children constitutes a government objective of surpassing importance." The Court upheld a criminal conviction for selling child pornography, even though the state had not shown the material was obscene under the First Amendment.

[75] Herman, Judith, Diana Russell, and Karen Trocki, "Long-term Effects of Incestuous Abuse in Childhood." *American Journal of Psychiatry* 143 (1986): 1293–1296, 1293. "Sexual abuse of children is now recognized as a serious mental health problem, both because it is so widespread and because of increasing evidence of its traumatic

likely to be severe.[76] Society has an extremely compelling interest in doing everything it can to prevent fathers and brothers from viewing their daughters and sisters in a sexualized manner. As Karst points out, "incest laws forbidding parent-child marriage are arguably sustainable even when the child is mature, on the theory that parental authority established during one's childhood may have a lasting impact, dominating what would otherwise be the child's freedom of choice."[77] Not surprisingly, the vast majority of criminal prosecutions for incest involve sexual abuse of children.[78]

Even the ban on incestuous marriage requires caveats, however. There are situations in which the fundamental right to marry might protect relatives who seek to wed. Karst asks:

> But what shall we make of the recent tragic case in which a brother and sister, who had grown up in separate adoptive families without knowing of each other's existence, found each other as adults, loved each other, and married? What the Commonwealth of Massachusetts made of it was a crime. The couple pleaded guilty, and were convicted of incest, fined $100 each and placed on probation.[79]

It is not unthinkable that such consenting adults might be entitled to Supreme Court protection of their marriage right, or that first cousins who did not grow up together in a family setting might have a valid constitutional claim to wed. As the Kansas Supreme Court has observed, "First-cousin marriages were not prohibited at common law...and

---

effects. Large-scale surveys of nonclinical populations yield current estimates that the risk of victimization may be as high as one in 10 for boys and greater than one in three for girls. Girls appear to be quite vulnerable to sexual abuse by family members; in a probability survey of more than 900 women, 16% reported sexual abuse by a relative and 4.5% reported sexual abuse by a father or stepfather before age 18."

[76] Ibid. "Clinical studies of child victims evaluated when sexual abuse is discovered consistently report a symptom picture of posttraumatic stress disorder. It is clear that for some victimized children these symptoms may persist over many years and into adult life. The resultant impairments of ego functioning and social relatedness increase the likelihood that victims of childhood sexual abuse will present at some point in their lives as psychiatric patients. Indeed, a very high percentage of psychiatric patients have been found to have a history of abuse."

[77] See Karst at 672.

[78] See Bratt at 257–258.

[79] See Karst at 672.

such marriages were not Biblically prohibited."[80] Thus, even those who
believe that the fundamental right to marry is limited to "traditional"
marriage might find merit to this claim.

The fundamental right to marriage, then, could be applicable even
to some limited categories of incestuous marriage. Still, this would not
lead to the wholesale collapse of prohibitions against such unions. It
would mean that these laws would be subject to heightened judicial
scrutiny, so states would be called upon to set forth their reasons for
them and to demonstrate that the prohibitions are connected to the
achievement of these objectives in the modern world. The prohibitions
would have to be based upon reasoned policymaking, not visceral an-
tipathy or force of habit. This is not so drastic, for there is nothing natural or inevitable about what is defined as incest in the United States;
Sweden, for example, allows marriage between half-siblings, even
though it is banned in the United States.[81] Requiring states to give a
reasoned explanation of their incest laws would probably be quite positive. If states are forced to take a fresh look at this issue, they might find
that although incest is sometimes defined too broadly, at other times it is
defined in a dangerously narrow fashion. Milton C. Regan Jr. observes
that anti-incest laws "often do not apply to stepparents and stepchil-
dren, to forms of abuse not involving marriage or sexual intercourse,
or to caretakers who may not be family members. One can easily argue,
then, that incest statutes are a crude form of regulation that sweeps both
too broadly and too narrowly."[82] Therefore, even if the courts apply
the right to marry to incestuous couples, there would merely be a productive rationalizing of the law. The prohibition on close relatives marrying would doubtless be upheld under nearly all circumstances. Some
first cousin marriages might be protected, particularly if the relationship began during adulthood, but states would also be forced to take
a fresh look at their incest laws and modify them to emphasize protection against child abuse. Many sexual relationships that currently are
not always defined as incestuous, such as relationships between step-
siblings, would probably be banned once states modified their laws to
emphasize child protection as the governmental interest at stake.

[80] *In the Matter of the Estate of Owen C. Loughmiller,* 629 P. 2d. 156, 158 (1981).
[81] Regan at 1523.
[82] Ibid. at 1525.

To some, even limited tolerance of certain instances of what is currently defined as incest, or the earlier discussion of polygamy, is shocking or repulsive. Yet the Constitution has a well-established history of protecting that which most people find shocking and repulsive. If the fundamental right to marry did not protect some things that shock and repulse most people, it would be a uniquely narrow right. The right to religious freedom protects not only "traditional" religions and religious practices, but also practices that many people find more repulsive than anything the Mormons ever practiced. The Court has protected the right of practitioners of the Santeria religion (often conflated with "voodoo") to commit animal sacrifices.[83] Nazism is one of the most despicable ideologies in the history of the world, but the right of jack-booted Nazis to march in a town populated largely by Holocaust survivors is protected pursuant to the rights of free speech and free association.[84]

The point is not to argue for the merits of polygamy or incest, any more than it is to argue for the merits of animal sacrifice or Nazism. Constitutional liberties are often exercised in ways that are disturbing or unwise. But when the government is legislating in the areas of human aspiration that the Court has defined as our fundamental rights, among them speech, religion, and marriage, we must take a second look at things that shock us. We must ask hard questions about what we are trying to prevent, and whether current laws achieve those goals.

Conclusion

Although marriage is a public act, marriage is among the most personal of all decisions. It is difficult to conceive of ourselves as morally autonomous human beings without the freedom to marry the person we love; thus, it is not surprising that marriage has long been considered one of our fundamental rights. With the great rights of freedom of speech, of religion, and of protection from unreasonable incursions into our homes, it limits government interference with our basic choices.

---

[83] *Church of Lukumi Babalu Aye, Inc. v. Hialeah*, 508 U.S. 520 (1993).
[84] *Collin v. Smith*, 578 F.2d 1197 (7th. Cir. 1978).

Because marriage is so important, it arouses intense feelings in many people. It is a subject about which emotions often overpower our capacity for analysis. The argument in this chapter might appear inflammatory to some readers, but it is no more than a straightforward set of conclusions that logically stem from long constitutional protection for the fundamental right to marry. To summarize:

1. There is a well-established, fundamental constitutional right to marry that is not limited to child-bearing couples.
2. There is no reason that this right does not apply to same-sex marriage; at any rate, courts have not yet articulated such a reason.
3. One of the reasons that judges, legislators, and even many advocates of same-sex marriage have shied away from this argument is the fear that it could apply to polygamy and incest.
4. This fear is greatly exaggerated. There is no reason that the Court should not apply the same strict scrutiny to any form of prohibited marriage that it has applied to laws banning marriage involving interracial couples, felons, or people in arrears on child support. Doing so will not lead to marital anarchy. It will mean simply that states will have to explain and rationalize more thoroughly their restrictions on marriage, as they must for restrictions on speech and association. Some restrictions, including the same-sex marriage ban, would probably be struck down. Others, such as incest restrictions, would undoubtedly be upheld, although there might be some changes at the margins that would probably result in greater protection for children.

The central argument of this book – that the Constitution has, does, and should protect everyone's fundamental right to marry the person of his or her choice – does not require gays and lesbians to ask for "special" rights or protections, or to shape their arguments into gender-bias claims. It allows them to frame their arguments in terms of equality instead of difference, in terms of aspiration instead of victimhood. Gays and lesbians are asking for nothing more than what heterosexuals have long since granted to themselves: freedom to marry the person they love, regardless of what anyone else thinks.

This argument gives rise to key questions. Was the Court correct in finding a right to marry in the Constitution? Where in the Constitution does it originate? Would strong judicial intervention in the same-sex marriage debate be appropriate in a democratic society? Even if the answer is "yes," would it be wise? What would be the likely effect of such intervention in the world beyond the courtroom? This book shall take up these questions in the next two chapters.

PART III

RIGHTS AND EQUALITY

6

Should Courts Create New Rights?

We have seen there is ample, longstanding precedent for the right to marry and that nothing in the reasoning of these Supreme Court decisions excludes same-sex marriage. But are these *good* decisions? Just because the Court says something does not make it right. Posner correctly warns against freely attacking the validity of disliked precedents and merely assuming the validity of favorable cases. He calls this the "'heads I win, tails you lose' kind of argument," in which "if a judicial decision favors the arguer's position, the decision is treated as having intrinsic authority, quite apart from the soundness of its reasoning."[1] Defenders of racial segregation in schools who simply relied upon state and federal Court decisions upholding that practice were not making much of an argument, even before the Supreme Court overturned those decisions in *Brown v. Board of Education*.

Advocates of the fundamental right to marry must do more than point out the Court has said there is such a right. This is no easy task. Posner made his criticism of "heads I win, tails you lose" regarding Eskridge's use of a case involving freedom of speech. Although freedom of speech is a very controversial issue, the Court's free speech jurisprudence is well developed and articulated; as I shall argue, it is the model the Court should follow in developing fundamental rights. Unfortunately, the same cannot be said for the Court's fundamental rights jurisprudence. Prior to any reasonable analysis of whether

[1] See Posner at 55.

marriage should be considered a fundamental right, it is therefore necessary to sort through this constitutional quagmire and see if there are actually any agreed upon standards for addressing this question.

Defining Fundamental Rights and Their Origins

The Court's fundamental rights jurisprudence is a shambles in just about every possible way, as the justices have been unable to articulate a consistent theory to explain which rights qualify as fundamental. Discussing *Moore v. East Cleveland*,[2] Joseph Grano writes that the decision "demonstrates both how elusive the search for sources of fundamental rights can be and how unsatisfying the Court's attempts at demonstration necessarily are."[3] In *Moore*, Justice Lewis Powell averred that the fundamental right to define one's own family structure "is deeply rooted in the Nation's history and tradition."[4] Grano points out that "the Court could not have intended to become constitutionally committed to every practice rooted in our history and tradition. In particular, progress toward racial and sexual equality depends upon success in freeing ourselves from the yoke of history and tradition."[5]

Struggling mightily to define what is a fundamental right, the Court has vacillated among at least four separate tests. Justices have asked whether the right is "deeply rooted in this Nation's history and tradition," as they did in *Moore*. They have also asked whether the right is "explicitly or implicitly protected by the Constitution" and whether the right is "implicit in the concept of ordered liberty."[6] Finally, the Court has said the delineation of fundamental rights is a matter of "reasoned judgment."[7] All these standards are extremely vague; Socrates himself would no doubt struggle to tell us what rights are "implicit in ordered liberty" or are products of "reasoned judgment." Not surprisingly, many commentators have "criticize[d] fundamental rights analysis [as]

---

[2] 431 U.S. 494 (1977).
[3] See Grano at 1337.
[4] *Moore v. East Cleveland*, 431 U.S. 494, 503 (1977).
[5] See Grano at 1337.
[6] See, respectively, *San Antonio Independent School District v. Rodriguez*, 411 U.S. 1, 17 (1973); *Palko v. Connecticut*, 302 U.S. 319, 325 (1937). See Clark.
[7] *Planned Parenthood v. Casey*, 505 U.S. 833, 849 (1992).

being too subjective, allowing judges to protect those rights that they deem important."[8]

Furthermore, the justices have been unable even to settle upon what part of the Constitution they are ostensibly interpreting when they declare something to be a fundamental right. Sometimes the Court finds fundamental rights in the due process clause of the Fourteenth Amendment;[9] sometimes it finds them in the equal protection clause;[10] and sometimes it cannot agree upon the source. Ira Lupu sums up the Court's confusion in his article, "Untangling the Strands of the Fourteenth Amendment":

Which new rights properly derive from the liberty strand, and which from the equality strand? Sometimes the Court tells us; other times it does not. Often, members of the Court agree upon the preferred status of an interest but disagree about its textual source. On occasion, members of the Court concede that an interest has no textual source, yet battle still over which strand of the fourteenth amendment protects it from state interference.[11]

Sometimes the justices put aside the Fourteenth Amendment altogether and find a fundamental right in "penumbras" of Amendments in the Bill of Rights, as they did when they found a fundamental right to "privacy" in *Griswold v. Connecticut*.[12] This approach has been widely derided. Lupu accuses the *Griswold* Court of having "tortured the Bill of Rights into yielding a protected zone of privacy that would not tolerate a law banning contraceptive use by married couples."[13] Another commentator describes the *Griswold* Court as having "skipped through the Bill of Rights like a cheerleader – 'give me a P . . . give me an R . . . an I . . .' and so on, and found P-R-I-V-A-C-Y as a derivative or penumbral right."[14]

For reasons having more to do with history and political strategy than with any jurisprudential theory,[15] the Court has simply bounced

---

[8] Clark at 603, citing John Hart Ely, *Democracy and Distrust: A Theory of Judicial Review*. Cambridge: Harvard University Press, 1980, and Alexander Bickel, *The Least Dangerous Branch*. Indianapolis: Bobbs-Merrill, 1962.

[9] *Roe v. Wade*, 410 U.S. 113 (1973).

[10] *Eisenstadt v. Baird*, 405 U.S. 438 (1972).

[11] Lupu at 984.

[12] See discussion in Chapter 4, supra.

[13] Lupu at 994.

[14] Dixon at 84.

[15] This section draws heavily upon Ira C. Lupu's excellent article, "Untangling the Strands of the Fourteenth Amendment" supra.

from clause to clause of the Constitution in order to protect various nontextual rights. During *Lochner*-era enforcement of laissez-faire capitalism, it derived fundamental rights from the due process clause, which says states cannot "deprive any person of life, liberty or property without due process of law." Under the doctrine of "substantive due process," the justices construed liberty to include a variety of economic freedoms as well as the right to marry. They generally ignored the equal protection clause, and when they did mention it, they did so contemptuously, dismissing it in one case as "the usual last resort of constitutional argument."[16]

Much of the subsequent history of fundamental rights can best be understood as various incarnations of the Court switching back and forth over the decades between the due process and equal protection clauses to distance themselves from the reputation and direction of the previous Court. As discussed, history has not kindly judged the *Lochner* Court, which is notorious for having "worked a reign of terror on attempted regulation of wages, hours of labor, and unionization."[17] After the Court's defeat at the hands of President Franklin Roosevelt in the court-packing battle, it entered a period of relative passivity until the 1950s.[18] Except for *Skinner*, a case that involved forced sterilization, the justices did little with the due process clause or the equal protection clause except for "occasional matters of race."[19] Then the Warren Court ushered in a second age of fundamental rights, built on the foundation of equal protection rather than liberty and due process. Under Chief Justice Earl Warren, the Court used the equal protection clause to find several fundamental rights, including the right to interstate travel in *Shapiro v. Thompson* and the right to vote in *Harper v. Virginia Board of Elections*.[20] All too eager to repudiate the substantive due process cases of the *Lochner* era, the Court declined even to mention the due process clause in *Shapiro* or *Harper*. This was especially striking in the latter case because it involved a poll tax, which could easily be seen as a process issue.

---

[16] *Buck v. Bell*, 274 U.S. 200, 208 (1926).
[17] Lupu at 986.
[18] Ibid. at 989.
[19] Ibid.
[20] Respectively, 394 U.S. 618 (1969) and 383 U.S. 663 (1966).

Indeed, to protect itself from charges of "Lochnerism,"[21] the Warren Court was willing to go to seemingly any length to avoid reliance upon the dreaded due process clause. In *Bolling v. Sharpe* in 1954, the Court held it unconstitutional for the federal government to segregate schools by race. Yet unlike its decision in *Brown*, which invalidated school segregation by states, as opposed to the federal government, the Court's decision could not rely upon the Fourteenth Amendment, because that Amendment applies only to the states. The Fifth Amendment applies to the federal government and includes a federal version of the due process clause, but not of the equal protection clause. Justices were therefore forced to rely on the Fifth Amendment's due process clause. But, to avoid substantive due process, they essentially grafted the equal protection clause onto the Fifth Amendment:

the Equal Protection Clause of the Fourteenth Amendment prohibits the states from maintaining racially segregated public schools. The legal problem in the District of Columbia is somewhat different, however. The Fifth Amendment, which is applicable in the District of Columbia, does not contain an equal protection clause, as does the Fourteenth Amendment, which applies only to the states. But the concepts of equal protection and due process, both stemming from our American ideal of fairness, are not mutually exclusive. The 'equal protection of the laws' is a more explicit safeguard of prohibited unfairness than 'due process of law,' and, therefore, we do not imply that the two are always interchangeable phrases. But, as this Court has recognized, discrimination may be so unjustifiable as to be violative of due process.[22]

In numerous cases after *Bolling*, "with little serious discussion since, the Court held that the due process clause of the 5th Amendment has an 'equal protection' component that restricts the national government in a manner virtually identical to the Fourteenth Amendment's equal protection restrictions upon the states."[23] Thus, the Warren Court reinvigorated the fundamental rights doctrine, and did so by relying upon the equal protection clause, even when it was striking down federal legislation to which the clause did not apply under its own terms.[24] The

---

[21] Despite the best efforts of the Warren Court, "The Court's equality commitment . . . never quite escaped the charge that it was Lochnerism reincarnated." Lupu at 992.

[22] 347 U.S. 497, 499 (1954).

[23] Lupu at 995.

[24] The Court has also applied most of the Bill of Rights to the states even though the text makes it applicable only to the federal government. The Court has held that the due

Warren Court moved aggressively, perhaps as aggressively as did the *Lochner* Court, in creating and enforcing rights that are not explicitly in the Constitution. "The language and relatively untroubled history of the equal protection clause combined to render acceptable a species of judicial intervention that, had it rested on the due process clause, would have been intolerable," Lupu writes.[25]

Further, the Court was expanding the reach of the equal protection clause in ways that were even more far-reaching than was the recognition of new fundamental rights. This continued even after Warren resigned from the Court and was replaced by Chief Justice Warren Burger in 1969. Most significantly, the Court began expanding the number of "suspect classifications" that trigger strict scrutiny regardless of whether a fundamental right is affected (as discussed in Chapters 2 and 3, if a law discriminates on the basis of race, the Court will subject that law to heightened scrutiny). In the late 1960s and early 1970s the Court began treating other classifications, such as gender, illegitimacy, and citizenship status, as suspect classifications.[26] All these were significant constitutional developments. But what threatened to herald a constitutional revolution was the Court's repeated implication that it might consider "wealth" to be a suspect classification.

When the Warren Court struck down a poll tax in *Harper*, it did more than declare that voting was a fundamental right; it held that "Lines drawn on the basis of wealth or property, like those of race, are traditionally disfavored."[27] Three years later, the Court stated that "a careful examination on our part is especially warranted where lines are drawn on the basis of wealth or race, two factors which would independently render a classification highly suspect and thereby demand a

process clause of the Fourteenth Amendment "incorporates" these liberties. *Duncan v. Louisiana*, 391 U.S. 145 (1968); *Malloy v. Hogan*, 378 U.S. 1 (1964).

[25] Lupu at 996.

[26] See, respectively, *Reed v. Reed*, 404 U.S. 71 (1971); *Levy v. Louisiana*, 391 U.S. 68 (1968) and *Graham v. Richardson*, 403 U.S. 365 (1971). This sentence simplifies a very complex set of precedents. The Warren Court did not actually claim to be treating gender and illegitimacy differently from other classifications, although it clearly was. Citizenship status was supposedly subject to strict scrutiny, although it never really was. Gender, illegitimacy, and citizenship status ended up being subjected to varying, poorly defined, intermediate levels of scrutiny in the 1970s. For a more complete explanation, see chapter 3 of *The Constitutional Underclass*.

[27] 383 U.S. at 668.

more exacting scrutiny."[28] By the early 1970s, enough state and federal judges were convinced that the Court had made wealth a suspect classification that several of them struck down school finance systems on this basis. Most states financed schools through local property taxes, which meant that poor children usually went to schools that were poorly financed. Several courts held that this system discriminated on the basis of wealth and was unconstitutional.[29] This was a monumental development. If the trend continued and the justices applied strict scrutiny to all laws that burdened the poor more than the wealthy, the reach of the Court would be greatly expanded; all manner of welfare, tax, and property laws would have to come under intense Court investigation. As the Court later noted, "if wealth were a suspect classification, virtually all local fiscal arrangements would be subject to strict scrutiny."[30]

The Court was on the brink of a phase of judicial activism that could surpass that of the *Lochner* Court, except that this one would be premised upon equal protection rather than substantive due process. But by 1973 the Court had changed. In 1972 two conservative appointees of President Richard Nixon's, Justices Powell and William Rehnquist, joined the Court.[31] With two relatively recent Nixon appointees, Burger and Justice Harry Blackmun, and Justice Potter Stewart, an Eisenhower appointee, they formed a relatively conservative majority. As we will see, this Court could be quite adventurous in its own way, yet it was not willing to go down the road that the Warren Court and its holdovers paved.

In 1973 the new Burger Court majority slammed the door on adventurous interpretations of the equal protection clause, especially on

---

[28] *McDonald v. Board of Electors*, 394 U.S. 802, 807 (1969). Oddly, this case had no direct connection to the issue of wealth as a suspect classification. It concerned the constitutionality of denying absentee ballots to jail inmates.

[29] *Serrano v. Priest*, 487 P.2d 1241 (Calif. 1971), *cert. denied* 432 U.S. 907 (1997); *Van Dusartz v. Hatfield*, 334 F. Supp. 870 (D. Minn. 1971); *Robinson v. Cahill*, 303 A.2d 273 (N.J.), *cert. denied* 414 U.S. 976 (1973); *Miliken v. Green*, 203 N.W.2d 457 (Mich. 1972), *vacated*, 212 N.E. 2d 711 (Mich. 1973); *Rodriguez v. San Antonio School District*, 337 F. Supp. 280 (W.D. Tex.1971), *reversed*, 411 U.S. 1 (1973).

[30] *San Antonio School Independent District v. Rodriguez*, 411 U.S. 1, 41 (1973).

[31] I am defining the Warren Court as having lasted, for all practical purposes until 1972, when Powell and Rehnquist joined the Court. Although Warren had stepped down in 1969, the liberal core of his Court remained a majority until Powell and Rehnquist were sworn in.

any possibility that wealth would be a suspect class. In *San Antonio Independent School District v. Rodriguez,* the Court took on the school financing issue and held, for the first time, that strict scrutiny would protect only groups that are so hated and powerless as to need a special shield:[32]

Appellees' suit asks this Court to extend its most exacting scrutiny to review a system that allegedly discriminates against a large, diverse, and amorphous class, unified only by the common factor of residence in districts that happen to have less taxable wealth than other districts. The system of alleged discrimination and the class it defines have none of the traditional indicia of suspectness: the class is not saddled with such disabilities, or subjected to such a history of purposeful unequal treatment, or relegated to such a position of political powerlessness as to command extraordinary protection from the majoritarian political process.[33]

Justices also took the opportunity to rein in the fundamental rights doctrine under the equal protection clause. Based on two points, the plaintiffs from the poor school districts had maintained that the equal protection clause protected equal education as a fundamental right. They argued that the Court emphasized the issue of education even more than race in *Brown,*[34] and that education is a necessary prerequisite to effective use of other constitutional rights, such as freedom of speech. The Court rejected these arguments in no uncertain terms:

It is not the province of this Court to create substantive constitutional rights in the name of guaranteeing equal protection of the laws. Thus, the key to discovering whether education is "fundamental" is not to be found in comparisons of the relative societal significance of education as opposed to subsistence or housing. Nor is it to be found by weighing whether education is as important as the right to travel. Rather, the answer lies in assessing whether there is a right to education explicitly or implicitly guaranteed by the Constitution.[35]

The language of *Rodriguez* appeared to be a harbinger of an era of judicial restraint. It turned out to be nothing of the sort, however; it

---

[32] The Court did not explain why, if powerlessness and a history of discrimination are prerequisites to judicial protection, it protects white men by applying strict scrutiny to affirmative action programs. See Gerstmann, Evan, *The Constitutional Underclass,* at 84–90.

[33] *San Antonio Independent School District v. Rodriguez,* 411 U.S. at 28.

[34] 387 U.S. 483 (1954).

[35] 411 U.S. at 33.

merely represented another round of the constitutional carousel, this time turning back to substantive due process and away from equal protection.

Also in 1973, the Court decided one of the most controversial cases in its history, *Roe v. Wade*,[36] holding that there is a fundamental constitutional right *under the due process clause* to abort a fetus during the first two trimesters of pregnancy. The Court recognized that it could have found the right to an abortion in the Ninth Amendment as well as in the due process clause, but it never mentioned the equal protection clause. This development was especially striking because abortion issues uniquely affect women, so a very defensible equal protection rationale was available. In fact, Justice Ruth Bader Ginsberg later argued that the Court would have been better off "linking reproductive choice to disadvantageous treatment of women on the basis of their sex."[37]

After *Rodriguez* and *Roe*, the Court continued to contract the scope of equal protection doctrine and to rely upon due process,[38] with significant consequences. Most importantly, the practice allowed the Court, even in decisions such as *Roe*, to write decisions with more limited future applications than they could using equal protection. *Roe* is in some ways a very activist decision, yet it is also very limited. Removed from concerns for the equality of women, *Roe* does not protect pregnant women against discrimination in contexts other than abortion.[39] Nor has the Court applied the autonomy right implicit in *Roe* to other areas of personal decision making, including protection for homosexual activity even in the privacy of one's own bedroom, or for physician-assisted suicide by the terminally ill.[40] And *Roe* did not have anything resembling the nearly limitless potential applications that creating suspect classifications such as wealth would have had.

Finally, it appears that the Court today is ready to lurch in a new direction altogether, and hang fundamental rights upon a new hook: the "privileges and immunities" clause, which, like the due process and

---

[36] 410 U.S. 113 (1973).

[37] *The Washington Post*, p. C3 (June 20, 1993).

[38] See Gerstmann, *The Constitutional Underclass*, pp. 46–56, for a more complete history of the Court's post-*Rodriguez* cases that scaled back the equal protection doctrine.

[39] *Geduldig v. Aiello*, 417 U.S. 484 (1974).

[40] See, respectively, *Bowers v. Hardwick*, 478 U.S. 186 (1986); *Washington v. Glucksberg*, 521 U.S. 702 (1997).

equal protection clauses, is found in the Fourteenth Amendment.[41] In
Saenz v. Roe,[42] the Court suddenly relocated the fundamental "right to
travel" from the equal protection clause to the privileges and immunities clause. The case involved a California law that limited the max-
imum welfare benefits to newly arrived residents, a law that closely
resembled the one that the Supreme Court struck down in *Shapiro v.
Thompson* as violative of the equal protection clause. The Court never
explained why it now considered the equal protection clause to be an
ill-suited home for the right to travel. This is particularly remarkable
as the Court had never in its history relied upon the privileges and
immunities clause in any context, and had virtually read it out of the
Constitution.[43] It remains to be seen how serious the Court is about
this particular relocation of fundamental rights doctrine.

The Case for Equal Protection

We have seen that the Supreme Court has never advanced any real reason for grounding fundamental rights in the due process clause or the
equal protection clause. The Warren Court relied upon equal protection to escape the shadow of *Lochner*, and the Burger Court switched
fundamental rights back to due process to limit them and separate itself
from the Warren Court. The Court's repeated desire to break with its
past was in many ways understandable. The activism of the *Lochner*
and Warren Courts had, and continues to have, countless critics, and
there are many well-crafted arguments that these tribunals had gone
too far. But this unexamined wandering between due process and equal
protection has had its costs, one of the greatest being a lack of sustained
analysis of why we even have a doctrine of fundamental rights and of
what this doctrine really means. The Court has treated parts of the
Constitution as convenient coat hooks, hanging individual rights on
whichever clause serves its purposes. It is not surprising that justices
have failed to set forth any coherent theory of fundamental rights.

---

[41] "No State shall make or enforce any law which shall abridge the privileges or immunities of citizens of the United States."
[42] 526 U.S. 489 (1999).
[43] Technically, there is one exception. The Court relied upon the privileges and immunities clause in *Colgate v. Harvey*, 296 U.S. 404 (1935), but overruled that case just five
years later in *Madden v. Kentucky*, 309 U.S. 83 (1940).

This chapter argues that for several key reasons, fundamental rights are best understood as an essential part of the equal protection clause instead of the due process clause.[44] One reason is fidelity to the constitutional text. "Due process" and "equal protection" have often been described as "open-ended" phrases, meaning there are many different ways to interpret them without violating the text. But even open-ended text can be stretched only so far without violating its plain meaning.[45] The due process clause is actually less textually ambiguous than many other parts of the Constitution: it says that no state shall "deprive any person of life, liberty or property without due process of law." This language is obviously concerned with proper process and implies that "liberty" *can* be taken away if such process is given; any other interpretation unbearably strains the plain meaning of these words. *Roe* does not make sense as an application of this very clear language, for that decision simply has nothing to do with process. Finding the right to abortion in the due process clause violates its text.

This observation about what the text means is hardly original to this book, and two types of rebuttals are commonly offered. First, the framers of the Fourteenth Amendment intended the due process clause, text notwithstanding, to have a substantive component that goes beyond process issues. Divining the intent of the framers, who are long since dead and whose goals were far from uniform, is tricky business, though. There is often conflicting evidence about their intentions, and diligent scholars can usually find plausible grounds for a variety of interpretations of their intentions. Surveying the literature on this question, John Hart Ely concludes that, "[O]ne cannot absolutely exclude that some of [the 14th Amendment's framers], had the question been put, would have agreed that the Due Process Clause they were including could be given an occasional substantive interpretation."[46] But this is a thin reed upon which to place so much constitutional weight. And

---

[44] At the time of this writing it is still too early to seriously engage the Court's (so far) one time resuscitation of the privileges and immunities clause.

[45] See Ely. I recognize that some people will disagree with this assertion. See Whittington at pp. 68 et seq. for an excellent description and response to theories that text is inherently indeterminate. Obviously, this argument will not convince those who believe that text is so indeterminate there is never any such thing as a text's plain meaning.

[46] Ibid. at 16.

as Ely points out, "the most important datum bearing on what was intended is the constitutional language itself."[47]

The second response is the "parade of horribles" approach. Without a substantive component to the due process clause, the government might violate our most basic liberties so long as it gives us a fair trial before punishing us, according to this view. Justice John Harlan has stated this argument eloquently. "Were due process merely a procedural safeguard it would fail to reach those situations where the deprivation of life, liberty, or property was accomplished by legislation which by operating in the future could, given even the fairest possible procedure in application to individuals, nevertheless destroy the enjoyment of all three,"[48] Harlan wrote. The argument assumes that the only possible source of fundamental rights is the due process clause and that going against its text is therefore justified. But the Constitution has several open-ended phrases, such as the equal protection clause and the Ninth Amendment; the latter can easily accommodate fundamental rights, as it refers to "other" rights besides those "enumerat[ed] in the Constitution." Ely has argued that the Ninth Amendment is the best source of unenumerated fundamental rights.[49]

One reason to argue that the equal protection clause is most suitably interpreted as protecting certain fundamental rights is the crucial requirement that these rights be protected equally for all people. As I shall discuss in Chapter 8, this is central to the proper role of the federal courts in a democratic society. Another reason, upon which I shall elaborate in the next section, is that unlike due process, the concept of equal protection of the laws *inherently requires* substantive content to have meaning as a constitutional principle.

Equal Protection and the Necessity of Substantive Rights

This section begins with the assumption that legal equality is one of the most important goals of our constitutional democracy. Naturally, there are many disagreements about what this means or how

---

[47] Ibid. (italics omitted).
[48] *Poe v. Ullman*, 367 U.S. 497, 541 (1961).
[49] Ely limits these to what he believes are rights that ensure proper process or reinforce representation of marginalized groups. See discussion below.

we should give life to this ideal; yet this goal seems to be something on which everyone agrees. The Constitution commands it; the Declaration of Independence speaks of the self-evident truth that all men are created equal and endowed with certain inalienable rights; the presumptive goodness of legal equality pervades all manner of legal, scholarly, and public debate; and in the voluminous writing on constitutional law, there does not appear to be a single article challenging this ideal.

The law cannot literally treat every person equally, of course. Blind people, unlike sighted people, are not allowed to drive or pilot. Higher-income earners are forced to pay a greater percentage of their taxes than are lower-income earners. Second cousins, but usually not first cousins, are allowed to marry. Legal equality, then, must mean something else if it is to mean anything at all. Peter Westen has ably demonstrated that "equality" cannot have real meaning without a system of substantive rights. "[R]egardless of the categories and levels of scrutiny, equality analysis logically collapses into rights analysis."[50] This is so because it is logically impossible for equality to stand on its own feet as an analytic tool. "To say that two people are 'equal' and entitled to be treated 'equally' is to say that they both fully satisfy the criteria of a governing rule of treatment. It says nothing at all about the content or wisdom of the governing rule," Westen says.[51] Because all laws classify and treat people differently, we must have a notion of substantive rights to distinguish between classifications that violate equal protection of the laws and those that do not. Laws that punish those who criticize the government but not those who praise it violate legal equality because we have a constitutional right to free speech. Laws that punish those who refuse to pay taxes to the government but not those who pay taxes do not violate legal equality because we do not have a constitutional right to evade taxes.

Thus, we cannot coherently discuss equality without first asking, "equality with respect to *what*?" This imperative points to why the phrase "gay rights" is so counter-productive and misleading: the term implies that gays and lesbians are seeking rights that others do not share, a concern powerfully expressed in the oft-repeated charge that

---

[50] Westen at 560.
[51] Ibid. at 548–549.

homosexuals are seeking "special rights," not equal rights.[52] Expressing legal equality in the form of fundamental rights is a necessary re-
minder that gays and lesbians are not seeking a special right for themselves, but that in wishing to marry, they are seeking to exercise a right
that others enjoy.

Supporters of the same-sex marriage ban argue that the prohibition
does not deny legal equality because relationships between homosexuals and between heterosexuals are inherently different. Society is not
failing to treat like cases alike, they say; it is merely treating unlike
cases differently. If marriage is a fundamental right, however, the Court
should hold the state to a high standard of proof regarding this distinction. Calling certain rights "fundamental" means that the Court will
hold legislatures to a higher standard in distinguishing cases. Also, it
allows gays and lesbians to frame their arguments in terms of equality –
they want to be treated as everybody else is – and forces the government to demonstrate the difference between same-sex and dual-gender
marriage.

Equality cannot exist in a vacuum; it must be part of a framework
of substantive rights. But which rights? By what criteria should these
rights be chosen? The next section turns to these questions.

The Debate over Substantive Rights

One of the most important criticisms of fundamental rights is that they
represent nothing more than the values of electorally unaccountable
judges that are undemocratically imposed upon society. If judges can
read their own substantive values into the Constitution, this undermines democracy because it would empower "politically unaccountable judges [to] select and define the values to be placed beyond
majority control," Ely writes.[53] For this reason, it might be wise to
limit fundamental rights to those found in the Bill of Rights itself. The
"liberty" protected under the due process clause has long been understood as including most of the liberties in the Bill of Rights. If the concept of equality needs substantive flesh and blood, the Bill of Rights
could provide that substance without giving judges carte blanche to

[52] See Gerstmann, Chapter 5.
[53] Ely at 8.

read their own values into the Constitution. Under this theory, the equal protection clause would simply mean that the liberties set out in the Bill of Rights have to be protected equally for all people.

But such an approach would be radically narrow. For example, not even the right to vote in state or local elections would be protected. The right to vote in these elections is so important to a democratic society that many people incorrectly assume that it is explicitly protected in the Constitution. In fact, the document only prohibits the state and federal governments from denying suffrage on the basis of race or gender (the Fifteenth and Nineteenth Amendments, respectively) and lowers the voting age to eighteen (the Twenty-Sixth Amendment). As a result, the Supreme Court had to go beyond the explicit text of the Constitution to hold that there is a fundamental right to vote. When the justices struck down the poll tax widely used in the South, they had to begin by conceding, "While the right to vote in federal elections is conferred by Art. I, § 2, of the Constitution, the right to vote in state elections is nowhere expressly mentioned."[54] (The Twenty-Fourth Amendment prohibits poll taxes for federal, but not state, elections.) Still, the Court went on to hold that "a State violates the Equal Protection Clause of the Fourteenth Amendment whenever it makes the affluence of the voter or payment of any fee an electoral standard."[55] The Court has also relied upon the "fundamental right to vote" to strike down voting districts that give more legislative representation to small yet entrenched groups and to uphold the right of military personnel to vote in the states where they live.[56] If there were no fundamental rights beyond the explicit text of the Bill of Rights, all these protections of our right to vote would evaporate. State legislatures could even restrict voting to those with land or wealth.[57] Ironically, for the sake of reserving value judgments for the democratic process, we would

---

[54] *Harper v. Virginia Bd. of Electors*, 383 U.S. 663, 665 (1966).

[55] Ibid. at 666.

[56] See *Baker v. Carr*, 364 U.S. 898 (1960), and *Carrington v. Rash*, 380 U.S. 89 (1965), respectively.

[57] These specific practices are now banned under the 1965 Voting Rights Act, but without constitutional protection Congress could dilute or eliminate such protection, should there be partisan advantage in narrowing access to the vote. Also, given renewed Court interest in state sovereignty and limiting congressional power, it is not clear how far Congress could go in enforcing these provisions, were there not a constitutional dimension to these rights.

have severely weakened constitutional protection for our most vital democratic instrument.

Suggesting a well-known solution to this problem, Ely begins by recognizing that we need to look beyond the explicit text of the Constitution to give it meaning. Clauses such as those found in the Ninth and Fourteenth Amendments contain language "that [is] difficult to read responsibly as anything other than quite broad invitations to import into the constitutional decision process considerations that will not be found in the language of the amendment or the debates that led up to it."[58] The Court should distinguish between rights that incorporate substantive values and those rights that protect fair process and are "representation-reinforcing." For Ely, substantive rights should not be read into the Constitution, because except for the Thirteenth Amendment prohibition of slavery, the Constitution is devoted entirely to procedure and representation rather than substantive values. He argues that a careful examination of the Constitution shows "the selection and accommodation of substantive values is left almost entirely to the political process and instead the document is overwhelmingly concerned, on the one hand, with procedural fairness . . . and on the other with ensuring broad participation in the process and distributions of government."[59]

Ely argues that the Court should therefore protect rights that are "representation-reinforcing" – rights that clear the channels for political change and facilitate the representation of minorities. This would place great emphasis on freedom of speech and assembly and would seem to protect the right to vote despite the absence of that right from the text of the Constitution. In addition, the mandate to facilitate the representation of minorities would allow the Court to protect the rights of racial minorities (although not necessarily women), even though the Constitution has no language explicitly barring discrimination on the basis of race or ethnicity, apart from voting. The justices nonetheless should also recognize they should not seek to impose their own values on the Constitution nor attempt to divine what society considers to be fundamental values. This is an elegant theory, but the distinction between rights that protect "values" and those that preserve "process" or

---

[58] See Ely at 14.
[59] Ibid. at 87.

"representation" is a lot less clear than Ely's argument implies. He uses this lack of clarity to sneak certain fundamental rights back into the Constitution by framing them as "process rights" or "representation-reinforcing rights." In *Shapiro*,[60] the Warren Court held there is a "right to travel" that entitles indigent people to qualify for welfare benefits in a state immediately upon moving there (some states required a year of residency for welfare benefits). This decision would certainly appear to be an example of judges imposing certain values upon an unwilling majority. But Ely argues that this right to travel is really a process right because "the right to travel freely through the various states is critical to the exercise of our more obviously political rights."[61] He concedes, as he must, that most people travel from state to state for reasons utterly unrelated to political activity. The right to travel, however, is protected under his theory because those who wish to flout majoritarian norms ought to be able to leave the state in search of a more compatible community.

The right is one that fits quite snugly into the constitutional theory of this book. Precisely *because* the choosing of values is a prerogative appropriately left to the majority . . . a dissenting member for whom the 'voice' option seems unavailing should have the option of exiting and relocating in a community whose values he or she finds more compatible.[62]

Perhaps this is so, although the right to pack up and move is still a substantive right, not a procedural right. In addition, absolutely nothing in the text of the Constitution elevates the right of nonconformist citizens to relocate to another state (assuming a welcoming one can be found) over, say, the right to retreat to the privacy of their own homes. For all the criticisms of Justice Douglas's "penumbras," he was certainly correct that the Bill of Rights is explicitly concerned with protection of the home. There is not one word about interstate travel in the Constitution, so Ely is stretching awfully far for someone who is trying to remove value judgments from judges' decisions.

Obviously an admirer of the Warren Court, Ely dedicates *Democracy and Distrust* to Earl Warren, writing, "You don't need many heroes if you chose carefully." But Ely's reverence for the legacy of the Warren

---

[60] 394 U.S. 618 (1969).
[61] Ely at 178.
[62] Ibid. at 179.

Court highlights the futility of the distinctions he is trying to draw. There does not appear to be *even one* major Warren Court precedent besides privacy that he cannot describe as a valid process right. Moreover, the divide between substantive rights and rights that reinforce minority representation is even less clear. Ely argues that democratic process includes a notion of "virtual representation,"[63] which means the majority may enact whatever laws it likes so long as those laws do not single out minorities for different treatment. He thus calls for special judicial scrutiny of laws that discriminate against groups that are too stigmatized to defend their interests effectively in the regular democratic process. Laws that discriminate against gays and lesbians would be subject to strict scrutiny because "homosexuals for years have been victims of both 'first degree prejudice' and subtler forms of we-they stereotyping."[64] Thus, in the name of preventing judges from making value judgments, Ely's theory tells us the Constitution requires states to provide welfare to new arrivals and respect the rights of gays and lesbians, among other things. These might be good policy ideas, but they obviously represent value judgments.

It is inherently impossible to avoid substantive value judgments even if judges exhibit the most rigid fidelity to the text of the Constitution. Consider the First Amendment command that "Congress shall make no law . . . abridging freedom of speech." The Amendment cannot mean "no law," for that would prohibit laws against perjury, libel, threats, extortion, and so forth. To apply the text to the real world, judges must make value judgments about what speech the states may censor. Is soft-core pornography protected under the First Amendment? What if it is held to be great art? What if it has a political theme? What if children might be exposed to it? Judges obviously cannot answer these questions without making some value judgments.

Although judicial restraint is a laudable goal, there is simply too much inherent flexibility in the constitutional text, and the world is too complicated a place, to allow for value-free interpretation. As Harlan explained in his concurring opinion in *Griswold*:

While I could not more heartily agree that judicial 'self restraint' is an indispensable ingredient of sound constitutional adjudication, I do submit that the

---

[63] Ibid. at 82.
[64] Ibid. at 162.

formula suggested for achieving it is more hollow than real. 'Specific' provisions of the Constitution, no less than 'due process', lend themselves as readily to 'personal' interpretations by judges whose constitutional outlook is simply to keep the Constitution in supposed 'tune with the times'.[65]

There is virtual unanimity on the goal of legal equality, which cannot be pursued meaningfully without reference to some substantive values beyond those expressed in the text of the Constitution. From where are these values to come? Is it reasonable for this substantive content to include the right to marry? If so, should that right be broad enough to include same-sex marriage? I shall take up these questions in the next chapter.

[65] 381 U.S. at 501.

7

Identifying Fundamental Rights

In the previous chapter, we saw that the promise of legal equality cannot be fulfilled without some substantive content. This chapter attempts to set forth a plausible account of what that content might be and whether it should include the fundamental right to marriage. Four factors are set out for identifying nontextual fundamental rights, none of which are novel. All four are criteria familiar to many judges, lawyers, and legal scholars and all four have been used by the U.S. Supreme Court from time to time in various contexts. The problem has been that the Court has used these criteria too sporadically and often implicitly rather than explicitly. As a result, as the Court has lurched from clause to clause in its fundamental rights jurisprudence, it has failed to systematically set out its criteria for identifying fundamental rights. What follows is not grand theory, but merely an explicit identification of criteria the Court has used that helps lay the foundation for reasoned discussion about which nontextual rights should be considered fundamental. It will be shown not only that each of these factors support the Court's holdings that marriage is a fundamental right, but also that the right to marry should be construed as sufficiently broad to include same-sex marriage. In identifying these four criteria, I assume that most people agree upon the following goals:

1. Leave most policy decisions to the democratic process.
2. Expect judges to refrain from simply reading their own values and policy preferences into the equal protection clause.

3. Hold judges accountable by setting out comprehensible standards for what is a fundamental right – standards that would guide (not eliminate) judicial discretion.
4. Don't leave individuals or less powerful groups completely at the mercy of the majority.
5. Limit fundamental rights to those rights that courts, given their institutional limitations, realistically can enforce.
6. Take into account that law changes incrementally, not radically.

It must be emphasized that this is not an attempt to lay out a definitive system for identifying fundamental rights. Rather it sets out a framework for reasoned discussion of whether something is a fundamental right by clarifying certain criteria that the Court has historically used and that are useful in achieving the goals mentioned above. Setting out these criteria is an important task for several reasons. As discussed in Chapter 6, the Court has been maddeningly vague and inconsistent in developing intelligible criteria for fundamental rights. Also, this chapter is intended to lay down the gauntlet to critics of same-sex marriage. The argument here is that all of the criteria for identifying fundamental rights point to protecting marriage, including same-sex marriage. The challenge is to opponents of such a right to identify alternative criteria that are not excessively vague or hopelessly radical that exclude or limit same-sex marriage as a fundamental right.

Before laying out the four factors that I believe are most helpful in identifying fundamental rights, a certain amount of ground clearing is necessary. Much of the literature on constitutional interpretation suggests standards that are too vague to be useful on a practical level. Therefore, the following section identifies those standards that I argue *cannot* be usefully relied upon in discussing fundamental rights.

Fundamental Rights and the Problem of Overly Vague Standards

The approach I shall describe is unabashedly "positivist" in nature; that is, it assumes that fundamental rights come from judges and are not ordained by God or any other transcendental source.[1] This is not to

---

[1] See Dworkin for an excellent discussion of positivist law in contrast to natural law.

contradict Thomas Jefferson's famous declaration that we are endowed by our creator with certain inalienable rights; it is merely to say that the justification for what follows does not rely upon anything that is not plainly comprehensible to the average thoughtful citizen. This discussion assumes that any approach to fundamental rights must be *pragmatic*, in the sense that it should avoid reliance upon standards that are excessively vague. Therefore, it does not rely upon "natural law," which, as John Hart Ely points out, can support an "almost infinite" list of causes, including everything from anarchy to strict paternalism and from universal suffrage to rigid limitations on who can vote.[2] "It has thus become increasingly evident that the only propositions with a prayer of passing themselves off as 'natural law' are those so uselessly vague that no one will notice – something along the 'no one should needlessly inflict suffering' line."[3]

Similarly, a pragmatic approach to equal protection does not rely upon concepts such as Michael Perry's moral "prophecy." Perry has argued famously that when a court needs to go beyond the values of the framers in interpreting the Constitution, it should

deal with those political issues that are also fundamental moral problems in a way that is faithful to the notion of moral evolution (and, therefore, to our collective religious self-understanding) – not simply by invoking established moral conventions but by seizing such issues as opportunities for moral reevaluation and possible moral growth. That is the sense in which I mean that noninterpretive review in human rights cases represents the institutionalization of prophecy. Such review is an enterprise designed to enable the American polity to live out its commitment to an ever-deepening moral understanding and to political practices that harmonize with that understanding.[4]

The impracticality of Perry's approach has been noted elsewhere. Perry understands that this vagueness could lead to "false prophecy" – the Court imposing values out of keeping with the present and future morals of America. This requires him to recommend powerful hedges against judicial power when the Court engages in "noninterpretive review," the application of the Constitution in a way that goes beyond the original intent or plain meaning of the text. Helen Garfield has noted

---

[2] See Ely at 51.
[3] Ibid.
[4] See Perry at 101–102.

that this requires Perry drastically to restrict judicial independence from Congress:

[Perry] does [not] believe that the fallibility of the Court – the possibility of false prophecy – is a sufficient reason to 'reject the whole enterprise.' Instead, to ensure some measure of political control over noninterpretive review, he would concede that Congress has unlimited power to limit the jurisdiction of the federal courts in noninterpretive cases. This would subject most modern decisions dealing with human rights to the rarely used and much disputed power of Congress to limit federal court jurisdiction, even though Perry believes that such decisions constitute 'the most important constitutional function of the Court.' Surely Perry concedes too much.[5]

Perry suggests that the Court discern fundamental rights by looking forward, but the more influential suggestion is that the courts look backward, toward "tradition." The Court itself has suggested that a fundamental right is one that is "deeply rooted in this Nation's history and tradition."[6] Again, a pragmatic approach cannot rest upon so vague a standard. Is affirmative action deeply rooted in the history or traditions of the United States?[7] What of sexual privacy in one's own bedroom?[8] The multifaceted nature of the American experience (not to mention justices' lack of qualification as social historians or social scientists)[9] makes it extremely unlikely that history and tradition can provide practical guidelines for discerning fundamental rights. As Perry puts the problem, "the so-called American tradition, to the extent it is determinate or concrete at all, is severely fragmented; there are several American traditions, and they include denial of freedom of expression, racial intolerance, and religious bigotry."[10] Ely makes a like point, noting that the "problems [with tradition] are obvious. The first is that people have come to understand that 'tradition' can be invoked in support of almost any cause. There is obvious room to maneuver."[11]

---

[5] See Garfield at 327–328.

[6] *Moore v. East Cleveland*, 431 U.S. 494 (1977).

[7] See a discussion of this question in Ely at 61.

[8] For the Court, the answer appears to be "yes for heterosexuals, but no for gays and lesbians." See, respectively, *Griswold v. Connecticut*, 381 U.S. 479 (1965), and *Bowers v. Hardwick*, 478 U.S. 186 (1986).

[9] See, e.g., Albertson.

[10] See Perry at 93.

[11] See Ely at 60.

In addition, a pragmatic approach cannot rely on such judicial standards as whether a right is founded upon "reasoned judgment"[12] or "implicit in the concept of ordered liberty."[13] These standards are too vague to serve as anything more than rhetorical devices. The same is true for Ronald Dworkin's reliance upon human "dignity."[14] As Keith Whittington notes, "features that have led to elevation to the bench include no particular talents or skills that suggest greater capacity for moral reasoning than that which is common to other public agents."[15]

A pragmatic approach to equal protection must also avoid the theory of "originalism," under which the Court should implement the value choices of the people who originally drafted and/or ratified the Constitution.[16] Robert Bork, a leading exponent of this theory, argues that "a Court that makes rather than implements value choices cannot be squared with the suppositions of a democratic society."[17] This theory of original intent will be discussed further in the next chapter. For now, it suffices to note that the theory is tremendously impractical because it would require the erasure of much of modern constitutional law, along with the political and social institutions that have developed in accordance with that law.[18] The framers of the Constitution envisioned a society vastly different from that of the twenty-first century, and a federal government far more limited than our post – New Deal government. Originalism would have drastic effects upon the economic

---

[12] See *Planned Parenthood of Southeastern Pennsylvania v. Casey*, 505 U.S. 833, 849 (1992). "The inescapable fact is that adjudication of substantive due process claims may call upon the Court in interpreting the Constitution to exercise that same capacity which by tradition courts always have exercised: reasoned judgment. Its boundaries are not susceptible of expression as a simple rule."

[13] See *Bowers v. Hardwick*, 478 U.S. 186 (1986).

[14] See Dworkin at 127. "If Hercules [Dworkin's metaphorical super-judge] sits in the abortion cases, he must decide that issue and must employ his own understanding of dignity to do so."

[15] Whittington at 38.

[16] There are different versions of originalism. One version looks to the intentions of the framers themselves. Another looks at the intentions of the people who ratified the Constitution and its Amendments. This distinction will not affect my analysis.

[17] Bork, Robert, "Neutral Principles and Some First Amendment Problems." *Indiana Law Journal* 47 (fall 1971): 1–35, 6.

[18] It has also been frequently argued that the theory of original intent is impractical because there is no way to know what framers, who lived long in the past and had many disagreements among themselves, really meant. That argument will not be addressed here.

system. For instance, the Constitution gives Congress the power to *coin* money, not to *print* paper money. To avoid the absurd result of outlawing legal tender, originalists have to backpedal furiously and assume the Court will be selective in the actual application of their theory. According to Whittington, one of the most thorough and thoughtful recent defenders of originalism,

> Even if the correct originalist interpretation would question the legality of legal tender laws, this would not itself make such laws the subject of serious controversy. Even if the bench were filled with originalist judges, it is exceedingly unlikely that there would be a host of litigants queuing up to have legal tender overthrown. Not every constitutional error must be, or can be, corrected by the courts.[19]

But the assertion that no one would challenge paper money is quite dubious. If currency speculators had a chance of successfully challenging the legality of paper money, presumably they would purchase large quantities of coin or alternative currencies and then would indeed be "queuing up to have legal tender overthrown." Whittington acknowledges this in an endnote, adding a caveat to the above quotation: "This is somewhat overstated, for one difficulty with the courts as policy-making institution is that the threshold for filing suits is relatively low and thus marginal political movements can gain exaggerated influence through litigation."[20] So will the courts get rid of paper money? Whittington says that averting this embarrassing outcome might "require some discretion by the courts not to leap to respond to marginal litigants,"[21] although he does not specify what would make a litigant "marginal" or what theory of the Constitution would allow the Court to reject these plaintiffs.[22] Finally, he grants that if there were sufficient historical evidence that the Constitution was not intended to allow paper money, "the courts would be compelled to begin the process of

[19] Whittington at 172–173.
[20] Ibid, at 284, n.36.
[21] Ibid.
[22] A plaintiff has standing to bring a case if he or she has a non-trivial injury that the court can remedy through the requested relief. *Frothingham v. Mellon*, 262 U.S. 447 (1923). The hypothetical money speculators would meet this requirement because the allegedly unconstitutional printing of paper money devalues their assets. It is difficult to think of what constitutional principle could be invented to keep them out of court, even if it were desirable to do so.

shifting doctrine to the correct position."[23] Yet it is hard to believe that the Court would or should turn the United States into the only nation in the world without the power to print its own legal tender.

A better-known example of the devastating potential of originalism is the problem of *Brown v. Board of Education*. Bork admits the framers of the Fourteenth Amendment probably had no objection to racially segregated schools, which means *Brown* cannot be reconciled with the original understanding of the Constitution.[24] Because this result would undoubtedly be fatal to any chance of the Court's taking originalism seriously, Bork tries desperately to find a way out. He defines the equal protection clause as guaranteeing "black equality," notes that in 1954 segregated public facilities were generally unequal, and argues that the Court would have faced a huge administrative burden in attempting to assure the genuine equality of all such facilities. "Endless litigation, aside from the burden on the courts, also would never produce the equality the Constitution promised. The Court's realistic choice, therefore, was either to abandon the quest for equality by allowing segregation or to forbid segregation in order to achieve equality," he writes.[25]

The problem with Bork's suggestion is that one could make the equivalent argument for many practices besides segregated schools. It can be very plausibly argued that the Court will never be able to purge racism from the imposition of the death penalty, the use of warrantless "stop and frisks" by the police, or the making of peremptory challenges[26] of prospective jurors by prosecutors, among many other

---

[23] Whittington at 284, n.36.
[24] There is strong evidence that the framers of the Fourteenth Amendment believed that racially segregated schools did not violate that Amendment. See Berger at 117–133. Alexander Bickel has disputed this argument in *Politics and the Warren Court*. New York: Harper & Row, 1965 at pp. 256–261, but this just highlights the problem with originalist jurisprudence. I believe the great weight of evidence is the side of Berger, and that, for various reasons, people are loath to concede that the Fourteenth Amendment's framers would have disapproved of *Brown*. But if that that is not true, and we really cannot tell what the framers thought of so basic and important an issue, then what use is originalism?
[25] Bork, *The Tempting of America*, at 82.
[26] These are challenges that allow the removal of a prospective juror for no stated reason. The Court has struggled mightily with how to purge race-based challenges from the judicial system. See *Batson v. Kentucky*, 476 U.S. 79 (1986) and the line of cases that followed it.

practices. If the Court is free to strike down any practice that it believes will not be applied equally, then Bork's approach reads tremendous judicial discretion right back into the Constitution.

Bork also suggests that the Court should decline to overrule certain precedents even though those cases were wrongly decided, if they are "fundamental to the public and private expectations of individuals and institutions."[27] It is difficult to think of a mission for which the Court is less suited than deciding what decisions over the past century have become "fundamental to public and private expectations of individuals and institutions." Again, this is an invitation to virtually boundless judicial discretion, far beyond anything ever dreamed of by the *Lochner* or Warren Courts.

Four Standards for a Pragmatic Approach to Equal Protection

If all these approaches are too vague to be useful, then what is left? This section sets out four criteria to determine whether something should be considered a fundamental right under the equal protection clause. No grand theory unifies them, although they should be looked at collectively. I shall argue that as a whole, they do not unduly trample upon the democratic prerogatives of the majority of the day. They protect individuals and less powerful groups. They are reasonably realistic about the institutional limitations of the Court.

It must be emphasized that these standards are not meant to be dispositive, merely useful. Nor are they meant to change radically the ways in which the Court interprets the Constitution. In fact they are as much descriptive as they are normative. The Court often uses them, albeit with such inconsistency and lack of clarity or explicitness that these standards are diluted or undermined in practice.

Finally, it also must be emphasized that these standards do not come from any a priori source. They are merely practical and useful standards for achieving the goals set out above.

To determine whether a right is fundamental, the Court should consider whether it squares with precedent; whether it is inherently connected to other rights; whether government exercises monopoly power over it; and whether it runs afoul of the political question doctrine. In

---

[27] Bork, *The Tempting of America*, at 158.

the next four sections, I shall examine the criteria, by which marriage is indeed a fundamental right.

Precedent

A pragmatic approach to equal protection must begin by recognizing that the Court will never be starting with a constitutional tabula rasa. It would be neither practical nor wise for the justices to throw out centuries of precedent and declare that they were deciding from scratch everything from freedom of speech to whether Congress has the power to enact civil rights laws. The rule of *stare decisis* – that the Court follows its own precedents – is fundamental to the judicial process.[28]

Respect for precedent serves several purposes: "to promote legal stability, to protect honest reliance [upon settled law], to preserve efficient judicial administration, to maintain similar treatment of persons similarly situated, and to promote public confidence in courts," Lief H. Carter says.[29] All these purposes are important, but that of treating people equally bears special notice. As we saw in Chapter 4, a long line of precedents declares marriage to be a fundamental right, none of which hold that the ability or willingness to procreate is essential to the exercise of that right. When gays and lesbians who want to exercise the right confront the courts, judges with mainstream values naturally will be sorely tempted to question whether decisions such as *Zablocki v. Redhail* and *Turner v. Safley* were good ideas. But for a justice system, is any promise more worthwhile than its pledge to treat the most marginalized citizens according to the rules by which other members are judged? Without stable, public, and consistently applied precedents, the promise of the rule of law is a hollow one.[30]

Stare decisis is not the same as stasis; it is vital to the incremental progress of law. Respect for precedent requires courts to articulate a defensible view of the principles at the core of decisions so they can be applied to new situations. In fundamental rights jurisprudence,

[28] See *Planned Parenthood of Southeastern Pennsylvania v. Casey*, 505 U.S. 833 (1992).
[29] Carter at 99.
[30] The question of whether precedents, and the legal principles contained therein, can actually protect legal equality will be discussed extensively in Chapter 8.

though, the justices' undisciplined veering from clause to clause of the Constitution has prevented them from developing any coherent set of principles regarding the derivation and application of these rights. Consequently, the development of law in this area has been unusually disjointed.

There are, of course, limits to stare decisis – precedent can be ambiguous, or there can be conflicting precedents. There are, however, many situations in which precedent is perfectly clear and without serious conflict, such as that of a person arrested for writing a letter to the President objecting to his policies but not threatening him. There is no doubt that the First Amendment protects that writer. To the extent that such an example seems trivial, that is only because the relevant precedent is so clear. Marriage is another example. There is no doubting whether there is a fundamental right to marry, because the Court has long said so, even if the contours and limits of this right will never be fully settled.

Another objection to precedent is that prior decisions might be very poor ones, as measured by any number of standards. Justice William O. Douglas warned over a half century ago: "A judge looking at a constitutional decision may have compulsions to revere past history and accept what was once written. But he remembers above all else that it is the Constitution which he swore to support and defend, not the gloss which his predecessors may have put on it."[31] Whittington cautions that judges must recognize not only that their predecessors might be mistaken, but also that they themselves might be mistaken. "Judges should not assume their own infallibility," he declares.[32] Stare decisis cannot be absolute, or we would be forced to live forever with our mistakes, among them the justices' validation of the repugnant "separate but equal" doctrine in *Plessy v. Ferguson*.[33]

The Court has spelled out four "prudential and pragmatic" reasons for which it might ignore stare decisis:

We may ask whether the rule has proven to be intolerable simply in defying practical workability, whether the rule is subject to a kind of reliance that would

---

[31] "Stare Decisis," 4 *Record of the Association of the Bar of the City of New York* 152, 153–54 (1949) (cited in Carter, supra, at 127).

[32] Whittington at 169.

[33] 163 U.S. 537 (1896).

lend a special hardship to the consequences of overruling and add inequity to the cost of repudiation, whether related principles of law have so far developed as to have left the old rule no more than a remnant of abandoned doctrine or whether facts have so changed, or come to be seen so differently, as to have robbed the old rule of significant application or justification.[34]

None of these reasons indicates the Court should abandon the precedents holding that there is a fundamental right to marriage. As discussed, there is nothing unworkable about constitutionally protecting the right to marry, nor have related constitutional principles changed to the point that the right is "no more than a remnant of an abandoned doctrine." Quite the opposite: we have seen in previous chapters that the right to marry is part of an array of Court decisions restricting governmental power to homogenize the definition of "family." Nor have "any facts changed or come to be seen so differently" that the Court would need to examine whether marriage should still be considered a fundamental right.

A distinction should be made between single cases and long lines of precedent. Occasionally overruling a single case obviously is less threatening to legal stability than wiping out lengthy strings of precedents that have been supported and elaborated upon over the years. Also, when precedents are part of these strings, the problem of the justices' thwarting democratic decision-making is mitigated. The Court's precedents on abortion provide one of the most important, if controversial, examples. Legions of commentators have questioned or attacked the legitimacy of *Roe v. Wade*, many wielding powerful and convincing arguments. Still, the Court has refused to overturn the decision, based almost entirely upon respect for more than a quarter century of precedent, during which justices of varying philosophies and political affiliations have affirmed *Roe*. The democratically accountable branches of government have had many opportunities to place pro-life justices on the Court, but have often chosen not to do so, because the President or the Senate majority supported abortion rights or made other concerns a priority.[35]

---

34 *Planned Parenthood*, supra, at 854 (citations omitted).
35 For example, although President Reagan was strongly pro-life, he prioritized nominating the first woman, Sandra Day O'Connor, for the Supreme Court, despite concerns that she might be pro-choice.

By these standards, the line of cases upholding the fundamental right to marry is as well grounded as any precedent can be. As discussed in Chapter 4, it stretches back almost as far as the fundamental-rights doctrine itself.

Connection to Other Rights

Lines of precedent involving freedom of speech and control over one's children support the right to marry and argue for its application to same-sex marriage. Meaningful protection for established rights sometimes requires protection of other rights, as Justice Douglas argued in his much-criticized exposition on the Constitution's penumbras in *Griswold v. Connecticut*. The problem with Douglas's opinion was in the application of the penumbra theory, not with the theory itself. He used penumbras to create a hydra of impossibly vague "zones of privacy" that covered everything from the individual to the home to a person's thoughts.[36] Worse, he never explained how any of these zones applied to that case, because no one was arrested for using contraceptives personally or for having them in their home. Although Douglas warned of "allow[ing] police to search the sacred precincts of the marital bedroom to search for telltale signs of the use of contraceptives," *Griswold* had nothing to do with police searches of the home or with the use of contraceptives, but with their distribution to the public. The defendants were officers of the Planned Parenthood League of Connecticut, and it would be difficult indeed to explain how their "privacy" was violated.

But the idea that the existence of certain rights requires the recognition of other rights is indisputable. Without such extrapolations, there would not be a constitutionally protected right to vote in state or local elections, as we have seen. Also, as Douglas demonstrates in the better-crafted part of his opinion, freedom of association, both in public and in private, relies upon these extrapolations:

The association of people is not mentioned in the Constitution, not in the Bill of Rights ... [but in] *NAACP v. Alabama* we protected the "freedom to associate and privacy in one's associations," noting that freedom of association was a peripheral First Amendment right. Disclosure of membership lists of a

---

[36] Douglas did not use the phrase "privacy of a person's thought," but it is strongly implied in his opinion.

constitutionally valid association, we held, was invalid "as entailing the like-lihood of a substantial restraint upon the exercise by petitioner's members of their right to freedom of association." In other words, the First Amendment has a penumbra where privacy is protected from governmental intrusion. In like context, we have protected forms of "association" that are not political in the customary sense but pertain to the social, legal, and economic benefit of the members.... Those cases involved more than the 'right of assembly'... and while [the right of association] is not expressly included in the First Amendment its existence is necessary in making the express guarantees fully meaningful.

This lengthy passage is worth quoting in full because it has much to say about the right to marry and its application to same-sex marriage. A major aspect of marriage is its expressive component of love and public commitment; yet the government can punish gays and lesbians merely for participating in a wedding ceremony, even when that cere-mony is nothing more than an expression of love or of the participants' religious or spiritual beliefs. In *Shahar v. Bowers*,[37] the Court upheld the decision of the Georgia Attorney General's Office to withdraw a job offer to Robin Shahar for the sole reason that she participated in a wedding ceremony with her female lover that was performed by her rabbi and was announced to the congregation at her Atlanta syna-gogue. Shahar had committed no crime. She was penalized solely for publicly expressing her commitment to someone of her own gender. The lack of legal protection for her is glaring because even government employees normally retain their rights to express unpopular or contro-versial beliefs.[38] Furthermore, employees usually cannot be fired for off-the-job "immoral" conduct.[39]

Even if there were no right to marry, the implications of the same-sex marriage ban on same-sex couples' freedom of expression and religion seems obvious. By banning same-sex marriage, the government is pro-hibiting gays and lesbians from publicly expressing their love and life-long commitment for one another. *Shahar* also helps demonstrate why

---

[37] 114 F.3d 1097 (11th Cir. 1997); (cert. denied), 522 U.S. 1049 (1998).

[38] For instance, in *Rankin v. McPherson*, a deputy county constable, on hearing that President Reagan had been shot, said to a co-worker, "if they go for him again, I hope they get him." She was fired, but the Court held the firing violated her First Amendment rights. 483 U.S. 378 (1987).

[39] Federal courts have ruled that a police officer cannot be fired for refusing to answer questions about his unmarried cohabitation, and that a teacher cannot be fired for having a man stay overnight with her. See cases cited in Karst at 675, n.236 (1980).

the right to marry is best understood as applying to same-sex couples. Recall that in *Turner*, the Court gave its most thorough explication of the purposes that marriage serves, which led justices to protect even the right of a prison inmate to marry, for marriages "are expressions of emotional support and public commitment."[40] The Court also noted that "the commitment of marriage may be an exercise of religious faith as well as an expression of personal dedication."[41] If this is true for heterosexual felons in *Turner*, it is also true for gay and lesbian couples. These factors clearly apply as much to Shahar and her life partner as they do to dual-gender couples. As for the Court's note that "marital status often is a pre-condition to the receipt of government benefits," in Shahar's case, far from receiving governmental benefits after marriage, she was denied a government job that she had won on her merits.

The right to marry is also closely related to recognized constitutional rights of a parent to control over the upbringing of his or her children. "An essential element in maintaining a system of limited government is to deny state control over child rearing, simply because child rearing has such power," Bruce C. Hafen writes.[42] Therefore, it is not surprising that despite the constitutional silence on this issue, the Court has found a broad right to parental autonomy in child rearing.[43] Because of the same-sex marriage ban, though, gays and lesbian parents, unlike heterosexual parents, do not have the power to make their life partners the stepparents, or even adoptive parents, of their own children.[44] This deeply undermines the power of gay and lesbians to choose who will raise their children should they suddenly pass away, or to choose who has the power to make medical decisions about their children if they cannot be contacted in emergencies.

Even if there were no precedents for a fundamental right to marriage, the freedoms of expression, of association, and of parental control over the upbringing of one's children would strongly point to such a right. At a minimum, these considerations show that the right to marry protects

---

[40] 482 U.S. at 95.

[41] Ibid. at 96.

[42] Hafen at 480–481.

[43] See *Pierce v. Society of Sisters*, 268 U.S. 510 (1925); *Wisconsin v. Yoder*, 406 U.S. 205 (1972); *Troxel v. Granville*, 120 S.Ct. 2054 (2000).

[44] There are many substantial, often insurmountable, obstacles to an adult who seeks to adopt the child of a same-sex partner. See Hedges at 884.

other constitutional rights that are as important to gays and lesbians as they are to others, and that the right to marry cannot be restricted to heterosexuals without diminishing these other rights for same-sex couples.

Considerations of "Monopoly"

Several commentators have argued that the government owes its citizens greater procedural protections when it is acting as a monopoly. "When the government acts as a 'monopolist' [then] the due process constraint is properly applied to balance the power of the government over the individual's life," Timothy Terrell writes.[45] This is equally applicable to fundamental rights analysis. Courts should be (and in fact often are) more willing to apply increased scrutiny to governmental decision making when the decision affects a benefit over which the state has a monopoly. For instance, this would make the Court more inclined to hold that eligibility to apply for a driver's license is a fundamental right.

Perhaps it sounds odd to equate a driver's license with such constitutional rights as freedom of speech and association. Suppose, however, that the government issued a rule denying driver's licenses to people over sixty, based upon the presumption that older people are usually incompetent drivers. This would not be very different from what Massachusetts did when it enacted a policy forcing police officers to retire at 50, based upon the assumption that older adults are not physically capable of police work. In *Massachusetts v. Murgia*,[46] the Court upheld that retirement policy against an equal protection challenge. One can question the wisdom of that decision, but at least Mr. Murgia could take his skills to another employer. If he were denied a driver's license because of his age the restraint upon his freedom of movement would be severe.

In fact, the Court has probably acted upon this monopoly principle without explicitly recognizing it. In *Bell v. Burson*,[47] justices invalidated a Georgia law that automatically suspended the license

[45] Terrell at 902–903.
[46] 427 U.S. 307 (1976).
[47] 402 U.S. 535 (1971).

of any uninsured driver involved in an accident unless the motorist could post a security bond to cover the damages. The opinion emphasized that "continued possession [of the license] may become essential in the pursuit of a livelihood." Why was the Court so concerned about Mr. Bell's livelihood, but not Mr. Murgia's? One explanation would be that the Court considers a driver's license more "important" than a job, and there are scholars who interpret *Bell* as representing "the high-water mark of [the] approach [that] whether an interest deserved . . . protection involved a simple pragmatic assessment of its 'importance' to the individual."[48] In fact, one year after *Bell*, in *Weber v. Aetna Casualty and Security*,[49] the Court implied that it considered itself in the business of balancing the importance of a right to an individual against the state interest furthered by the law.

But the Court retreated from this position one year later in the school funding case, *Rodriguez*, which was probably fortunate, for it is difficult to see how the Court would be qualified to make ad hoc determinations of how "important" various rights are to people. As the majority opinion in *Rodriguez* noted, people's interests in food and shelter are certainly important, but this does not mean that the Court should turn government housing and food programs into fundamental rights, subject to strict judicial scrutiny. The more practical way to reconcile *Bell* and *Murgia* is the criterion of monopoly power: The government has that power over driver's licenses, but not jobs. "Foreclosure of state-monopolized opportunities leaves the individual with absolutely no alternative source of redress," Ira Lupu succinctly argues.[50]

The monopoly issue obviously applies to marriage. Indeed, one of the few times that the Court has ever expressly relied upon the rationale of state monopoly was in the context of a marriage-related issue. In *U.S. v. Kras*,[51] an indigent debtor asked the Court to waive the filing fee required in United States Bankruptcy Court because he could not afford it. He argued that his situation was the same as that of the indigent party in *Boddie v. Connecticut*, in which the Court had held that divorce courts had to waive filing fees for indigent parties. The

---

[48] Monaghan at 407.
[49] 406 U.S. 164 (1972).
[50] Lupu at 1007.
[51] 409 U.S. 434 (1973).

Justices rebuffed the debtor, holding that *Boddie* turned on the state monopoly on the power of divorce:

Nor is the Government's control over the establishment, enforcement, or dissolution of debts nearly so exclusive as Connecticut's control over the marriage relationship in Boddie. In contrast with divorce, bankruptcy is not the only method available to a debtor for the adjustment of his legal relationship with his creditors. The utter exclusiveness of court access and court remedy, as has been noted, was a potent factor in Boddie.[52]

Monopoly cannot serve as the *sole* criterion for whether something is a fundamental right, of course. The government has monopoly power over vanity license plates, for example, but that does not make access to such plates a fundamental right. Nonetheless, the monopoly theory has several virtues. Explaining *Bell* and *Murgia* better than the Court itself has, just as it distinguishes between the holdings of *Boddie* and *Kras*, the theory puts some logic into what the Court has been doing. It encourages the Court to apply heightened scrutiny to areas in which individuals truly are at the mercy of the state. Further, Richard Epstein points out that when the state has a monopoly on certain privileges, it is less reasonable to construe a government grant of access to those privileges to an unpopular group as government endorsement of that group.[53]

The monopoly theory suggests the Court should apply strict scrutiny to the ban on same-sex marriage because it deprives gays and lesbians the opportunity to marry their life partners. When the government has exclusive power, as it does over marriage and divorce, the Court has indicated that it must be more protective of individual rights than it would when the state merely delays or burdens the exercise of rights. In *Sosna v. Iowa*, for example, the justices rejected a challenge to the one-year state residency requirement for filing for a divorce:

In *Boddie v. Connecticut*...this Court held that Connecticut might not deny access to divorce courts to those persons who could not afford to pay the required fee. Because of the exclusive role played by the State in the termination of marriages, it was held that indigents could not be denied an opportunity to be heard 'absent a countervailing state interest of overriding significance.' But the gravamen of appellant Sosna's claim is not total deprivation, as in *Boddie*, but only delay. The operation of the filing fee in *Boddie* served to exclude

---

[52] Ibid. at 445.
[53] See discussion in Chapter 2, supra.

forever a certain segment of the population from obtaining a divorce in the courts of Connecticut.[54]

Same-sex couples face an even more complete obstacle to marriage than Mr. Boddie faced in getting divorced. Maybe Boddie somehow could have come up with the money; but same-sex couples are barred from marriage no matter what measures they take. In fact, even when one member of a same-sex couple goes so far as to undergo a sex-change operation, courts still refuse to let the two legally marry.[55] The monopoly theory indicates that the marriage right should receive powerful judicial protection, and that this protection should extend to same-sex couples.

The Political Question Doctrine

Legal equality should not be confused with broader notions of libertarianism or egalitarianism. The *Lochner* Court was notorious for enforcing a strict economic libertarianism in which workers were "free" to work under whatever dangerous conditions, brutal hours, and low pay the employer could impose. Because the *Lochner* era has been so thoroughly vilified, the drawbacks of turning laissez-faire libertarianism into a constitutional mandate need no elaboration. However, "a broadly conceived egalitarianism was the main theme to which the Warren Court marched," Alexander Bickel notes.[56] The idea that "the judiciary can proceed to the relief of poverty . . . by requiring the political branches to affirmatively satisfy the basic needs of the most impecunious"[57] has had its defenders.[58] Frank Michelman suggested in 1969 that courts should assure that government satisfy the "just wants" of the poor,[59] and for a time, the Warren Court appeared to be heading in that direction.

---

[54] 419 U.S. 393, 410 (1975).

[55] See *In re Estate of Marshall G. Gardiner*, 42 P.3d 120 (kan. 2002); *Littleton v. Prange*, 9 S.W.3d 223 (Tex. Civ. App. 1999), cert. denied 148 L. Ed. 2d 119, 121 S. Ct. 174 (2000); *In re Ladrach*, 32 Ohio Misc. 2d 6, 513 N.E.2d 828 (1987).

[56] Bickel, Alexander. *The Supreme Court and the Idea of Progress* New York: Harper and Row, 1970.

[57] Wilkinson at 945.

[58] See Tushnet, "And Only Wealth Will Bring You Justice – Some Notes on the Supreme Court. 1972 Term," *Wisconsin Law Review* 1974 (1974): 177–197.

[59] Michelman at 15–16.

Several cases implied that the Court might consider welfare a fundamental right. As noted, it struck down a one-year state residency requirement, although it cast the violated right as the "right to travel," and overturned a law denying welfare to households of unrelated individuals.[60] The Warren Court never explicitly held that welfare or any other form of wealth redistribution is a constitutional right, though, and the Burger Court subsequently moved away from this idea altogether. The Court was wise not to dive into these waters. Good policy aims are not necessarily good constitutional or judicial aims. Decisions about income and wealth distribution "engage in what is indisputably the most basic of all legislative functions – from whom and to whom to raise and distribute revenue," Judge J. Harvie Wilkinson III writes.[61] Granting greater freedom of speech or freedom of religious exercise to one person does not mean taking some of those rights from another person; but money for food, shelter, and other basic needs for one person must come from another. The question of how to meet these needs is fundamentally political. "When extended sufficiently, judicial reduction of economic disparities reduces politics almost to a nullity."[62]

The Court has elaborated a doctrine that nicely spelled out the factors distinguishing between legal and political questions. Straightforward and sensible, the "political question" doctrine is superior to the vague formulations justices have usually offered about due process and equal protection. Unfortunately, it has fallen into disuse. Over the past ten years the Court has rarely uttered the phrase "political question,"[63] and only once, in a case involving impeachment of a federal judge, has it conceded that something was a political question rather than an issue to be solved by judicial expertise.[64]

Justice William Brennan spelled out the elements of the doctrine in his opinion for the Court in *Baker v. Carr* in 1962.[65] A controversy

---

[60] *USDA v. Moreno*, 413 U.S. 528 (1973).

[61] Wilkinson at 1010.

[62] Ibid. at 1011.

[63] A Lexis-Nexis search reveals that from 1991 to 2001, the Court used the phrase "political question" only eleven times, and even then usually only in passing or in dissenting or concurring opinions.

[64] *Nixon v. U.S.*, 506 U.S. 224 (1993).

[65] 369 U.S. 186 (1962).

involves a political question when there is a "textually demonstrable constitutional commitment of the issue to a coordinate political department; or a lack of judicially discoverable and manageable standards for resolving it."[66] The veto and a declaration of war are examples of the former. The Constitution clearly commits these powers to the President and the Senate, respectively, so the Court would never order the chief executive to veto a bill or tell senators to declare war. Justices have also held that Senate standards in trying impeachments involve a political question because the Constitution states, "The Senate shall have the sole power to try all Impeachments."[67] An example of lack of judicially discoverable and manageable standards is the question of how long a proposed constitutional amendment remains open to ratification. The Court refused to rule on this issue because it would have meant the "appraisal of a great variety of relevant conditions, political, social and economic, which can hardly be said to be within the appropriate range of evidence receivable by a court of justice."[68] Similarly, for the Court to decide issues of welfare policy and of redistribution of wealth, it would have to pretend to a range of expertise on political, social, and economic decisions that it does not possess.[69] And what judicial standards would it apply to decide how much wealth redistribution is sufficient?

By contrast, the right to marry is not a political question. That states have traditionally regulated marriage does not make it a political question because "it is the relationship between the judiciary and the coordinate branches of the Federal Government, and not the federal judiciary's relationship to the States, which gives rise to the 'political question,'" the Court said in *Baker*.[70] Moreover, giving same-sex couples the right to marry does not make it any more difficult for other couples to marry, so the Court does not have to engage in distributive questions that belong to the democratic process, including those involving social policy such as welfare. Same-sex marriage might cost the public some money as a result of additional people qualifying for the

---

[66] *Baker v. Carr*, 369 U.S. at 217.
[67] U.S. Constitution, Art. I, Sec. 2[6].
[68] *Coleman v. Miller*, 307 U.S. 433, 453 (1939).
[69] See Albertson on the Court's lack of ability or training to analyze social scientific data.
[70] *Baker v. Carr*, 369 U.S. at 210.

financial benefits of marriage, but as Wilkinson notes, "Any constitutional decision, of course, may require public spending as a by product of compliance,"[71] which alone cannot convert something into a political question. Allowing same-sex marriage might make some people feel that government recognition of their dual-gendered marriage is worth less, yet this is true of many constitutional rights. Supporters of laws banning hateful speech against minorities have long argued that allowing such speech diminishes the power of minorities' speech.[72] The Court has never accepted their theory, however.

The other standards for determining what is a political question are inapplicable to marriage because they are concerned primarily with military or foreign affairs. They are

[whether an issue can be decided] without an initial policy determination of a kind clearly for nonjudicial discretion; or the impossibility of a court's undertaking independent resolution without expressing lack of respect due coordinate branches of government; or an unusual need for unquestioning adherence to a political decision already made; or the potentiality of embarrassment from multifarious pronouncements made by various departments on one question.[73]

Justices have refused to decide whether the President can abrogate a treaty without Senate consent.[74] Also, in *Gilligan v. Morgan*, they refused to review the training procedures of the Ohio National Guard, stating that "trained professionals" under control of civilian officials must evaluate these methods. "It would be inappropriate for a district judge to undertake this responsibility in the unlikely event that he possessed requisite technical competence to do so."[75]

In sum, nothing in the political question doctrine prevents the Court from continuing to hold that marriage is a fundamental right. As the above discussion should make clear, that a decision requires value judgments does *not* make it a political question; virtually all decisions regarding the Bill of Rights and other fundamental rights involve value judgments.

[71] Wilkinson at 1010.
[72] See, e.g., MacKinnon, *Only Words*.
[73] Baker at 217.
[74] *Goldwater v. Carter*, 444 U.S. 996 (1979).
[75] 413 U.S. 1, 8 (1973).

Conclusion

These criteria, leaving room for disagreement among reasonable people, will not satisfy everybody. Two judges applying them could come to very different conclusions about, say, whether education is a fundamental right. The precedent is ambiguous.[76] Education is strongly related to the right to freedom of speech, but a good education is not an absolute requirement to exercise free speech. Government does not have a monopoly on education, but private school is beyond the reach of many Americans.

Yet these criteria are clearer and more useful than such standards as "reasoned judgment," tradition, and so forth, and unlike such blunderbuss theories as original intent, they do not require the courts to take on matters beyond their competence or overturn a century's worth of precedent. For my purposes, the most important thing about these criteria is their challenge to those who believe the Court would be going too far in holding that there is a constitutional right to same-sex marriage. We have seen that there is long-standing precedent for a fundamental right to marry; that this right is closely tied to other long-standing rights, including freedom of expression and control over one's children; that the government has a monopoly on access to marriage, which places a higher obligation on the state not to block access to it without good reason; and that marriage is not a political question, as that term has been defined by the Court.

As discussed in Chapters 4 and 5, precedents such as *Zablocki* and *Turner* provide a firm foundation for the right to same-sex marriage. The arguments of Chapters 6 and 7 are that marriage is at least as well-grounded in the Constitution as any other nontextual right, and that it should be applied to new and controversial cases such as same-sex marriage as vigorously as the Court has applied the principles of freedom of speech to controversial cases. If one believes there is no constitutional right to vote or to freedom of association, one is unlikely to believe the Court should protect same-sex marriage. But the views that there are no such things as nontextual rights and that the Constitution means only what its framers or ratifiers meant it to say are

---

[76] Compare *San Antonio Independent School District v. Rodriguez*, 411 U.S. 1 (1973), with *Plyler v. Doe*, 457 U.S. 202 (1982).

radical opinions that courts have not accepted. Nor would most people embrace these cramped ideas of constitutional rights. The fundamental right to marriage, even to same-sex marriage, fits comfortably in mainstream standards of constitutional law, a point obscured by the Court's terrible lack of clarity in fundamental rights jurisprudence and the strong visceral reaction of many people to the idea of gays and lesbians marrying one another.

That people might hate the idea of gays and lesbians getting married does not make judicial protection of same-sex marriage usurpative; after all, many hate the idea of Nazis marching in Jewish neighborhoods or of guilty criminals going free because police did not read them their Miranda rights. Public opposition cannot be an objection to judicial action; many of what are considered the Court's finest moments came in the face of virulent popular objection. Nevertheless, in a democratic society there is still something disturbing about an unaccountable institution creating a right to same-sex marriage, which cannot be found in the constitutional text, when there is a strong popular sentiment against it. Also, some fear that if the Court protected same-sex marriage in the face of opposition not only by the public but also by Congress and the state governments, such a right might do more harm than good. I shall address these concerns in Part IV.

PART IV

RIGHTS IN A DEMOCRATIC SOCIETY

8

Democracy, Neutrality, and Consistency of Principle

No matter how strong the legal case for same-sex marriages may be, there are still legitimate questions about whether the Court should require states to sanction them. We are a democratic society and thus expect that we will resolve controversial social issues by democratic means such as legislation by electorally accountable representatives, or by referenda. This chapter suggests that the Court fulfills its proper role in a constitutional democracy when it protects the rights of unpopular individuals and minorities even if that frustrates the will of the majority. Although this point may seem obvious to some, the tenor of the debate over same-sex marriage has often ignored this crucial point.

There are many reasons for the judiciary to be cautious about taking the issue of same-sex marriage away from the people and legislatures. Pure majoritarianism can oppress dissenting individuals and minorities, but indiscriminate antimajoritarianism can easily slip into antidemocratic elitism. Writing on the same-sex marriage issue, G. Sydney Buchanan warns, "We are in danger of developing an attitude of distaste, suspicion and even hostility toward majority action per se, of viewing majority action as a lower form of political action that is invariably the product of unsophisticated thinking and selfish motivation."[1]

Judicial humility can be a virtue and the Court's own history shows that it ought to be reluctant to impose its own views on civil rights upon the American public. Throughout much of American history, the Court

---

[1] Buchanan at 552.

has been a less reliable defender of minority rights than Congress has. "It was after all, the Court's decisions in *The Civil Rights Cases* and *Plessy v. Ferguson* that played a major role in vitiating the civil rights legislation enacted by Congress in the post-Civil War period."[2] Some believe that the modern Court is still a poor protector of individual minority rights due to the intense partisanship of the confirmation process for Supreme Court nominees. Stephen Griffin concludes, "it can be argued that the Court has lost its comparative advantage over Congress and the President creating and enforcing constitutional rights."[3]

Even when the Court is on the "right" side, there is little evidence that it has the persuasive power to bring the public along with it.[4] Alexis de Tocqueville warned that those who wish to change the decisions of the people "must either change the Nation's opinion or trample them under foot."[5] But the Court frames its orders in terms of decrees, which are poorly suited for bringing about democratic dialogue or a genuine change of the public's heart. Griffin argues that the increased politicization of the Supreme Court nomination process makes it even more "unlikely that the Court can perform a special function in educating the citizenry or assum[e] a vanguard role to promote a national dialogue on rights."[6]

If the Court holds that the fundamental right to marry includes same-sex marriage it would be running well ahead not only of public opinion, but also of the federal and state legislatures. Richard Posner argues that no matter how strong the legal arguments are for same-sex marriage, both prudence and respect for democratic process counsel against the Court taking the lead:

Reasonable considerations also include the feasibility and desirability of allowing the matter to simmer for a while before the heavy artillery of constitutional rightsmaking is trundled out. Let a state legislature or activist (but elected, and hence democratically responsive) state court adopt homosexual marriage as a policy in one state, and let the rest of the country learn from the results of its experiment. That is the democratic way, and there is no compelling reason to supersede it merely because intellectually sophisticated people of secular inclination will find Eskridge's argument for same-sex marriage convincing.

---

[2] Ibid. at 553, n.52.
[3] Griffin at 693.
[4] This will be elaborated upon in Chapter 9.
[5] Quoted in Glendon, Mary Ann, *A Nation Under Lawyers*, 1994.
[6] Griffin at 698–699.

Sophisticates aren't always right...and judges must accord considerable respect to the deeply held views of the democratic majority.[7]

Even many people who support equal rights for gays and lesbians in other areas balk at the idea of gay marriage. After a close Senate vote on the Employment Non-Discrimination Act, which would have barred employment discrimination against gays and lesbians, Senator James Jeffords opined that public support for same-sex marriage was sparse. "People don't want to go too far on changing marriage and traditional relationships. But the feeling is that when someone wants to work someplace, they ought to be able to get a job."[8] If the courts rule in favor of same-sex marriage, that would move the issue ahead of ending workplace discrimination, which has greater public and legislative support.

When the Supreme Court of Hawaii moved toward constitutionalizing same-sex marriage, the democratic counter-reaction was swift and decisive. Hawaiians voted to amend the state Constitution. Congress quickly passed the Defense of Marriage Act ("DOMA"), which barred federal recognition for as-of-then nonexistent same-sex marriages. Thirty-nine state legislatures debated equivalent legislation at the state level. Proponents of the same-sex marriage movement successfully opposed some of these state "mini-DOMA's," but even they concede that "the mere fact that thirty-nine state legislatures spent time discussing whether same-sex couples should be allowed to marry makes clear that this is an issue that strikes fear in the hearts of middle-America."[9]

Others argue that aggressive judicial intervention would not only be anti-democratic, but would also be unwise because it would prevent the public's conflicting passions from working themselves out in the give and take of politics. Cass Sunstein and Mark Tushnet are among a recent wave of prominent law professors who accept the importance of individual rights but argue for greater democratic give and take in their development. The Court's inaction so far allows for legislative compromise. Legislatures can keep marriage dual gendered while maintaining

---

[7] Posner at 1585–1586.
[8] Stoddard at 990.
[9] Cox at 157. By October 2000, thirty-four states had adopted "mini-DOMA's." See also Eskridge at 862.

flexibility to accommodate same-sex couples in terms of benefits and protection from discrimination.

Same-sex marriage is situated on a fault line of tectonic friction between majority rule and minority rights because both the constitutional argument in its favor and the public's reaction against it are so strong. Not everyone believes that principle should triumph over popular passion under such circumstances. Alexander Bickel taught that when principle and unchanging public passion conflict, the popular passion must prevail if it cannot be persuaded to change:

Having been checked, should the people persist; having been educated, should the people insist, must they not win over every fundamental principle save one – which is the principle that they must win? Are we sufficiently certain of the permanent validity of any other principle to be ready to impose it against a consistent and determined majority, and could we do so for long? Have not the people the right of peaceable revolution, as assuredly, over time, they possess the capacity for a bloody one?[10]

These are all serious concerns. Courts cannot simply ignore public opinion. However, many of these arguments exaggerate the extent to which judicial action would preempt democratic debate and legislative action. If the Court ruled in favor of same-sex marriage a relatively small number of people who have been excluded would become eligible to marry. Yet the democratically accountable branches of government would not lose the power to take any number of steps to strengthen the institution of marriage. They could augment the legal and financial benefits of marriage, make the divorce process more demanding, or require counseling prior to marriage. In fact, the only option the majority would lose would be the power to "defend" marriage by imposing restrictions that only affect gays and lesbians.

Also, the public would still have many ways to express its belief that homosexuality is not morally equivalent to heterosexuality. The Court has held that private organizations such as the Boy Scouts and veterans groups can exclude gays and lesbians from membership and participation in parades.[11] State and federal legislatures

---

[10] Bickel at 27–28.
[11] See, respectively, *Boy Scouts of America v. Dale*, 120 S.Ct. 2446 (2000); *Hurley v. Irish-American Gay, Lesbian and Bi-Sexual Group of Boston*, 115 S.Ct. 2338 (1995).

remain free to grant or withhold support from such institutions. School boards can make whatever decisions they wish regarding what children are taught about alternative families, lifestyles and sexual practices. States can make their own decisions about adoption by same-sex couples.

There is no reliable way to predict what the effect of judicially enforced same-sex marriage would be on the democratic debate over issues of marriage and homosexuality. But the virtue of fundamental rights doctrine is that it promotes judicial protection of certain specific freedoms for unpopular groups and individuals while allowing democratic decision making for the vast majority of issues.

Further, it is the job of the courts to enforce rights even when those rights are very unpopular. Interracial marriage was unpopular in the South in the 1960s, which is why in sixteen states and the District of Columbia such marriages were a criminal offense at the time the Court decided *Loving v. Virginia* in 1967. Yet few would argue that the Court should have deferred to the majority in those states.

Posner suggests that the difference is that in *Loving*, as well as *Brown v. Board of Education*, the Court was opposed by a regional rather than a national majority. Even if that is a relevant distinction, the Court often bucks national majorities as well. It has protected groups that are far more unpopular than gays and lesbians, such as pornographers, Nazis, and the Ku Klux Klan,[12] even though the great majority of Americans do not support the free speech of these unpopular groups.[13] As the previous chapters demonstrated, broad constitutional protection for the right to marry has a well-established history as a fundamental constitutional right. It is at least as well grounded in constitutional law as is broad freedom of expression for pornographic or racially hateful speech.

There is nothing unusual about the Court acting counter to the popular will. The Court overrides the will of local and national majorities when it prohibits school prayer, requires the exclusion of illegally

---

[12] See *Hustler Magazine v. Falwell*, 485 U.S. 46 (1988); *Collin v. Smith*, 578 F.2d 1197 (7th Cir.), cert. denied, 439 U.S. 916 (1978); *Brandenburg v. Ohio*, 395 U.S. 444 (1969).

[13] See Erikson and Tedin at 142–146.

obtained evidence against criminal defendants, or protects the free association of groups like the Klan. None of those decisions were specifically mandated by the text of the Constitution.[14]

The resistance of legal luminaries such as Sunstein and Posner to judicial protection of same-sex marriage, even though they both concede that there are strong constitutional arguments in its favor, reveals an underlying discomfort with the institution of judicial review. Every time the Court strikes down a democratically enacted law, it must deal with what Bickel called the "countermajoritarian" problem[15]: the fact that a democratically unaccountable Court is striking down a law that the majority of people presumably support.[16]

The attention scholars and judges pay to the countermajoritarian problem has waxed and waned over the decades. It reached an apex in the years after the *Lochner* era and the Court's battle with President Roosevelt, when John Jackson concluded that there is a "basic inconsistency between popular government and judicial supremacy."[17]

This book's argument that the Court should not be afraid to protect same-sex marriage is perhaps out of tune with the times. There appears to be a renewed interest in the idea that the Court should not be the final arbiter of the Constitution. "The prospect of constitutionalism outside the courts has attracted increasing attention from constitutional theorists over the past several years."[18] In *Taking the Constitution Away from the Courts*, Mark Tushnet argues that "judicial review basically

---

[14] See Alexander and Schauer at 470–471. "With a text as indeterminate as the American Constitution, however, it is far more common to find disputes with a constitutional dimension in which the text itself provides no settlement for that dispute. Does the establishment clause prohibit teacher-organized non-denominational prayer in the public schools or student-led nondenominational prayer at public school graduations? Does the equal protection clause prohibit states from maintaining single-sex colleges and universities? Does the Fourth Amendment's warrant requirement prohibit use at trial of probative evidence obtained without a warrant? Does the free speech clause encompass speech explicitly encouraging racial violence?"

[15] Bickel at 3.

[16] This of course assumes that legislative enactments are generally supported by the majority of voters. That is not an obviously correct proposition. See Farber and Frickey, *Law and Public Choice*.

[17] Jackson at vii.

[18] Whittington, "Commentaries on Mark Tushnet's *Taking the Constitution Away from the Courts*," at 519.

amounts to noise around zero" and questions whether America would be better off de-emphasizing it.[19]

Tushnet has two major criticisms of judicial review. One is that it allows legislatures to pass the buck on difficult constitutional questions to the Court when they should be wrestling with these questions themselves. But Tushnet offers no evidence that eliminating judicial review would effectively encourage the legislature to seriously engage constitutional issues. Even without judicial review legislatures would still be able to pass difficult constitutional issues on to other institutions that operate well out of the light of public scrutiny. "Simply removing the power of judicial review may not force legislators to be any more conscientious in carrying out their responsibilities. Congress has passed a wide variety of political hot potatoes to institutions other than the courts in the past, including the executive bureaucracy. . . . The institutional alternatives to the judicial involvement in constitutional decisions may be even less attractive."[20]

Tushnet also argues that judicial review is antidemocratic. As noted, this is a long-standing objection to judicial power. But Tushnet does not offer a developed alternative to judicial review, and no one appears to favor a regime of pure, unlimited majoritarianism.

The renewed attention to the countermajoritarian problem has also led to increased interest in originalism. Robert Bork argues that "only the approach of original understanding meets the criteria that any theory of constitutional adjudication must meet in order to possess democratic legitimacy. Only that approach is consonant with the design of the American Republic."[21]

Originalists argue that their approach successfully engages the countermajoritarian problem in two ways. First, "Originalism supports democratic values in the form of present majoritarianism by fostering judicial restraint."[22] If judges are restricted to the relatively narrow

---

[19] Tushnet, Mark. *Taking the Constitution Away from the Courts.* Princeton: Princeton University Press, 1999 at 153.

[20] Whittington, Keith E., "Commentaries on Mark Tushnet's *Taking the Constitution Away from the Courts*: Herbert Wechsler's Complaint and the Revival of Grand Constitutional Theory." *University of Richmond Law Review* 34 (2000): 509–543, 540.

[21] Bork at 143.

[22] Whittington at 43.

original understandings of the eighteenth and nineteenth centuries, then they have far less discretion to strike down laws.

Advocates of originalism also argue that it promotes democratic values because, "to the extent that judges do strike down government acts, they do so in the name of prior, popularly approved law."[23] These theories emphasize the concept of popular sovereignty, which requires that the people can only be limited by those constraints that previous sovereigns (i.e., past majorities of people acting in their sovereign capacity) have written into the Constitution: "Since 'We the People' ratify constitutional provisions and later generations govern themselves within the framework of that law, these later generations must follow the command of the 'People' unless one of those generations successfully amends the Constitution and so acts as the 'People' in its own right."[24]

The overwhelming practical problems with putting originalism into practice were discussed in the previous chapter. Even as a purely theoretical matter, though, originalism is a poor solution to the countermajoritarian problem. It is not clear how originalism respects the people's sovereignty more than any other theory does. Quite the contrary, it imposes centuries-old notions of individual rights and federalism upon modern Americans. Perhaps the original intent of the Constitution was to prohibit Congress from keeping guns out of schools or from penalizing rapists,[25] but when the Court strikes those laws down it is hardly empowering Americans as sovereigns.

Whittington refers to this as "the dead hand problem," which is that "originalism cannot be adopted as a method of constitutional interpretation because it renders the Constitution unduly rigid and burdens the present generation with the outmoded opinions of a previous generation."[26] He acknowledges that originalists have not sufficiently responded to the "dead hand" problem and attempts to fill the gap. He

---

[23] Ibid.
[24] See Flaherty, "History in Constitutional Argumentation." in *Encyclopedia of the American Constitution*, 2nd ed., 1290, 1291, Leonard W. Levy and Kenneth L. Karst eds., New York: Macmillan 2000), cited in Robert W. Scheef, "Note: 'Public Citizens' and the Constitution: Bridging the Gap Between Popular Sovereignty and Original Intent," *Fordham Law Review* 69: 2201. (April 2001).
[25] See, respectively, *United States v. Lopez*, 115 S.Ct. 1624 (1995); *United States v. Morrison*, 120 S.Ct. 1740 (2000).
[26] Whittington at 196.

attempts to demonstrate the absurdity of ignoring the original intention of, say, the commerce clause, by pointing out that, by the same logic, we also ought to ignore the original intention of much more recently passed constitutional amendments – a result he considers "strikingly incorrect."[27] But it is not clear why it would be so wrong to ignore even relatively recent original intent if that intent is already outdated. The Twenty-Sixth Amendment lowered the voting age to eighteen. It was ratified by the states in the late 1960s and early 1970s. Suppose it could be demonstrated that in those prefeminist days most voters intended that the states would be able to more easily disqualify young female voters than young male voters, or vice versa. (As late as 1975, some states had laws establishing different ages of legal dependency for men and women.)[28] Would it really be "strikingly incorrect" for the Court to follow the gender-neutral text of the amendment and ignore the original intent,[29] given the evolution in beliefs about gender equality over the past thirty years?

Whittington also argues that no one is willing to take the "dead hand" argument to its logical conclusion and completely ignore the intentions of the original constitutional ratifiers. "No advocate of living constitutionalism seems willing to embrace the complete rejection of intentions from constitutional interpretations."[30] But one can accept the importance of the framers' broad commitments without slavishly adopting their outdated specific beliefs. Ronald Dworkin helpfully distinguishes between the constitutional framers' *concepts* and their *conceptions*.[31] The framer enshrined the *concept* of cruel and unusual punishment in the Constitution. But their *conception* of what constitutes cruel and unusual punishment is quite different from what we believe today. The framers' forbade double jeopardy of "life or limb," so they apparently believed that some forms of mutilation of the limbs

---

[27] Ibid. at 199.
[28] See *Stanton v. Stanton*, 421 U.S. 7 (1975).
[29] Originalism does not treat the text as having independent meaning. The text only has meaning as an expression of authorial intention. See Dennis J. Goldford, "Does the Constitution Require Originalism?" Paper presented at the 2001 Annual Meeting of the Midwest Political Science Association, Chicago, IL. Therefore, originalism would apply the Twenty-Sixth Amendment in a gender-biased manner, despite its gender-neutral language, if it were clear that this was the original intent of the amendment.
[30] Whittington at 199.
[31] Dworkin at 134.

was not cruel and unusual, because if it were, a person could not have their limbs put in jeopardy even once.

Most people are mildly originalist in that they believe that the Constitution is concerned with concepts such as cruel and unusual punishment, due process, and legal equality and that judges should pay attention to that. This does not mean that judges must embrace centuries-old conceptions of what those phrases mean. Originalism would only restrain judges from imposing their own conceptions of equality, fair process, and so forth, if judges are required to follow the framers' specific eighteenth and nineteenth century conceptions of what these terms mean. Even if this were practical or desirable, it certainly would not make America any more democratic or deliberative.

The Constitution and the Protection of Individuals and Minorities

The most important response to the countermajoritarian problem is that the Constitution does not embrace democracy above all other values. Even if we assume that democratic decision making will consistently achieve utilitarian ends – lead to the greatest happiness for the majority of citizens – there are powerful currents in Western political thought that hold that majority rule is not the most important value. John Rawls writes that: "Each person possesses an inviolability founded on justice that even the welfare of society as a whole cannot override.... The Rights secured by justice are not subject to political bargaining or to the calculus of social interests."[32]

The rights that individuals and minorities have against the majority are not just the abstract concern of elite academics. They were a vital concern of the framers of the Fourteenth Amendment. While the founding fathers of the revolutionary era were largely concerned with protecting the rights of the majority against tyranny by an unpopular, centralized government, the framers of the Fourteenth Amendment were far more skeptical of democratic rule.[33] Political conditions in the pre – Civil War South amply demonstrated the tension between democracy and liberty. There was the issue of slavery of course. But

[32] Rawls at 3–4.
[33] The following discussion draws heavily on Amar, Akhil Reed, "A Tale of Three Wars: Tinker in Constitutional Context." *Drake Law Review* 48 (2000): 507–518.

suppression of liberty can rarely be quarantined to one corner of society. To maintain slavery, southern legislatures found it necessary to progressively abridge the liberty of more and more groups and individuals:

The Civil War was precipitated by extremely aggressive Southern attempts to stifle liberty. First, of course, the liberty of slaves was snatched away, requiring brutal repression, slave by slave. Then, it became necessary to oppress free blacks down South, because free blacks, by their very example of being free and walking around, were an incitement to slaves. Next, it became imperative to suppress anti-slavery Southern whites – and there were many such people: most white Southerners were not, in fact, slave owners. Finally, the Slave Power had to suppress Northerners who tried to come down South and preach against slavery – often, preach literally, because these were generally men and women of faith. Thus, in order to prop up slavery, the Slave Power had to resort to an ever-widening spiral of oppression. The Republican Party in 1860 was an outlaw party – it was, in effect, a crime in the Southern states to be a Republican; it was sedition.[34]

All this repression was accomplished by democratic means in that these laws were passed and enforced by electorally accountable officials. This taught the hard lesson that the Bill of Rights had to protect minorities and dissenting individuals against the majority just as it had to protect "the people" against the central government. The framers of the Fourteenth Amendment therefore needed to create "a new Bill of Rights, one against the periphery, and one that would balance the initial Bill of Rights against the center."[35]

Protecting minorities and individuals is a core command of the Fourteenth Amendment. The nineteenth-century framers had a different set of influences than the Revolutionary generation. The Civil War Amendments reflect the writings and beliefs of a new generation of Americans such as Ralph Waldo Emerson, Henry David Thoreau, and Harriet Beecher Stowe, as well as the influential Englishman John Stuart Mill. "This new birth of freedom in the Fourteenth Amendment helps redefine the entire American ethos to include more emphasis on the individual, and the need to protect him or her against majoritarian oppression and social intolerance, not just against unrepresentative government."[36]

[34] Ibid. at 513.
[35] Ibid. at 514.
[36] Ibid. at 515–516.

To some, it may seem obvious that the core purpose of the Four-teenth Amendment is protect minorities and individuals against ma-jority oppression, but this crucial point is often missed in the debate over judicial protection of fundamental rights, especially with regard to marriage. Several commentators have defended originalism against the charge that it would fail to protect the right to marry by arguing that the people would never vote for or tolerate the abolition of marriage. Robert Bork writes:

Once, after I had given a talk on the Constitution at a law school, a stu-dent approached and asked whether I thought the Constitution prevented a state from abolishing marriage. I said no, the Constitution assumed that the American people were not about to engage in despotic insanities and did not bother to protect against every imaginable instance of them. He replied that he could not accept a constitutional theory that did not prevent the criminal-ization of marriage. It would have been proper to respond that in any society that had reached such a degenerate state of totalitarianism, one which the Cambodian Khmer Rouge would find admirable, it would hardly matter what constitutional theory one held; the Constitution would have long since been swept aside and the Justices consigned to reeducation camps, if not worse. The actual Constitution does not forbid every ghastly hypothetical law, and once you begin to invent doctrine that does, you will create an unconfinable judicial power.[37]

Joseph Grano similarly dismisses concerns that an overly rigid the-ory of constitutional interpretation would eliminate the constitutional right to marriage:

I cannot conceive of a legislature prohibiting marriage, but the reason is that I cannot foresee the circumstances that would prompt such legislation. Presum-ably, however, such a decision would occur only after some event convinced a majority or super-majority of the population that marriage should be banned. Assuming such a society (again, one we cannot really conceive), it cannot be obvious that such a ban should be struck down as unconstitutional. "Ah!," you answer, "but suppose the legislature passes such a law without popu-lar support?" Anyone who believes that noninterpretivism or anything else in constitutional law, or in any other law, can safeguard society from such a legislature is welcome to his views, for I have nothing further to say to such a person.[38]

[37] Bork at 243.
[38] Grano at 1381, n.267.

Both Bork and Grano dismiss the constitutional right to marry as something that is needed only to salve the fears of paranoids and crackpots who imagine the United States turning into a bizarre society that would ban marriage. Their dismissals miss the point. The Fourteenth Amendment is not needed to prevent people from taking away their own right to marry; it is needed to prevent the majority from taking away *other people's* right to marry. Of course the majority of Americans will not support legislation that makes it impossible for them to marry. But they do support legislation that keeps it impossible for gays and lesbians to marry, just as state majorities in the South tolerated the ban on interracial couples marrying.

One of the greatest dangers of unchecked majoritarianism is that the majority will be tempted to place burdens on others that do not apply to themselves. In 1949, Justice Robert Jackson warned:

The framers of the Constitution knew, and we should not forget today, that there is no more effective practical guaranty against arbitrary and unreasonable government than to require that the principles of law which officials would impose upon a minority must be imposed generally. Conversely, nothing opens the door to arbitrary action so effectively as to allow those officials to pick and choose only a few to whom they will apply legislation and thus to escape the political retribution that might be visited upon them if larger numbers were affected. Courts can take no better measure to assure that laws will be just than to require that laws be equal in operation.[39]

While Jackson was writing over a half century ago, his concerns say much about the situation of same-sex marriage today. There is much in the news today about the sorry state of marriage in America and high divorce rates. Yet the public has shown no stomach for laws that would restrict their absolute freedom to marry or to divorce at will, even when children are involved. As Jackson warned, Congress and state legislatures have rushed to "defend" marriage from gays and lesbians while refusing to place even the slightest burden on the heterosexuals who form the great majority of the electorate.

To some degree this sort of behavior is inevitable, perhaps even desirable. The majority of people vote for legislation that taxes the inheritance of wealthy people while leaving their own inheritances untaxed.

---

[39] *Railway Express Agency v. New York*, 336 U.S. 106, 112–113 (1949).

People naturally prefer to place burdens on others rather than on themselves and it is not always unjust or bad policy to do so. The purpose of constitutional rights is to draw lines around certain liberties that cannot be treated unequally. The majority cannot vote to have free speech for themselves but not for others and cannot vote to place special burdens on minority religions. The central argument of this book is that because marriage is a long recognized fundamental right, the majority cannot take away the liberty for others to marry while retaining it for themselves.

Tushnet argues that Congress can actually be more protective of individual and minority rights than the Court. He highlights the Religious Freedom Restoration Act, which restored protections for religious exercise that the Court had limited in a 1990 decision.[40] The Court struck down that Act, holding that it violated the Supreme Court's prerogative as the ultimate interpreter of the Constitution. But this is not a good example of Congress protecting minority rights. America is a religiously plural society, composed of many powerful religious groups that consider themselves to be minority religions: Catholics, Jews, Mormons, Muslims, Southern Baptists, and so forth. This represents a powerful coalition of support for a bill and it is hardly surprising that Congress leapt to defend the interests of religious freedom. Other "minorities" protected by Congress, such as the elderly or disabled, are either represented by powerful lobbies or provoke sympathetic reactions from the majority of Americans. Also, every American has a likelihood of being disabled at some stage of their life and, hopefully, will live to become elderly. These examples merely demonstrate that Congress will take the lead when it is popular to do so. When it is popular to restrict individual rights, Congress and the President have not hesitated:

While the 1990s saw significant congressional action to protect individual rights, it also saw the passage of legislation that was severely criticized by legal liberals, such as the Illegal Immigration Reform and Immigrant Responsibility Act (IIRIRA), the Antiterrorism and Effective Death Penalty Act n19 (AEDPA), and the Prison Litigation Reform Act (PLRA). No less a civil libertarian than Anthony Lewis recently criticized President Clinton for signing all three laws

---

[40] *Employment Division v. Smith*, 494 U.S. 872 (1990).

and argued 'the years since 1992 have been as bad a period as any in memory for civil liberties in the United States.'[41]

In short, the academic pendulum may be swinging too far in terms of cynicism about the Court's willingness to protect unpopular minorities and trust for the elected branches of government to protect minority rights. It is worth remembering that the Supreme Court struck down Colorado's state constitutional amendment that permanently forbade legal protection for gays and lesbians at a time when President Clinton's Justice Department was unwilling even to file a brief in the case.

The question then is not whether the Courts should strive to protect the rights of individuals and minorities or whether there should be judicial review. The question is "what kind of judicial review can be justified in a deliberative democracy?"[42] The next section turns to that question.

The Courts, Consistency, and Principle

Alexander Bickel argued that the role of the Court was to inject principle rather than expediency into the political process. He understood that this was not always possible: sometimes difficult political situations require a certain degree of expediency. Nonetheless, even in those situations, the Court can pull the political process in the direction of principle and away from pure expediency. "The role of principle, when it cannot be the immutable governing rule, is to affect the tendency of policies of expediency. And it is a potent role."[43]

The role of principle restrains both the public and the courts. It restrains the public from having one set of rules themselves and another for the minority. Just as importantly, if taken seriously, it restrains judges from wantonly imposing their own values on the nation. In some areas of adjudication, the Court has taken the idea of principle very seriously indeed.

The constitutional area where the Court has taken principled adjudication most seriously is freedom of speech. There are numerous areas

---

[41] Griffin 686–687. It should be noted that Griffin also argues that the Court is "unlikely to hamper the operation of any of these laws." The question of whether the Courts can reliably protect individual rights will be taken up in the next section.

[42] Ibid. at 684.

[43] Bickel, *The Least Dangerous Branch*, at 64.

where the Court's free speech jurisprudence is still poorly developed. Nonetheless, the area of free speech is one where principle has most often triumphed over expediency. Here, the Court has been willing to set out its basic adjudicatory principles in a serious and straightforward manner. In *Chicago Police Department v. Mosley*,[44] the Justices clearly laid out the basic free speech principle of content neutrality:

Under the Equal Protection Clause, not to mention the First Amendment itself, government may not grant the use of a forum to people whose views it finds acceptable, but deny use to those wishing to express less favored or more controversial views. And it may not select which issues are worth discussing or debating in public facilities. There is an 'equality of status in the field of ideas,' and government must afford all points of view an equal opportunity to be heard. Once a forum is opened up to assembly or speaking by some groups, government may not prohibit others from assembling or speaking on the basis of what they intend to say. Selective exclusions from a public forum may not be based on content alone, and may not be justified by reference to content alone. Guided by these principles, we have frequently condemned such discrimination among different users of the same medium for expression.[45]

Principled adjudication means that the Court publicly sets out certain rights, defined by clear standards that it enforces evenhandedly. In the case of content neutrality, the Court has been willing to set out clear and stringent standards to enforce this general principle. In *Brandenburg v. Ohio*, the Court held that the government cannot censor speech it believes advocates illegal activity unless the speech is "directed to inciting or producing imminent lawless action and is likely to incite or produce such action."[46]

The clarity of this standard has successfully protected gays and lesbians at a time when they had few political or judicial friends. Even before *Brandenburg*, in 1958, a period of intense vilification of homosexuals,[47] the Supreme Court overturned a ruling that a homoerotic magazine incited illegal sexual activity.[48] In the 1970s many public universities tried to ban gay and lesbian student groups, arguing that they advocate illegal sexual activity. The gay and lesbian student groups

[44] 408 U.S. 92 (1972).
[45] 408 U.S. at 96.
[46] 395 U.S. 444, 447 (1969).
[47] See Gerstmann, *The Constitutional Underclass*, at pp. 62–63.
[48] *ONE v. Olesen*, 355 U.S. 371 (1958).

won every one of those cases, including five decisions at the federal
appellate court level, and none of those decisions were reversed by the
Supreme Court.[49] All of these cases applied the principle of content
neutrality and the standards laid out in *Brandenburg*.

These cases show that when legal principles and standards are clearly
set out by the Supreme Court they can not only protect individual and
minority rights, but they can also prevent the courts from basing their
decisions upon their own personal policy preferences. It is hardly likely
that in the 1970s the courts were packed with judges who wanted their
sons and daughters to attend colleges with a strong gay and lesbian
presence. In fact, in some of these cases, judges took the unusual step
of expressing their personal distaste for the rulings they had to make.
In one case, a federal judge wrote, "It is of no moment, in First Amendment jurisprudence that ideas advocated by an association may to some
or most of us be abhorrent, even sickening."[50]

It has been noted that "gay people have found far more success in
the courts than in Congress."[51] But these victories have not generally
come as the result of judicial policy preferences for pro – gay rights
results, or from any line of cases that are explicitly concerned with gay
rights at all. Rather, gays and lesbians have benefited enormously from
general principles that the Warren Court laid down regarding freedom
of speech and association, procedural due process, limits on police
enforcement practices, and the requirement that laws not be unduly
vague or discretionary. Reviewing William Eskridge's book *GayLaw*,
Richard Posner observes:

Another revelation is that the constitutional adventurism of the Supreme Court
under Earl Warren's chiefship, *an era when the Court seemed to go out of its way
to deny the existence of homosexual rights*, produced substantial legal gains for
homosexuals. The reason – this Eskridge does not stress – is that types of
legal regulation that the liberal Warren Court made more difficult were precisely the methods by which law enforcers silenced, harassed, and intimidated

---

49 For a list and further discussion of these cases, see Rubenstein, William B, "Since When
is the 14th Amendment Our Route to Equality: Some Reflections on the Constructions
of the Hate Speech Debate from a Lesbian/Gay Perspective." *Law and Sexuality* 2
(1992): 19–27, 23.
50 *Cyr v. Walls*, 439 F. Supp. 697, 701 n.3 (N.D. Tex. 1977).
51 Podhoretz at 33, quoting the executive director of the Lambda Legal Defense and
Education Fund.

homosexuals. Those methods included the enforcement of vagrancy laws, the prohibition of pornography, movie censorship, the discharge of tenured public employees, the enforcement of vague criminal statutes, the suppression of organizations that advocated 'immoral' practices, and police brutality and surveillance of disfavored groups.[52]

Thus, "homosexuals were the unintended beneficiaries of legal innovations made by judges who for the most part had rather little sympathy for them."[53] Judicial treatment of gays and lesbians indicates that when the Court does lay down clear principles and standards, these can help protect the legal equality of even the most unpopular groups.

This is why the Court's fundamental rights jurisprudence is so disappointing. As noted earlier, the Court's decisions on unenumerated fundamental rights are among the most incoherent and inconsistent in constitutional law. Because the Court has continually wavered and equivocated about where these rights come from and how they are derived and defined, the Court has been unable to apply any legal principles in a consistent fashion. Without clear principles to appeal to, the rights of gays and lesbians depend upon judicial attitudes rather than precedent.

The "right to privacy" is a case in point. As discussed earlier, the Court has held that both married and unmarried people have a fundamental constitutional right to access to contraceptives. These cases led many members of the legal community, including the Federal Appellate Court for the Eleventh Circuit, to conclude that the Court had found a principle of sexual privacy that protected, at a minimum, consenting adult sexual activity in the privacy of the home. In *Hardwick v. Bowers*, a Federal Circuit Court struck down a Georgia antisodomy law, holding, "The right to privacy extends to some activities that would not normally merit constitutional protection simply because those activities take on added significance under certain limited circumstances. In particular, the constitutional protection of privacy reaches its height when the state attempts to regulate an activity in the home."[54]

---

[52] Posner, "Ask, Tell," *The New Republic* 52, 53 (October 11, 1999), reviewing William N. Eskridge's *GayLaw: Challenging the Apartheid of the Closet* (emphasis added).
[53] Ibid.
[54] 760 F.2d 1202, 1212 (11th Cir. 1985).

In *Bowers v. Hardwick*, the Supreme Court reversed the Circuit Court in a 5–4 decision, holding that earlier precedents had only recognized constitutional protection for "family, marriage [and] procreation."[55] Many commentators have critiqued the Court's decision, but two particular criticisms merit attention here. *Eisenstadt v. Baird* explicitly held that the right to contraceptives is unrelated to marriage.[56] Regarding procreation, there is no doubt that the decision in *Eisenstadt* is concerned with the issue of birth control. But, as it has often been noted, the most effective form of birth control is abstinence. Contraceptives are not necessary to protect one's constitutional right to avoid unwanted pregnancy unless there is also a constitutional right to engage in non-reproductive sexual behavior. If the government had the power to ban recreational sexual intercourse, then contraceptives would be irrelevant.[57]

Also, even if the right to use contraceptives were solely an offshoot of reproductive freedom, then heterosexual sodomy should also be without constitutional protection. But even though the Georgia statute was just as applicable to heterosexual activities as to homosexual activities, the Court went out of its way to state that it was not deciding whether heterosexual sodomy is constitutionally protected. "The only claim properly before the Court, therefore, is Hardwick's challenge to the Georgia statute as applied to consensual homosexual sodomy. We express no opinion on the constitutionality of the Georgia statute as applied to other acts of sodomy."[58] But if there is no right to sexual privacy beyond issues of reproductive freedom, it should be absolutely clear that there is no constitutional difference at all between heterosexual and homosexual sodomy. While there is nothing wrong with a court addressing only the case before it, the Court's exclusively addressing

---

[55] 478 U.S. 186, 191 (1986).

[56] 405 U.S. at 453, "If the right of privacy means anything, it is the right of the individual, married or single, to be free from unwarranted governmental intrusion into matters so fundamentally affecting a person as the decision whether to bear or beget a child."

[57] Cases of rape are an exception, but none of the contraception cases involved such a situation. Norma McCorvey, a.k.a. "Jane Roe," of *Roe v. Wade*, initially claimed that she had been gang raped but later recanted. See Tribe, Laurence, *Abortion: The Clash of Absolutes*. New York: Norton, 1990. In any event, the issue did not affect the Court's analysis in *Roe*.

[58] 478 U.S. at 188. As this book went to press, the Court had heard oral argument but had not decided a case challenging the Texas sodomy law that banned only homosexual sodomy.

homosexuality is of a different order of magnitude because the Court expressly reserved judgment on a sexual act that the Court's reasoning unavoidably leaves unprotected. It is akin to the Court adding a caveat in a automobile warranty case that says, "we express no opinion on the constitutionality of the warranty statute when the purchasers are homosexual."

There is a burgeoning literature arguing that appellate courts decide cases based on judicial attitudes rather than legal principle or precedent.[59] This literature devotes too little attention to legal doctrine and there is a dearth of empirical research that studies the impact of clarity of doctrine on judicial outcomes. Therefore, little of the published work in this area distinguishes between highly principled areas of constitutional law such as the line of cases applying *Brandenburg*, and under-theorized areas such as privacy.[60] One of the few works that seriously looks at the impact of legal arguments on how judges decide cases is Lee Epstein and Joseph F. Kobylka's, *The Supreme Court and Legal Change: Abortion and the Death Penalty*, which studies the impact of legal argument on judicial willingness to change the law. They conclude:

Our finding, stated simply, is this: the law and legal arguments grounded in law matter, and they matter dearly. The justices that hear these cases and the groups and governments that bring them are relevant factors in their eventual outcomes and policies they produce, but it is in the arguments they hear and make that at least in the early stages of a doctrinal and decisional shift seem to influence most clearly the content and direction of the legal change that results.[61]

The free speech cases and the cases discussed by Posner show that courts often do protect the rights of gays and lesbians regardless of

---

[59] The leading books on this are *The Supreme Court and the Attitudinal Model*. New York: Cambridge University Press, 1993; *Majority Rule or Minority Will: Adherence to Precedent on the U.S. Supreme Court*. New York: Cambridge University Press, 1999, both by Jeffery A. Segal and Harold J. Spaeth.

[60] In fact, Segal and Spaeth do not discuss *Brandenburg's* impact on Supreme Court behavior at all because it is not listed as a "landmark" case in Elder Witt's *Guide to the U.S. Supreme Court* (Washington, D.C.: CQ Press, 1990). They remark that this omission is "surprising," but, as a result of it, they leave the case out of their analysis.

[61] Epstein, Lee, and Joseph F. Kobylka. *The Supreme Court and Legal Change: Abortion and the Death Penalty*. Chapel Hill: University of North Carolina Press, 1992, at 301–302.

judicial attitudes if the law at issue sets out clear legal standards. But as noted, free speech is an unusual area. The principle that the government cannot ban or punish speech is well established, as are the legal rules such as the *Brandenburg* test that courts use to enforce these principles. As a result, even unpopular groups such as Nazis and the Ku Klux Klan and marginalized groups such as gays and lesbians are frequently victorious in the judicial forum.[62]

As we have seen, there is a fundamental right to marriage that applies to same-sex marriage. Nonetheless, it would take a great deal of judicial courage to enforce such a right for gays and lesbians. When the courts are so uncertain as to what part of the Constitution the right to marry comes from or why there is a fundamental right to marry at all, it is not surprising that the courts are reluctant to apply that right to an unpopular group such as gays and lesbians. The "right to privacy" is also a poorly theorized area, with the Court uncertain about where privacy comes from and what it even really means. As with marriage, the Court has been unwilling to extend the protection of sexual privacy that it gives to others to gays and lesbians. Thus we have a Court that has been adventurous in expanding rights for the heterosexual majority, but then finds a safe harbor in an ostensible adherence to tradition when it comes to gays and lesbians.

The importance of clear, principled jurisprudence is missed by Cass Sunstein, who argues that the Court should often avoid principled decision making and should instead write "narrow" and "shallow" decisions that do little more than resolve disputes between parties. He argues in favor of "judicial minimalism," which is "the phenomenon of saying no more than necessary to justify an outcome, and leaving as much as possible undecided."[63] Sunstein specifically argues against the position that "urges principled consistency across cases."[64] Minimalism is the exact opposite of the Court's approach in *Brandenburg*. "Minimalists do not like to work deductively; they do not see outcomes as reflecting rules or theories laid out in advance."[65] Sunstein defends

---

[62] Of course, those same free speech rights can work against gays and lesbians as well when private groups argue that their rights of speech and association allow them to exclude gays and lesbians. See cases in note 11, supra.

[63] Sunstein. *One Case at a Time: Judicial Minimalism and the Supreme Court.* Cambridge: Harvard University Press, 1999, at 3–4.

[64] Ibid. at 7.

[65] Ibid. at 9.

minimalism as follows:

Why might anyone want an outcome to be unaccompanied by a reason? For one thing, an approach of this kind does not foreclose other decisions in other cases. Thus a mistaken ground for a decision will not produce later mistakes. If people are sometimes better at knowing *what* is right than knowing *why* it is right, this is an advantage. Such decisions take relatively less time to produce, since it can be far easier to come up with a decision than with an explanation.[66]

Sunstein assumes that it is possible for a Court to know what is right without knowing why it is right. But what does it really mean when a judge says, "I know it is right that the Constitution protects only heterosexual marriage, but I don't know why?" The requirement of principle and reason requires judges to articulate a basis other than their own prejudices and preferences, and therefore is the only true ally that unpopular minorities and individuals have in the courts.

Nonetheless, Sunstein's skepticism of principled decision making is shared by many. The argument that principled adjudication can protect the rights of unpopular minorities and individuals is out of favor in many academic circles. One reason for this is the belief, already discussed, that judicial decisions are primarily determined by judge's attitudes. As discussed above, this "attitudinal" model gives short shrift to the judicial protection given to gays and lesbians when the Court makes legal principles sufficiently clear. However, there are several other, significant, powerfully articulated objections to Bickel's proposition that the role of the Court is to inject principle into the public arena. These objections will be addressed in the following section.

Objections to the Role of Principle in the Courts

One line of objections to principled decision making is the perceived clash between principled outcomes and substantively "good" outcomes. This perceived clash is largely a result of the historical context in which the argument for principled adjudication gained national attention. In 1959, Herbert Wechsler, the Harlan Fiske Stone Professor of Law at Columbia University, delivered the high profile "Holmes

---

[66] Ibid. at 15 (emphasis in original).

lecture" to the Harvard Law School. His lecture was reproduced as an article in the same year,[67] and his written and published remarks received wide attention.

Wechsler argued that the difference between "ad hoc" politics and the judicial process is that the latter must be "genuinely principled, resting with respect to every step that is involved in reaching judgment on analysis and reasons quite immediately transcending the results achieved."[68] Decisions must be based on something more than the judge's opinion of what the desirable outcome is or who the more sympathetic party may be. And judges need to consider how the principle invoked to decide the current case will affect future cases. "Must [courts] not decide on grounds of adequate neutrality and generality, tested not only by the instant of application but by the others they imply?"[69] For Wechsler, this commitment to principle is what prevented courts from acting merely as a "naked power organ."

Unfortunately, Wechsler made this argument in the context of criticizing the Warren Court's decision in the great civil rights case, *Brown v. Board of Education*, which at the time was still a controversial and relatively recent case. Wechsler argued that although he agreed with the result in *Brown*, he did not believe that the Court had articulated a principled basis for its decision. *Brown*'s defenders struck back quickly and angrily, defending a sociological and political role for a Court that would bring about substantively desirable results:

Wechsler's approach, to those critical of it, bore too much similarity to the now bad old days of arid legal formalism. In an impassioned speech, Eugene Rostow, the dean of the Yale Law School, fairly spanked Wechsler and his cohort for their attack on the Court. 'Professor Wechsler's lecture . . . represents a repudiation of all we have learned about law since Holmes published his Common Law in 1881, and Roscoe Pound followed during the first decade of this century with his pathbreaking pleas for a result-oriented, sociological jurisprudence, rather than a mechanical one.' And Martin Shapiro remarked, 'This search for legal standards which the Justices are to discover by the process of collective legal reasoning is little more than the lawyer's nostalgia for the

---

[67] Wechsler at 1–35. Both the lecture and article are cited in Friedman, Barry, "Symposium: Defining Democracy for the Next Century: Neutral Principles: A Retrospective," 50 *Vanderbilt Law Review* 503–536, 511–514 (March 1997).
[68] Wechsler at 15.
[69] Ibid.

legal Court and the legal modes of discourse which prevailed before the advent of the political Court and political modes of discourse.'[70]

Cold abstractions of principle hardly seemed sufficient when contrasted with what was seen as the substantive goodness of the Warren Court's decisions. Bickel's call, three years after Wechsler's lecture and article, for principled adjudication met with similar resistance. "The Bickelian interpretative method was itself rejected almost as soon as it was offered. The increasing activism of the Warren Court . . . fed desires to loosen the constraints on the judiciary that Bickel had imposed and to provide an interpretive method that was more substantive than Bickel's rather vague call for principles."[71]

This perceived contrast between principled adjudication and substantively good outcomes is both illusory and unfortunate. It fails to appreciate the distinction between the short term and long term "goodness" of a result. When the Nazis wish to march in Skokie, Illinois, a neighborhood filled with holocaust survivors, the good result in the short term might be to protect the residents and ban the march.[72] For Wechsler, the Courts must look beyond the immediate result. Is society better off when the government has discretion to decide what groups' messages are too repulsive or incendiary to be expressed in public? What principle could be applied to the situation that might protect the holocaust survivors without giving the government carte blanche as censors? The job of Skokie's mayor and council members might be to represent the understandable desires of the townspeople to keep the Nazis out. But the job of the Court is to protect the free speech rights of the Nazis unless some principled distinction can be found between the Nazis' speech and other forms of unpopular speech.[73]

Even when there is a consensus as to what a good result is, the conflict is not between those substantively good results and cold abstract principles. The tension is between unrestrained, case by case,

---

[70] Friedman, supra, at 519–520 (citations omitted).

[71] Whittington, *Constitutional Interpretation*, at 21.

[72] For a careful analysis of the substantive burdens and benefits to the Skokie community of allowing the Nazis to march, see Downs, Donald A., *Nazis in Skokie: Freedom, Community and the First Amendment*. South Bend: Notre Dame Press, 1985.

[73] One such distinction might be between targeted racial vilification and other forms of speech. Downs suggested this possibility in *Nazis in Skokie*, supra, but has subsequently moved away from this position.

policymaking by judges and principled adjudication. In fact, the *Brown* Court was not particularly clear in its reasoning or as to what legal principle it was expounding.[74] Wechsler's call for a statement of principle led to a flurry of major scholarly work that helped set out the modern principles of antidiscrimination law. In response to Wechsler, influential figures such as Charles Black, Owen Fiss and Louis Pollak all wrote articles developing principles of antiracial subordination.[75]

Originalists such as Robert Bork criticize Wechsler from the opposite end, arguing that his "neutral principles" leave too much discretion for judges to read their own values into the Constitution. For Bork, principled adjudication addresses only half of the "Madisonian dilemma" of how to balance minority rights with majoritarian democracy.[76] Bork argues that principles must be neutral not only in application, but in derivation and definition to prevent judges from imposing their own personal values.[77] Meanwhile, scholars of the "critical legal studies" movement persuasively argue that no principle can truly be neutral in the way Bork demands. No principle can be substantively neutral; every legal principle represents value and policy judgments. For critical legal theorists, the law disguises these values and policies as being neutrally derived and defined, even though they really are skewed in favor of the dominant economic classes and racial groups. These theorists seek to strip away the pretense of neutrality and reveal the hierarchical values that lurk behind the supposedly neutral principles.[78]

Both Bork and the critical legal theorists are correct that nothing Wechsler wrote would create substantively neutral law. Nor did

---

[74] See *The Constitutional Underclass*, at 29–34.

[75] Pollak, Louis, "Racial Discrimination and Judicial Integrity: A Reply to Professor Wechsler." *University of Pennsylvania Law Review* 108 (1959): 1–39; Black, Charles L., "The Lawfulness of the Segregation Decisions." *Yale Law Journal* 69 (1960): 421–430; and Fiss, Owen, "Racial Imbalance in the Public Schools: The Constitutional Concepts." *Harvard Law Review* 78 (1965): 564–617; all cited in Klarman, Michael, "An Interpretive History of Equal Protection." *Michigan Law Review* 90 (1980): 213–318, 255.

[76] Bork, Robert. "Styles in Constitutional Theory." *South Texas Law Journal* 26 (1985): 383–395, 383–384.

[77] Bork, Robert. "Neutral Principles and Some First Amendment Problems." *Indiana Law Journal* 47 (1971): 1–35, 7.

[78] For an excellent set of examples of critical legal theory, ranging from constitutional law to business law, see Kairys, David, *The Politics of Law: A Progressive Critique*, rev. ed. New York: Pantheon Books, 1990.

Wechsler actually advocate such substantive neutrality, which is indeed impossible. It is perhaps unfortunate that Wechsler used the word "neutral," as it implies to many people the idea that the law should somehow be value free. A better term than "neutral" principles is *consistent* principles.[79] This has both retrospective and prospective meaning. Retrospectively, the Court should resolve disputes according to public, reasonably clear principles rather than engaging in ad hoc policy making. This is nothing less than the promise of "the rule of law." Prospectively, this means that when judges create new laws, they formulate them as general principles that they understand they will be obligated to apply consistently in future cases, regardless of their feelings towards the parties that come before them. This is nothing less than the promise of "equality before the law."

This does not vitiate the need for substantive value judgments by the courts in fashioning these principles. The free speech principle of content neutrality, embraced by *Brandenburg* and other First Amendment cases, is not substantively neutral. It embraces the values of dialogue, tolerance, and rationality, sometimes sacrificing values of tranquility, order, and the right of people to avoid contact with hateful ideas and epithets. The principle is not self-evidently right, nor is it inherently "required" by the Constitution. It needs to be defended on its merits, as it has been by Justices Oliver Wendell Holmes, Louis Brandeis, William O. Douglas, and Hugo Black and countless academic commentators and civil libertarians for nearly a hundred years.

Another line of criticism of principled adjudication is that it is naïve to assume that courts will ever act this way. This book holds up free speech as a highly principled area of constitutional law. Stanley Fish, in his well-known and provocatively titled book, *There's No Such Thing as Free Speech and It's a Good Thing Too*,[80] challenges this. Fish argues that "Free Speech, in short, is not an independent value but a political prize."[81] He claims that "Despite the apparent absoluteness of the First Amendment, there are any number of ways of getting around

---

[79] This term was suggested to the author by Mark Graber during a conversation at the 2000 Annual Meeting of the American Political Science Association in Washington, D.C.

[80] Fish, Stanley. *There's No Such Thing as Free Speech and It's a Good Thing Too*. New York: Oxford University Press, 1994.

[81] Ibid. at 102.

it ... the preferred strategy is to manipulate the distinction, essential to First Amendment jurisprudence, between speech and action."[82] Action, unlike speech, is not protected by the First Amendment, and Fish believes that the distinction between speech and action is easily manipulated. He asserts that "speech always seems to be crossing the line into action, where it becomes, at least potentially, consequential."[83] This is a very strong claim. If true, it would indeed be fatal to the argument that the Court has behaved in a principled fashion in this area. But Fish offers virtually no evidence for this enormously important assertion. Indeed, the only example he cites is a 1942 case, *Chaplinsky v. New Hampshire*, that predates the advent of modern First Amendment law and which the Supreme Court has never once relied upon since then.[84]

Mark Tushnet is another skeptic of principled adjudication. He argues that it is impossible for judges in a multimember body like the Supreme Court to apply principles in a consistent fashion:

The first institutional problem is that Supreme Court decisions are made by a collective body, which is constrained by a norm of compromise and cooperation. Suppose that in case 1 Justices M, N, and O have taken neutral principles theory to heart and believe that the correct result is justified by principle A. Justices P, Q, R, and S have done likewise but believe that the same result is justified by principle B. Justices T and V, who also accept principle A but believe it inapplicable to case 1, dissent. The four-person group gains control of the writing of the opinion, and the three others who agree with the result accede to the institutional pressure for majority decisions and join an opinion that invokes principle B. Now case 2 arises. Justices T and V are convinced that, because case 2 is relevantly different from case 1, principle A should be used. They join with Justices M, N, and O and produce a majority opinion invoking principle A. If principle B were used, the result would be different; thus, there are four dissenters.[85]

Although this may sound a bit more like an SAT question than an argument, Tushnet has a valid point. If Justices M, N, and O joined the other Justices in case 1, which set out a certain principle that they

---

[82] Ibid. at 105.

[83] Ibid.

[84] To be fair to Fish, he spends most of his time arguing that the way that free speech is currently conceptualized is not value neutral. As indicated above, I agree with that point.

[85] Tushnet, Mark, "Following the Rules Laid Down, A Critique of Interpretivism and Neutral Principles." *Harvard Law Review* 96 (February 1983): 781–827, 808–809.

do not believe in, then it would be unfair to criticize them for being unprincipled when they refused to apply that principle in future cases.

But this example certainly does not mean that principled adjudication is impossible. For one thing, some principles, such as content neutrality, are sufficiently widely accepted that they consistently command a majority of the Court. (Although there are often sharp disagreements among the Justices regarding how that principle applies to a particular case.) More significantly, in the first case, Justices M, N, and O were free to write a separate opinion that concurs with the result but makes clear that they do not endorse principle B. Also, if the Court is truly that fractured, it may be better not to take the case or, as Sunstein suggests, decide the case without stating a reason.[86] This would not lead future litigants to rely on a precedent that the majority of justices would not be willing to enforce in the future.

Tushnet also argues that applying consistent principles is beyond the capacity of mortal judges:

[E]ven if we confine our attention to cases in the same general area as the present one, this formulation of the neutrality requirement is obviously too stringent. We cannot and should not expect judges to have fully elaborated theories of race discrimination in their first cases, much less theories of gender, illegitimacy, and other modes of discrimination as well.[87]

This is certainly true, but it ignores the way that legal principles are actually developed. Legal principles do not emerge full-blown from a single case; they are developed over time. Neither *Brown* nor *Brandenburg* were bolts from the blue. Both were part of a long string of cases dealing with racial segregation and free speech. As detailed in Chapter 4, the right to marry evolved over many decades. Principled jurisprudence does not require a single judicial decision to serve as a complete guide to all future cases. It does demand that when a broad right to marry develops in the law, that courts take this seriously and not deny the right

---

[86] The Court routinely gives such opinions, called per curiam opinions. Some readers may question my own consistency here, as I previously criticized Sunstein's endorsement of minimalist jurisprudence. I do argue that it is better to give a reasoned decision than an unreasoned opinion. But it is also preferable to not give any reason than to give a reason that one does not actually believe and has no intention of abiding by in the future.

[87] Tushnet, Mark, "Following the Rules Laid Down, A Critique of Interpretivism and Neutral Principles." *Harvard Law Review* 96 (February 1983): 781–827, 810.

to gays and lesbians based upon the inadequate distinctions discussed in Chapter 5.

Tushnet also argues that principles are too subject to interpretation to require a specific outcome. He analogizes the application of legal principles to completing a string of mathematically related numbers:

Consider the following multiple choice question: 'Which pair of numbers comes next in the series 1, 3, 5, 7? (a) 9, 11; (b) 11, 13; (c) 25, 18.' It is easy to show that any of the answers is correct. The first is correct if the rule generating the series is 'list the odd numbers'; the second is correct if the rule is 'list the odd prime numbers'; and the third is correct if a more complex rule generates the series. Thus, if asked to follow the underlying rule – the principle of the series – we can justify a tremendous range of divergent answers by constructing the rule so that it generates the answer that we want. As the legal realists showed, this result obtains for legal as well as mathematical rules.[88]

There is some truth to this, but, again, principles are developed over time, and the more cases that develop them, the clearer their application to new cases becomes. To use Tushnet's number analogy, the longer the string, the clearer the principle is. The string: 1, 3, 5, 7 can be completed in a number of ways. But once the string skips 9 and 15, continuing: 11, 13, 17, then it becomes clear that it is a string of odd prime numbers and that the next number should be 19. With the right to marry, the principle also becomes clearer over time. After *Loving v. Virginia*, it would still have been possible to interpret the principle of that case as solely anti-racial subordination, with no relevance to marriage, although that would have been a stretch. After *Bodie v. Connecticut*, *Zablocki v. Redhail*, *Moore v. East Cleveland*, and *Turner v. Safely*, it became clear that these cases stand for a much broader principle of marital freedom that is not restricted to traditional families or procreation. As we saw in Chapter 5, no reasonable principle has been articulated that explains the holdings in those cases that does not also cover same-sex marriage. Gays and lesbians have been denied the right to same-sex marriage largely because neither the Court nor its critics have taken the norm of principled adjudication as seriously in Fourteenth Amendment jurisprudence as they have in First Amendment jurisprudence.

In order to appreciate the role of principled adjudication, we need not adopt a view of judges as automatons, mechanically applying

---

[88] Ibid. at 822.

principles to facts. Judges, and especially Justices, do have discretion. The question is what kind of discretion. Ronald Dworkin distinguishes between "strong" and "weak" discretion and uses a hypothetical sergeant to illustrate his point.[89] If a sergeant is told by his commanding officer to choose any five men for an unspecified assignment, then the sergeant has strong discretion. If the commanding officer is more specific about what kind of men the mission will require, the sergeant still has weak discretion in choosing the five men. Extending Dworkin's analogy to the question of protecting the rights of gays and lesbians, suppose there are three police sergeants, one who is very homophobic, one who is mildly so, and another who is not homophobic at all. Suppose also that among the men under the sergeants' command there is one gay police officer who is unusually strong and fit. If the sergeants have strong discretion, it is likely that the first two sergeants will not choose that officer to be among the five men selected, but the third one might. If the commanding officer tells the sergeants to choose the strongest and most fit five men the sergeants have at their disposal, both the mildly homophobic and nonhomophobic sergeants will probably choose the gay police officer. But since the words "strong" and "fit" are somewhat subjective, the very homophobic sergeant still has room to exclude the gay police officer. So more specific rules do not eliminate the role of attitudes and prejudices but they do *lessen* discretion, and they can guide outcomes, unless the negative attitudes of the decision makers are very strong. Thus, a norm of more principled adjudication in the area of fundamental rights, one akin to First Amendment adjudication, would not make attitudes irrelevant, but it could still provide substantial rights-based protection to gays and lesbians.

Some proponents of the attitudinal model of Supreme Court decision making argue that legal principles do not even accomplish that much. Spaeth and Segal assert that "the justices are rarely influenced" by legal precedent.[90] Their conclusions are based on their findings that when Justices dissent in a particular decision, they do not subsequently put those objections to the side and vote in accordance with that case in the future. But as Howard Gillman has pointed out, this hardly shows

[89] Dworkin at n.31.
[90] Segal, Jeffery A., and Harold J. Spaeth, at 288.

that the Justices are following their attitudes or political preferences rather than their best understanding of legal principles.[91] It does mean that they continue to disagree with the principle set forward or with how that principle was applied in the case from which they dissented. If Justices ignored First Amendment principles and simply relied upon their own attitudes and policy preferences, then we would expect to see familiar ideological groupings with the Court's liberals, moderates, and conservatives all tending to agree with their ideological counterparts. But that is not what actually happens. Eugene Volokh has measured how supportive the current Justices have been of First Amendment claims from 1994 (the last time the Court had a change in personnel) to 2000.[92] It turns out that a Justice's ideology is a poor predictor of his or her support for First Amendment claims. The three strongest supporters of First Amendment rights are Justices Kennedy, Souter, and Thomas. The three least supportive Justices are Rehnquist, O'Connor, and Breyer. The middle three are Ginsburg, Stevens, and Scalia. Unless the general perception of these Justices' ideologies is vastly off the mark, these groupings make it quite clear that they are doing something other than merely voting in accordance with their own ideologies.

Arguments from principle certainly have their limitations. It would be a significant exaggeration to claim that all judges would decide all cases the same way, even if they consistently applied the same legal principles. Justices Antonin Scalia and Ruth Bader Ginsburg are going to disagree at times no matter what. But legal principles are often clear enough that they will be applied the same way even by judges with very different views. Despite the deep divisions in the Rehnquist Court, it still delivers many unanimous or nearly unanimous opinions – a fact that is too often ignored by proponents of the "attitudinal" model of decision making. "Modern Courts have consisted of a mix of liberal, conservative and moderate justices. And yet, they consistently reach unanimous decisions in more than one-third of all decisions on the

---

[91] Gillman, Howard, "What's Law Got to Do with It? Judicial Behaviorists Test the 'Legal Model' of Judicial Decision Making." *Law and Social Inquiry* 26 (spring 2001): 465–498.

[92] Volokh, Eugene, "How the Justices Voted in Free Speech Cases, 1994–2000." *UCLA Law Review* 48 (2001): 1191–1202. Volokh's methodology for measuring supportiveness of First Amendment claims is clearly described in the article.

merits; in fact, in the 1995 term, 45% of the decisions on the merits were unanimous."[93]

It should also be noted that agreement even amongst the most principled judges depends upon shared cultural understandings. Western understandings of reason and rationality are not "neutral," nor are they shared by all cultures. A person who completed the string of numbers referred to above by "throwing bones" would probably not come up with '19' as the next number. Nor would an Islamic judge from Afghanistan be likely to conclude that same-sex marriage is a fundamental constitutional right, regardless of precedent. So no legal principle or decision is "objective"; they are products of reasoning in the Western legal tradition. But virtually all judges are trained and educated in this tradition. The problem realistically faced by unpopular minorities and individuals in America is not judges from the Taliban, it is judges who are themselves immersed in the cultural views that make these minorities and individuals unpopular in the first place. While a commitment to consistent principles is not culturally neutral, it does hold the promise of equality under the law in our society.

Levels of Generality

Perhaps the greatest challenge of principled adjudication is defining a legal principle's level of generality. Robert Bork correctly argues that if a judge "must demonstrate why principle X applies to cases A and B but not to case C... he must, by the same token, also explain why the principle is defined as X, rather than X minus, which would cover A but not cases B and C, or as X plus, which would cover all cases, A, B and C."[94] Much of the debate has been framed in terms of narrow or specific levels of generality versus broader levels. Justice Scalia claims to apply principles that are narrowly defined. For example, Scalia believes that whatever constitutional rights a father might have with regard to his biological son are limited to situations where the father

---

[93] Herbert Kritzer, J. Mitchell Pickerill, and Mark Richards, "Bringing the Law Back in: Finding a Role for Law in Models of Supreme Court Decision-Making." Paper delivered at the 1998 Annual Meeting of the Midwest Political Science Association, Chicago, IL.

[94] Bork, Robert, "Neutral Principles and Some First Amendment Problems." *Indiana Law Journal* 47 (1971): 1–35, 7.

is married to the boy's mother, because the liberty interest is narrowly defined by traditions that respect the nuclear family and do not tolerate adultery:

We do not understand why, having rejected our focus upon the societal tradition regarding the natural father's rights vis-à-vis a child whose mother is married to another man, [the dissenting Justices] would choose to focus instead upon 'parenthood.' Why should the relevant category not be even more general – perhaps 'family relationships'; or 'personal relationships'; or even 'emotional attachments in general'? Though the dissent has no basis for the level of generality it would select, we do: We refer to the most specific level at which a relevant tradition protecting, or denying protection to, the asserted right can be identified.[95]

Scalia argues that his approach limits judicial discretion by keeping principles narrow. But, as observed in Chapter 6, "tradition" is a very poor way to restrain judges since American traditions are so varied and ambiguous and are often in tension with one another. Laurence Tribe and Michael Dorf argue that the better way to prevent purely result-driven legal decisions is to insist that judges adequately describe the principle they are applying before they even discuss the present case:

the requirement that distinctions among prior cases and historical traditions be principled provides one check on result-orientation. Result-orientation would be further limited by a requirement that the asserted level of generality provide an appropriate description of already-protected rights without reference to the newly asserted rights. Judges should ask whether the abstraction is a bona fide tradition or "a mere concoction for litigational purposes." First, the Court must determine what concerns actually motivated the prior decisions. Only after the Court has selected the appropriate level of abstraction at which to describe these concerns should it test the asserted specific right against that abstraction.[96]

It is not particularly helpful to define rights as "broad" or "narrow." It implies one-dimensionality, when rights actually exist along multiple axes. The right to marry is broad in that it applies to nontraditional couples such as gays and lesbians. It is narrow in that it would not protect the legal rights of gays and lesbians in any other area besides marriage.

---

[95] *Michael D. v. Gerald H.*, 491 U.S. 110, 128, n.6 (1989).
[96] Tribe, Laurence, and Michael Dorf, at 1103.

There is no helpful formula for defining levels of generality. Every principle is defined by the reasons that the Court protects it in the first place, and these reasons will always be open to argument. If the sole reason for freedom of speech were to protect political debate, then only political speech would be protected by the First Amendment. (An approach endorsed by Bork.[97]) Tribe and Dorf argue that this insistence on articulating the reasons that stand behind a legal principle in order to define its contours is the best way to limit judges' ability to impose their own values. "This program does not eliminate judicial value-choice, but it does limit choice considerably more than does [Scalia's approach]. It does so by requiring that, in characterizing its prior cases, the Court look not only to what those cases held, but also to the essential reasons for those holdings."[98]

This means that the Court should protect same-sex marriage unless it can articulate a principle that explains the Court's prior holdings but does not extend to same-sex marriage. As discussed in Chapter 5, the distinctions given so far, such as "same-sex couples cannot have children," cannot meet even a minimum requirement of rationality.

Conclusion

Principled enforcement of the equal protection clause is not incompatible with democracy. As Justice Scalia observes, the equal protection clause "requires the democratic majority to accept for themselves and their loved ones what they impose on you and me."[99] It prevents the heterosexual majority from telling same-sex couples that they cannot marry because they cannot have children while preserving their own unlimited right to marry regardless of whether they can have children, can support their children, or even have convictions for child molestation (or even if they are still *serving their sentences* for child molestation). As noted, it is natural for a majority to want to impose burdens on others rather than themselves.

Citing James Madison's Federalist 51, Tribe and Dorf observe, "Perhaps in a perfect world, elected legislatures would accomplish the

---

[97] Bork, Robert, "Neutral Principles and Some First Amendment Problems." *Indiana Law Journal* 47 (1971): 1–35.
[98] Tribe and Dorf at 1103.
[99] *Cruzan v. Missouri Department of Health*, 110 S.Ct. 2841, 2863 (1990).

generalization of rights. But the Framers understood all too well that this is not a perfect world. Like it or not, judges must squarely face the task of deciding how abstractly to define our liberties."[100]

The example of First Amendment jurisprudence shows that when the Court takes the norm of principled adjudication seriously, it can fulfill this crucial role and protect the rights of unpopular minorities such as gays and lesbians. For the most part, gays and lesbians enjoy the same freedom of speech that heterosexuals have. Unfortunately, the Court has not behaved this way with its Fourteenth Amendment jurisprudence. It has extended abundant sexual and marital freedom to heterosexuals but denied that freedom to gays and lesbians. If the Court protected the right of gays and lesbians to marry, it would not be antidemocratic. Rather, it would be fulfilling the Court's highest mission of protecting the fundamental rights of all Americans equally.

The reliance upon consistent principles does place a great deal of faith in rationality. Many would argue that such faith is naïve. But without faith in reason, what is left but force? In fact, some worry that if the Court protected same-sex marriage, others would turn to force, either engaging in increased violence against gays and lesbians or in refusing to cooperate in enforcing the law. Others worry that people would turn to the force of numbers and amend the Constitution. These concerns will be taken up in the final chapter.

[100] Tribe and Dorf at 1099.

9

Principles and Practicalities

We have seen so far that there is a powerful rights-based argument for same-sex marriage, and that enforcing such a right would be well within the Court's proper role in a constitutional democracy. There is still one more issue to address. Is it really possible for the Supreme Court, which lacks "sword" and "purse," to alter a basic institution such as marriage in the face of public opposition? Many have suggested that it is not. Whittington notes that "rights theories are particularly prone to abstractions that do not give adequate weight to actual political settlements."[1] Posner warns:

An overwhelming majority of the American people are strongly opposed to it.... A complex and by no means airtight line of argument would be necessary plausibly to derive a right to homosexual marriage from the text of the Constitution and the cases interpreting that text – a tightrope act that without a net constituted by some support in public opinion is too perilous for the courts to attempt. Public opinion may change ... but at present it is too firmly against same-sex marriage for the courts to act.[2]

In a similar vein, Cass Sunstein says that the Court should stay away from same-sex marriage on prudential grounds:

Suppose, for example, that the ban on same-sex marriage is challenged on equal protection grounds. Here, ongoing judicial supervision of complex institutions

---

[1] Whittington at 29.
[2] Posner at 1585.

is not really at issue. Nonetheless, there is reason for great caution on the part of the courts. An immediate judicial vindication of the principle could well jeopardize important interests. It could galvanize opposition. It could weaken the anti-discrimination movement itself. It could provoke more hostility and even violence against gays and lesbians. It could jeopardize the authority of the judiciary. It could well produce calls for a constitutional amendment to overturn the Supreme Court's decision.[3]

This fear of the parade of horribles that would follow such an act by the Court is the result of several factors, including the vote in Hawaii to amend the state Constitution rather than accept gay marriage, as well as the swift passage of the Defense of Marriage Act by Congress and equivalent legislation by many states.

The reaction of the Hawaiian voters in particular surprised many, including Andrew Sullivan, one of the leading advocates of same-sex marriage. Prior to the vote, he averred that "Hawaii is a remarkably tolerant, predominantly Democratic State," that would reject the proposed amendment.[4] Yet it passed by a two-to-one margin. This reaction has led scholars such as Sunstein to fear that if the Supreme Court recognized that the fundamental right to marry extends to gays and lesbians, the voters might respond with violence or a constitutional amendment.

Another reason for skepticism about the Court's power to allow same-sex marriage is widespread influence of Gerald Rosenberg's seminal book, *The Hollow Hope: Can Courts Bring About Social Change?*[5] That book argued that the Court is "constrained" in its ability to achieve social change and usually requires the help of other branches of government or of the market to do so. Under this constrained model, courts can bring about social change only when there is a fairly low level of public opposition, when there is an incentive for compliance, and when either the market forces or the support of other public officials can overcome obstacles to enforcing judicial decisions.

The popularity of *The Hollow Hope* is based in part upon the clarity of its writing and the persuasiveness of its central case study, the implementation of school desegregation in the wake of *Brown*

---

[3] Sunstein at 25.

[4] "Hawaiian Aye: Nearing the Altar on Gay Marriage," in *Same-Sex Marriage*, Robert Baird and Stuart Rosenbaum, eds. Amherst, MA: Prometheus Books, 1997.

[5] Chicago: University of Chicago Press, 1991.

v. Board of Education. Rosenberg offers substantial evidence not only that the Court was unable to desegregate the schools without substantial help from the President and Congress, but that *Brown* actually may have *hurt* the civil rights movement. "By stiffening resistance and raising fears before the activist phase of the civil rights movement was in place, *Brown* may actually have delayed the achievement of civil rights."[6]

The Hollow Hope also fit well with the increasingly skeptical tenor of the times regarding judicial efficacy. This increasing skepticism is illustrated by the ever-growing interest in Robert Dahl's article, "Decision-Making in a Democracy: The Supreme Court as a National Policy-Maker,"[7] which argued that the Court is virtually useless as a protector of individual liberties against a national law-making majority. Despite the fact that the article has various methodological flaws, dubious assumptions and unfounded logical leaps,[8] it has been cited with increasing frequency every decade since it was first published in 1957.[9]

We live, then, in an age of what Jane Schacter calls "law skepticism," which doubts the capacity of the law to secure legal equality.[10] As a result many advocates of same-sex marriage have praised the more cautious approach of the Vermont Supreme Court in *Baker v. State*, which held that same-sex couples are entitled to "obtain the same benefits and protections afforded by Vermont Law to married opposite-sex couples."[11] The *Baker* Court did not decree a particular remedy, but instead sent the issue to the state legislature to craft appropriate legislation. The legislature responded by creating a new status open to same-sex couples called "Civil Unions."

Although this approach continues to deny gays and lesbians the right to marry, it does grant them broad legal rights and, because it defers to the legislation for the specifics of how these rights are defined, it fits

---

[6] Rosenberg at 156.

[7] *Journal of Public Law* 6 279: (1957).

[8] See Gerald Rosenberg, "The Road Taken: Robert Dahl's Decision-Making in a Democracy: The Supreme Court as a National Policy-Maker," *Emory Law Journal* 50: 613 (2001).

[9] Ibid.

[10] Schacter at 686.

[11] 744 A.2d 864, 886 (1999). The *Baker* decision was based upon the "Common Benefits Clause" (ch.I, Article 7) of the Vermont Constitution.

better with the law skepticism of our times. Greg Johnson argues:

Baker was not the first case to find in favor of same-sex couples seeking the rights, benefits, and protections of marriage, but Baker is unique in that it was the first time a high court ruled unanimously in favor of the plaintiffs in a same-sex marriage case. Baker is also the first decision of a state supreme court holding a state marriage statute unconstitutional. The real distinction of Baker is its sober recognition that 'judicial authority is not ultimate authority.' By bringing the legislature into the process, the Court acted not so much as the dictator of a result, but as a catalyst for change. In her dissent Justice Johnson criticizes the Court for declaring a right without providing a remedy and for throwing the plaintiffs into 'an uncertain fate in the political cauldron.' While that cauldron proved fiery indeed, we know now that the result was a positive one. Rather than creating a combative atmosphere between the two branches, the Vermont Supreme Court's collaborative approach empowered the legislature to fashion its own just and constitutional remedy.[12]

There is much to support Johnson's argument. In response to *Baker*, the Vermont legislature created a system of Civil Unions that gives same-sex couples a wide variety of rights that they were previously denied. These include the right to receive maintenance and support from their partners, access to state courts and rules for division of property and child custody upon divorce, priority of inheritance if their partners die without wills, the option of holding property as tenants in the entirety, the right to bring lawsuits for wrongful death of their partners, visitation and notice rights when their partners are hospitalized, the joint care and parenthood of children born to one of the partners during the union, and the right to adopt children jointly with their partners, or adopt the children their partners bring to the union.[13]

Furthermore, the *Baker* decision did not trigger the type of backlash that the Hawaii decision did. Vermont's governor, who signed the Civil Unions bill into law, survived a reelection challenge against an opponent who ran largely on the Civil Unions/gay marriage issue.[14] A small number of state legislators lost their seats, apparently as a result of their

---

[12] Johnson at 36–37 (citations omitted).

[13] Vt. Stat. Ann. tit. 15, 1204(d) (1991). All cited in Eskridge, "Equality Practice: Liberal Reflections on The Jurisprudence of Civil Unions," *Albany Law Review* 64: 853–881, 866 (2001).

[14] Eskridge at 873 (2001).

support for same-sex unions,[15] although U.S. Senator James Jeffords was reelected despite his support for Civil Unions. Proposed amendments to the state Constitution that would have nullified *Baker* were defeated in the Vermont Senate, with the help of substantial numbers of Senate Republicans.[16]

The early political success of Civil Unions has led some to favorably compare *Baker*'s cautious approach to the cautious tack the U.S. Supreme Court took in addressing interracial marriage. Although the Court's 1954 decision in *Brown v. Board of Education* made it obvious that segregation at the marriage altar is unconstitutional, the Court avoided the issue for thirteen years until it decided *Loving v. Virginia* in 1967. For Eskridge, the combined lesson of Hawaii, Vermont, and *Loving* is that it is preferable for courts to sometimes deny unpopular groups their rights, at least for a substantial period of time, in order to more effectively enforce those rights at some time in the future. He argues:

There is a broader lesson for the modern state: its constitution may promise liberal rights that its political system cannot immediately deliver and that its judiciary dare not insist upon. Different-race marriage was such a right in the 1950s and 1960s, and same-sex marriage is such a right today. That the political and judicial system cannot practically implement such rights immediately does not mean that they are entirely empty. Justice delayed is not always justice denied. Sometimes rights come on little cat's feet.[17]

But there are strong reasons to reject the Vermont approach. Gays and lesbians are being asked to be uniquely patient. It is difficult to think of any other area where so many legal scholars have called upon the courts to deliberately refuse to enforce constitutional rights for prudential reasons. Despite *The Hollow Hope*'s widely cited argument that *Brown* did not advance, and indeed may have retarded, school desegregation, it is virtually impossible to find a modern scholar or lawyer who argues that the Court should have avoided or substantially delayed taking the case. The Court is actively involved in many areas where they are strongly opposed by the public. California voters amended the California Constitution to eliminate affirmative action

[15] Ibid.
[16] Johnson at 34.
[17] Eskridge, supra, at 876.

programs, but there is no call for the Court to reverse its decision in *Regents of the University of California v. Bakke*,[18] lest voters amend the Constitution to ban that practice.

Further, Civil Unions fall far short of marriage. Because it is a state rather than federal creation, it has no impact on federal laws. There are more than one thousand federal legal rights and benefits for married couples covering everything from social security survivor benefits to immigration eligibility for spouses of American citizens.[19] As noted earlier, the Defense of Marriage Act makes it abundantly clear that no state law can grant same-sex couples access to these important federal rights.

Also, Civil Unions are most likely not portable from state to state. As Eskridge notes, Civil Unions are less likely to be recognized by hostile states than are same-sex marriages:

Another way in which civil unions will constitute a separate-but-unequal regime for same-sex couples is their relative lack of portability. As of October 2000, thirty-four states have adopted junior-DOMAs, that is, statutes providing that their courts should not recognize same-sex marriages validly entered into in another jurisdiction or state.... In at least some states that have not adopted junior DOMAs, or whose statutes are loosely drafted or found to be unconstitutional, a Vermont same-sex marriage would probably be recognized.[20]

So same-sex couples who want to keep their Civil Union rights are virtually prisoners in the state of Vermont. For example, if a same-sex couple moves from Vermont to New Hampshire, the person who is currently the legally recognized parent of his or her partner's children would abruptly lose that status. Recall that the Supreme Court has held that it violates a person's constitutional rights to be denied welfare for one year upon moving to another state.[21] Juxtaposing that with the fact that gay and lesbian couples would permanently lose *all* the legal rights of a Civil Union immediately upon leaving the state of Vermont

---

[18] 438 U.S. 265 (1978).
[19] General Accounting Office, Report to the Honorable Henry J. Hyde, Chairman, Committee on the Judiciary, House of Representatives: The Defense of Marriage Act, GAO/OCG 97-16 (1996).
[20] Eskridge, William, "Lecture: Equality Practice: Liberal Reflections on the Jurisprudence of Civil Unions." *Albany Law Review* 64 (2001): 853–881, 862.
[21] *Shapiro v. Thompson*, 394 U.S. 618 (1969).

highlights the unique burden that gays and lesbians are being asked to bear.

Further, no discussion of legal rights can adequately describe the enormity of the gap between marriage and Civil Unions. What, after all, is the purpose of granting gays and lesbians the legal rights of marriage while withholding access to the institution itself? If the government, for example, told Jews or Muslims or Hindus that they could have all the legal protections and religious freedoms enjoyed by Christians as long as they did not hold themselves out as "religions," the stigma inherent in such an offer would be obvious. Freedom to marry, like freedom to practice religion, is more than a bundle of legal privileges.

The Supreme Court has repeatedly held that marriage is "one of the basic civil rights of man." To deny this right to gays and lesbians then, is to say that they are somehow less than fully human. As Andrew Sullivan points out, "marriage is not merely an accumulation of benefits. It is a fundamental mark of citizenship."[22] Denying gays and lesbians access to marriage, despite giving them a grab bag of marriagelike rights, is to deny them full citizenship and is a form of government-endorsed stigmatization.

The argument that allowing gays and lesbians to marry will weaken the institution of marriage depends entirely upon the view that no one wants to share a societal institution with despised groups. Sullivan asks:

How exactly does the freedom of a gay couple to marry weaken a straight couple's commitment to the same institution? The obvious answer is that since homosexuals are inherently depraved and immoral, allowing them to marry would inevitably spoil, even defame, the institution of marriage. It would wreck the marital neighborhood, so to speak, and no one would want to live there.[23]

Thus, Civil Unions fall far short of marriage. What then of the argument that this is the best that the courts can do as a practical matter? There is less to this argument than there may seem to be. The practical problems with enforcing same-sex marriage are greatly overstated and lack empirical support. Despite the plethora of warnings that recognizing the right of same-sex marriage would undermine support for the Supreme Court or trigger a backlash, we actually know very little about

---

[22] Sullivan, "State of the Union," at 22.
[23] Ibid. at 21.

how Court decisions affect public opinion. "Surprisingly, we have little systematic empirical research on the important question of judicial impact on public opinion."[24] As Lee Epstein and Jack Knight recently noted, "we know of no explicit empirical evidence that Americans take legitimacy norms seriously."[25] As will be discussed below, there is good reason to believe that the Supreme Court could influence the terms of the public debate in the way that would help advocates of same-sex marriage. But we do not have anywhere near the knowledge about the Courts and public opinion to justify the calls for the Court to deliberately fail to enforce the constitutional rights of gays and lesbians.

Public reaction is difficult to predict or even understand. Neither social scientists nor lawyers should pretend that we have a greater ability to predict public reaction than we actually do. If the nation's leading experts had been asked in mid-2000 how the public would likely react to a 5–4 decision by the Supreme Court that abruptly stayed a crucial vote recount in Florida and placed the candidate who undisputedly received fewer popular votes nationally in the White House based on legal reasoning that has been almost universally derided, it seems safe to say that most experts would have seriously missed the mark.

One might have thought that there would be a fierce public backlash against *Loving v. Virginia*'s declaration that all states must recognize interracial marriages. While it is true that after World War II the number of states that banned interracial marriage significantly declined, it is important not to sugarcoat the virulence of American racism at the time of *Loving* or the overwhelming public opposition to interracial marriage. In 1968, the year after *Loving*, 72 percent of the American public disapproved of interracial marriage, while only 20 percent supported it.[26] Despite this, the Court encountered little public resistance to *Loving*, nor was there a serious move to amend the Constitution.[27]

The reaction to *Loving* cautions us against overestimating our ability to predict public reaction to Court decisions. Public opposition to interracial marriage at the time of *Loving* was actually far greater than

---

[24] Gregory Caldeira, "Courts and Public Opinion," in *The American Courts: A Critical Assessment*, eds. John B. Gates and Charles A. Johnson (Washington, D.C.: CQ Press, 1991), 305.

[25] Epstein and Knight at 158.

[26] *New York Times*, Information Bank Abstracts, August 30, 1978.

[27] Coolidge at 226–227.

public opposition is to same-sex marriage today. A May 2000 poll conducted by ICR of Media, Pennsylvania of 1,012 Americans found that only 51% opposed same-sex marriage, while 34% approved of it. (11% didn't know and 3% refused to answer.) Polls can be somewhat misleading, of course, as people sometimes answer as they think they are supposed to, and other polls have shown opposition to same-sex marriage to be closer to 70%.[28] Even so, the 72% opposition to interracial marriage at the time of *Loving* was at least as great as, and quite possibly greater than contemporary opposition to same-sex marriage.

The ease of enforcing *Loving*, in contrast with the Court's ineffectiveness in *Brown*, indicates why judicial protection of same-sex marriage would not be a "hollow hope." Unlike with school desegregation, there is not very much that the Court has to do in order to enforce decisions opening marriage to new parties. There are no masses of school children to bus, or lumbering educational bureaucracies to cope with. As noted earlier, numerous religious orders already conduct ceremonial same-sex marriages, so there would be no problem finding ministers and rabbis willing to preside over the marriages. Even if some county clerks illegally refused to issue marriage licenses to gay couples, those couples would be free to go to a friendlier venue to get married and return as a legally married couple. Indeed, there would be a great deal of money to be made by the businesses of any city that chose to hold itself out as a place that is friendly to same-sex marriages.[29] Even the relatively pessimistic *Hollow Hope* concludes that "Courts may effectively produce social reform when judicial decisions would be implemented by the market."[30] When one thinks of the money that could be made by, for example, cruise lines that were willing to have their captains marry same-sex couples, it is obvious that this condition of judicial effectiveness would not be difficult to meet.

---

[28] For example, polls showed that California's Proposition 22, which bans same-sex marriage, had the support of just over 50% of California voters but it passed with just over 61% of the vote. This may be due in part to the fact that the competitive Republican primary contest between John McCain and George W. Bush skewed turnout toward Republican voters. See "Activists partly blame McCain for passage of gay-union ban," *Houston Chronicle,* March 9, 2000.

[29] See Halpern, Jake, "Out for a Buck," *The New Republic* (May 8, 2000, p. 23) on the enthusiasm of many Vermont entrepreneurs and businesses for the gay and lesbian business expected to be generated by Civil Unions.

[30] Rosenberg at 33.

It is true that legal marriage can provide rights and benefits, but not necessarily the social acceptance that comes with heterosexual marriage. Such acceptance may truly be beyond the power of the courts to grant. Thomas B. Stoddard, for example, notes that on paper, New Zealand is a legal paradise for gays and lesbians, yet the reality is far different. He argues that the courts, whether in New Zealand or in the United States, have limited ability to truly change culture.[31] But it is not the job of the courts to change culture; the courts' high duty is to protect the legal rights of even unpopular groups. The fact that much of the public would continue to disapprove of same-sex marriage is not a reason for the Court to withhold marriage from gays and lesbians. In fact, even after *Loving*, public approval of interracial marriage has been remarkably slow in coming. In 1978, eleven years after that landmark decision, 54 percent of the American public continued to disapprove of interracial marriage, while only 36 percent approved of it.[32] Even as late as 1991, only a slim plurality of Americans approved of interracial marriage, by a 48–42 percent margin.[33] Yet the glacial pace of public opinion on interracial marriage has not led us to declare *Loving* a failure or a hollow hope. There is no reliable way to know how much of the public would accept same-sex marriage in the decades after a supportive Supreme Court decision, but we do know that same-sex marriage already has as much or more public support as interracial marriage had when the Court entered that breach.

There is also concern that voters might respond to a Supreme Court decision in favor of same-sex marriage by attempting to amend the Constitution, as Sunstein warns.[34] There no doubt would be such a move, but that is hardly a reason to withhold constitutional rights from an unpopular group. Many Supreme Court decisions have led to serious attempts to amend the Constitution. For example, after the Supreme Court held that dissidents have the First Amendment right to

---

[31] Stoddard at 967–991.

[32] Gallup poll of 1,555 adults in 700 U.S. communities, reported in *The New York Times*, Information Bank Abstracts (August 30, 1978).

[33] Gallup poll reported in *St. Louis Post-Dispatch* (August 16, 1991).

[34] There is some irony here. As discussed in Chapter 8, it has been argued that it would be antidemocratic for the Supreme Court to decide the same-sex marriage issue. The argument that the public might amend the Constitution is the opposite argument – that the democratic process of constitutional amendment could too easily be used to override the Court.

burn the American flag, there were numerous, very serious attempts to amend the Constitution and these attempts are continuing. In 2001, the United States House of Representatives passed a proposed flag burning amendment for the fourth time in a six-year period.[35] Yet no one suggests that the Court should relent on the flag burning issue in order to avoid the possibility of a constitutional amendment.

The constitutional amendment process is notoriously difficult and lengthy. (The most recent Amendment, the Twenty-Seventh, was finally ratified *203 years* after it was originally submitted in 1789.) A Supreme Court decision that the fundamental right to marry protects same-sex marriage would doubtless energize the movement for an anti-same-sex marriage amendment, but it would also shift the terms of the debate in a profound manner. For the first time, opponents of same-sex marriage would be put in the position of having to acknowledge that they were trying to take a fundamental constitutional right away from gays and lesbians. This would be an enormous political hurdle. Flag burning is even more unpopular than same-sex marriage. *The Christian Science Monitor* reported that: "Most surveys have shown that a majority of Americans support the amendment. Between 1989 and 1999, five Gallup polls found that between 62 and 71 percent of Americans, depending on the year, supported an amendment that would let Congress prohibit flag burning."[36] Yet, every attempt to pass such an amendment has failed.

While the public is generally ignorant of what the Supreme Court says and does,[37] the Congress is not. Gordon Silverstein has shown that Supreme Court precedent can have a powerful framing effect on how Congress debates and deliberates on issues. For example, after the Court held that campaign donations are a form of speech,[38] the debates in Congress began to take the connection between money and the First Amendment for granted – a shift that obviously favored one side of the debate over the other. After the Court declared that monetary contributions are a form of speech, "the doctrinal link between money and

---

[35] "House Approves Flag Amendment," *The Arizona Republic* (July 18, 2001).

[36] "Push Persists to Protect Stars and Stripes," *The Christian Science Monitor* (July 19, 2001).

[37] See Marshall, Thomas R., *Public Opinion and the Supreme Court*. Boston: Unwin Hyman, 1989.

[38] *Buckley v. Valeo*, 424 U.S. 1 (1976).

speech seemed unshakable in the [Congress]...the fight was not over the doctrinal foundation but over how and when it is permissible to restrict speech."[39]

The issue framing effect of a Supreme Court decision recognizing that the fundamental right to marry extends to gays and lesbians could be profound. Same-sex marriage would be an established constitutional right. Its opponents would be in the position of seeking to amend the Constitution away from a specific targeted group. It could no longer be argued that it is "obvious" or "natural" that marriage is exclusively dual-gendered, or that the advocates of same-sex marriage represent a "fringe" movement.

Finally, it should be emphasized that this book does not attempt to suggest that it is desirable or inevitable for advocates of same-sex marriage to rely *solely* upon the Court. This is a book about constitutional law and theory, and therefore it is focused upon the role of law and courts. This book is *not* intended as a political blueprint for achieving same-sex marriage. The argument here is that marriage is a long-recognized constitutional right and that it is the role of the Court to protect such rights for all people, however unpopular. Nonetheless, many people are, of course, concerned with practical questions, and as noted, many advocates of same-sex marriage have argued that it is better to pursue this issue politically rather than legally. But the two avenues are not mutually exclusive. Legal and political advocacy can go hand in hand. Greg Johnson has convincingly argued that the Vermont Supreme Court's decision encountered less public backlash than the decision in Hawaii (as well as in Alaska, where the voters also amended the state Constitution to avoid same-sex marriage) because activists in Vermont laid the political groundwork for *Baker*. Johnson notes that in Hawaii and Alaska, same-sex marriage activists did little political groundwork to make sure that judicial victories could stick. He continues:

Contrast this with Vermont, where significant grassroots and legislative work was occurring a full decade before the suit was even filed. Even though Vermont is thought of as the last state in the second wave of marriage cases, work began on the suit well before Hawaii's Supreme Court issued its ruling in 1993.

[39] Gordon Silverstein, "Bridging the Gap, Political Science and the Law." Paper presented at the 2001 Annual Meeting of the American Political Science Association, San Francisco, CA, at 23.

In 1985, the Vermont Coalition for Lesbian and Gay Rights (VCLGR) was formed. It was initially organized 'to provide social activities for [gay/lesbians] who felt isolated in rural Vermont, but [it] soon developed a political identity/consciousness.' In 1986 Vermont Governor Madeleine Kunin established 'Co-Liaisons to the Governor' for gay and lesbian issues. The positions were filled by VCLGR members. The liaisons 'nurtured personal relationships' with the governor and other elected officials. They sat in on legislative hearings, and 'spoke up in [the] legislature in support of issues of importance to non-gay groups (e.g., Commission on Women, Human Rights Commission), thereby gaining respect and support of non-gay allies.'[40]

As a result of this and other political efforts, political activists "created a positive media buzz about the issue of same-sex marriage even before the suit was filed."[41]

Even those who are very concerned about judicial efficacy need not wait until an effective grassroots political movement has taken hold before pursuing federal judicial action. Just as grassroots activism can augment judicial efficacy, favorable judicial decisions can enhance political efficacy. For example, in a well-known study, Michael McCann found that favorable court decisions in the area of gender pay equity galvanized the political movement in that area.[42]

The relationship between public opinion and Supreme Court decisions is extremely complicated and, as noted, poorly understood. The abortion controversy and the public's attitude toward *Roe v. Wade*,[43] which held that abortion is a fundamental constitutional right, show the complexity of how the public thinks about constitutional rights. A June 2000 poll by the *Los Angeles Times* shows that "while 57 percent of [the American public] say they consider abortion to be murder, more than half of that group agree that a woman should have the right to choose an abortion."[44]

The American public is quite capable of supporting the Supreme Court's decisions and the constitutional rights protected by those decisions, even while continuing to oppose the very actions protected by

---

[40] Johnson at 27–28 (citations omitted).
[41] Ibid. at 30.
[42] McCann, Michael. *Rights at Work: Pay Equity Reform and the Politics of Legal Mobilization.* Chicago: University of Chicago Press, 1994.
[43] 410 U.S. 113 (1973).
[44] "Americans Narrowing Support for Abortion," *Sunday Los Angeles Times* (June 18, 2000).

those rights and decisions. According to the same *Los Angeles Times* poll, nearly two-thirds of Americans believe abortions should be illegal after the first three months of pregnancy. *Roe* held that a woman's right to abortion extends well past the first three months of pregnancy, so one would think that public support for that decision would be slim. Yet, polls have shown that public support for *Roe* peaked just when the decision was under the greatest political attack. "In the last decade ... previous polls show support for Roe peaking at 56% around 1991, when the decision was under attack across the country."[45]

As discussed in Chapter 3, same-sex marriage advocates have advanced various constitutional theories including the claim that gays and lesbians should receive heightened protection. However, a Court decision holding that gays and lesbians are simply entitled to the same fundamental freedom to marry as everybody else would have unique power in terms of its framing effects on public discourse. One of the greatest obstacles that gays and lesbians face in the political arena is the public perception that they are seeking "special rights," rather than equal rights.[46] While the public is usually not very aware of constitutional doctrine, opponents of antidiscrimination laws protecting gays and lesbians have made very effective rhetorical use of Supreme Court doctrine to further that perception.[47] A Court decision that held that gays and lesbians deserve heightened judicial scrutiny would lend further credence to this argument. But a decision that held that gays and lesbians are merely seeking the same fundamental rights as everyone else has the potential to have the opposite effect. Opponents of same-sex marriage would be cast in the position of seeking to limit constitutional rights. If even people who believe that abortion is murder can support the right to an abortion, it is certainly reasonable to believe that opponents of same-sex marriage could come to tolerate a practice that causes no direct harm to anyone.

It must be emphasized that none of this is intended as *proof* that the Supreme Court can or cannot successfully protect same-sex marriage. The argument is that it would be wrong for the Court to deny gays and lesbians their constitutional rights out of fear of public backlash and

---

[45] Ibid.
[46] See Gerstmann at 91–114 for extensive discussion of this point.
[47] Ibid.

that the high degree of cynicism regarding the Court's ability to protect the fundamental right of marriage for gays and lesbians is unwarranted. To summarize:

1. We know very little about how public opinion is affected by Supreme Court rulings, and neither social scientists nor lawyers have any sort of established track record of successfully predicting public reaction to judicial decisions.

2. The Court encountered little resistance to interracial marriage, even though it was even more unpopular at the time than same-sex marriage is today.

3. There are few bureaucratic obstacles to enforcing same-sex marriage, and powerful market forces in its favor, making it a very different situation from *Brown*.

4. Although there may well be a move to amend the Constitution, there are tremendous institutional and political obstacles to such amendments and even extremely unpopular Supreme Court decisions, such as the one protecting flag burning, have not resulted in a constitutional amendment.

5. Judicial protection of same-sex marriage would shift the terms of debate in Congress, so that opponents would be put in the position of having to argue for depriving gays and lesbians of a fundamental constitutional right that other Americans have.

6. Although this book focuses on the role of law and courts, there is no reason for advocates of same-sex marriage to rely solely on the Supreme Court.

7. As Vermont shows, political advocacy can lower barriers to enforcing the Court's decision.

8. The public is capable of distinguishing between what they believe is good public policy and what they recognize as being an individual right, as they apparently have on the issue of abortion.

9. A judicial decision that marriage is a fundamental right that extends to gays and lesbians would aid grassroots political activism in favor of same-sex marriage by making it more difficult for opponents to argue that gays and lesbians are seeking special rights.

In sum, calls for the Court to fail deliberately to enforce the constitutional rights of same-sex couples are not warranted by either empirical evidence or by our current abilities to predict judicial efficacy.

Conclusion

Same-sex marriage is an issue that truly tests America's commitment to genuine legal equality. Many have raised concerns that America's focus on groups and group rights threatens our unity and democracy.[48] If we hope to move past the current discourse of "gay rights" as well as "women's rights," "minority rights," and so forth, then we must be willing to take a fresh look at the question of what rights we *all* share as people and as Americans. Although reasonable people can disagree on the merits of same-sex marriage, the legal response to the claims of same-sex couples has been callow and dismissive. The courts' repeated reliance upon reasons that have so little analytic substance does serious damage to the ideal that all are equal before the law. At an absolute minimum, the courts must refrain from relying upon arguments that they would never accept in other contexts. The same is true for the heterosexual majority. If we find it charming when eighty-year-olds marry, we cannot turn around and tell same-sex couples that they cannot marry because they cannot have children or because marriage is reserved for traditional families.

The question of legal equality based upon shared fundamental rights has been obscured by the current skepticism about legal principles and judges' willingness to make good faith attempts to apply those principles fairly with respect to unpopular groups. Too little attention has been paid to the role of clear, well-developed legal principles in protecting legal equality, especially by law-skeptical social scientists. The current state of equal protection and fundamental rights is a travesty. The Court has drifted between different parts of the Constitution in deriving these rights as if they were so many coat hooks for the Court to use which-ever one is convenient. The various standards set out by the Court for deriving these rights are so vague as to be virtually useless. It is small wonder that these "standards" are of little use in protecting the legal equality of unpopular groups.

The Court should follow the example of its own First Amendment jurisprudence. While that area is far from perfect, it is a model of clarity compared with the Fourteenth Amendment. This clarity has more than academic benefits. As discussed earlier , First Amendment rights

---

[48] See, e.g., Elshtain.

have a long track record of protecting gays and lesbians even in the face of a hostile judiciary. The fundamental right to marry, which has a powerful expressive component, deserves similar treatment by the Court. However, while judges have internalized the imperative of principled adjudication in the area of the First Amendment, the Fourteenth Amendment remains a hodgepodge of underdeveloped ideas.

We can do better than this. Neither our personal beliefs about sexuality, nor cynicism about legal principles, nor doubts about judicial efficacy should prevent judges, lawyers, professors, teachers, and engaged citizens from vigorously engaging the question of what rights we all share and what the contours of those rights should be. Rights-based discourse is not the *only* form of reasoned discussion and should not replace religious, moral, and other forms of discourse. The Court's protection of the rights of dissidents to burn the American flag did not stop millions of Americans from proudly flying that flag in the wake of the terrorist attacks of 2001, nor did it diminish the power of the flag in the hearts of the people. Nor would judicial protection of same-sex marriage diminish the power of marriage in American life. But it would stand as a potent symbol of the depth of our commitment to genuine equality under the law.

Bibliography

Ackerman, Bruce. "Beyond Carolene Products." *Harvard Law Review* 98 (1985): 713–746.

Albertson, Bethany. "Victorian Courtship: The Restrained Relationship between Social Science and the Court." Paper presented at the American Politics Workshop at the University of Chicago, May 30, 2001.

Alexander, Larry, and Frederick Schauer. "Defending Judicial Supremacy: A Reply." *Constitutional Commentary* 17 (winter 2000): 455–482.

Alfange, Dean. "On Judicial Policymaking and Constitutional Change: Another Look at the 'Original Intent' Theory of Constitutional Interpretation." *Hastings Constitutional Law Quarterly* 5 (1978): 603–606.

Amar, Akhil Reed. "A Tale of Three Wars: Tinker in Constitutional Context." *Drake Law Review* 48 (2000): 507–518.

Berger, Raoul. *Government by Judiciary.* Cambridge, MA: Harvard University Press, 1977.

Beschle, Donald. "Defining the Scope of the Constitutional Right to Marry: More Than Tradition, Less Than Unlimited Autonomy." *Notre Dame Law Review* 70 (1994): 39–64.

Bickel, Alexander. *The Least Dangerous Branch.* Indianapolis: Bobbs-Merrill, 1962.

Politics and the Warren Court. New York: Harper & Row, 1965.

The Supreme Court and the Idea of Progress. New York: Harper & Row, 1970.

Blake, Jennie Holman. "Religious Liberty Book Review Symposium: The History and Evolution of Marriage from Sacrament to Contract: Marriage, Religion, and Law in the Western Tradition." *Brigham Young University Law Review* (1999): 847–857.

Bonauto, Mary, Susan M. Murrat, and Beth Robinson. "The Freedom to Marry for Same-Sex Couples: The Reply Brief of Plaintiffs Stan Baker, et al. in *Baker, et al. v. State of Vermont.*" *Michigan Journal of Gender and Law* 6 (1999): 1–41.

Bork, Robert. "Neutral Principles and Some First Amendment Problems." *Indiana Law Journal* 47 (1971): 1–35.

The Tempting of America. New York: Simon & Schuster, 1990.

"Stop Courts from Imposing Same-Sex Marriage." *Wall Street Journal,* September 21, 2001.

Bratt, Carolyn S. "Incest Statutes and the Fundamental Right of Marriage: Is Oedipus Free to Marry?" *Family Law Quarterly* 18 (fall 1994): 257–297.

Buchanan, G. Sydney. "Same-Sex Marriage: The Linchpin Issue." *University of Dayton Law Review* 10 (1985): 541–573.

Caldeira, Gregory. "Courts and Public Opinion." In *The American Courts: A Critical Assessment.* Ed. John B. Gates and Charles A. Johnson. Washington, D.C.: CQ Press, 1991.

Carter, Leif H. *Reason in Law.* 5th ed. New York: Longman, 1998.

Carter, Stephen. "'Defending' Marriage: A Modest Proposal." *Howard Law Journal* 41 (1998): 215–228.

Chambers, David. "What If? The Legal Consequences of Marriage and the Legal Needs of Lesbian and Gay Male Couples." *Michigan Law Review* 95 (1996): 447–491.

"Polygamy and Same Sex Marriage." *Hofstra Law Review* 26 (fall 1997): 53–83.

Chapman, Steve. "Two's Company; Three's a Marriage." *Slate On-Line,* June 4, 2001.

Christensen, Craig W. "If Not Marriage? On Securing Gay and Lesbian Family Values by a 'Simulacrum of Marriage.'" *Fordham Law Review* 66 (1998): 1700–1746.

Clark, Sarah Harton. "Substantive Due Process in a State of Flux: Should the Courts Develop New Fundamental Rights for Alien Children?" *Boston University Law Review* 72 (1992): 579–606.

Coolidge, David Ogden. "Law and the Politics of Marriage: *Loving v. Virginia* After Thirty Years." *Brigham Young University Journal of Public Law* 12 (1998): 201–238.

Corwin, Edward S. *Liberty Against Government.* Baton Rouge, LA: Louisiana State University Press, 1948.

Courrie, David P. *The Constitution and the Supreme Court.* Chicago: University of Chicago Press, 1985.

Cox, Barbara J. "Symposium: Toward a Radical and Plural Democracy: The Lesbian Wife: Same-Sex Marriage as an Expression of Radical and Plural Democracy." *California Western Law Review* 33 (spring 1997): 155–167.

Damslet, Otis R. "Note: Same-Sex Marriage." *New York Law School Journal of Human Rights* 10 (1993): 555–592.

Destro, Robert A. "Law and the Politics of Marriage: *Loving v. Virginia* After Thirty Years Introduction." *The Catholic University Law Review* 47 (1998): 1207–1230.

Dixon, Robert. "The New Substantive Due Process and the Democratic Ethic: A Prolegomenon." *Brigham Young Law Review* 1976 (1976): 43–84.

Downs, Donald A. *Nazis in Skokie: Freedom, Community and the First Amendment*. South Bend: Notre Dame Press, 1985.

Duncan, Richard F. "Homosexual Marriage and the Myth of Tolerance: Is Cardinal O'Connor a 'Homophobe'?" *Notre Dame Law Journal of Ethics and Public Policy* 10 (1996): 587–607.

 "Symposium: *Romer v. Evans*: The Narrow and Shallow Bite of Romer and the Eminent Rationality of Dual-Gender Marriage: A [Partial] Response to Professor Koppelman." *William and Mary Bill of Rights Journal* 6 (winter 1994): 147–166.

Dworkin, Ronald. *Taking Rights Seriously*. Cambridge: Harvard University Press, 1977.

Ely, John Hart. *Democracy and Distrust: A Theory of Judicial Review*. Cambridge: Harvard University Press, 1980.

Elshtain, Jean Bethke. *Democracy on Trial*. New York: Basic Books, 1995.

Epstein, Lee, and Jack Knight. *The Choices Justices Make*. Washington, D.C.: CQ Press, 1998.

Epstein, Lee, and Joseph E. Kobylka. *The Supreme Court and Legal Change: Abortion and the Death Penalty*. Chapel Hill: University of North Carolina Press, 1992.

Epstein, Richard A. "Caste and the Civil Rights Laws: From Jim Crow to Same Sex Marriages." *Michigan Law Review* 92 (August 1994): 2456–2478.

Erikson, Robert S., and Kent L. Tedin. *American Public Opinion*. 6th ed. New York: Longman, 2001.

Eskridge, William. "Lecture: Equality Practice: Liberal Reflections on the Jurisprudence of Civil Unions." *Albany Law Review* 64 (2001): 853–881.

 "Comparative Law and the Same-Sex Marriage Debate: A Step-by-Step Approach Toward State Recognition." *McGeorge Law Review* 31 (spring 2000): 641–670.

 The Case for Same-Sex Marriage: From Sexual Liberty to Civilized Commitment. New York: The Free Press, 1996.

 "Why Gay Legal History Matters." (book review) *Harvard Law Review* 113 (June 2000): 2035–2060.

 "Symposium: Constructing Family, Constructing Change: Shifting Legal Perspectives on Same-Sex Relationships: Panel Two: Same-Sex Marriage: Article: Three Cultural Anxieties Undermining the Case for Same-Sex Marriage." *Temple Political & Civil Rights Law Review* 7 (1998): 307–318.

Ettelbrick, Paula L. "Youth, Family, and the Law: Defining Rights and Establishing Recognition: Article: Wedlock Alert: A Comment on Lesbian and Gay Family Recognition." *Journal of Law and Policy* 5 (1996): 108–160.

Farber, Daniel, and Philip Frickey. *Law and Public Choice: A Critical Introduction*. Chicago: University of Chicago Press, 1991.

Farrell, Megan E. "*Baehr v. Lewin*: Questionable Reasoning; Sound Judgment." *Journal of Contemporary Health Law & Policy* 11 (spring 1995): 589–616.

Finnis, John M. "Law, Morality, and 'Sexual Orientation.'" *Notre Dame Law Review* 69 (1994): 1049–1076.

Fish, Stanley. *There's No Such Thing as Free Speech and It's a Good Thing Too*. New York: Oxford University Press, 1994.

Flaherty, Martin S. "History in Constitutional Argumentation." *Encyclopedia of the American Constitution*. (2000): 1290–1291.

Foster, Sheila Rose. "Symposium: Constructing Family, Constructing Change: Shifting Legal Perspectives on Same-Sex Relationships: Panel Two: Same-Sex Marriage: Article: The Symbolism of Rights and the Costs of Symbolism: Some Thoughts on the Campaign for Same-Sex Marriage." *Temple Political & Civil Law Review* 7 (1998): 319–328.

Garfield, Helen. "Privacy, Abortion, and Judicial Review: Haunted by the Ghost of Lochner." *Washington Law Review* 61 (April 1986): 293–365.

George, Robert P., and Gerard V. Bradley. "Marriage in the Liberal Imagination." *Georgetown Law Journal* 84 (December 1995): 301–320.

Gerstmann, Evan. *The Constitutional Underclass: Gays, Lesbians and the Failure of Class-Based Equal Protection*. Chicago: University of Chicago Press, 1999.

Glendon, Mary Ann. *Rights Talk*. New York: The Free Press, 1991.

  A Nation Under Lawyers: How the Crisis in the Legal Profession is Transforming American Society. New York: Farrar, Straus and Giroux, 1994.

Grad, Frank B. "Communicable Disease and Mental Health: Restrictions of the Person." *American Law Journal and Medicine* 12 (1986): 318–383.

Graff, E. J. *What Is Marriage For?* Boston: Beacon Press, 1991.

Grano, Joseph. "Judicial Review and a Written Constitution in a Democratic Society." *Wayne Law Review* 46 (2000): 1305–1402.

Griffen, Stephen. "Has the Hour of Democracy Come Round at Last? The New Critique of Judicial Review." *Constitutional Commentary* 17 (2000): 683–693.

Gunther, Gerald. "Forward: In Search of Evolving Doctrine on a Changing Court: A Model for a Newer Equal Protection." *Harvard Law Review* 86 (1972): 1–48.

Hafen, Bruce C. "The Constitutional Status of Marriage, Kinship and Sexual Privacy: Balancing the Individual and Social Interests." *Michigan Law Review* 81 (January 1983): 463–509.

Hedges, Rebra Carrasquillo. "The Forgotten Children: Same-Sex Partners, Their Children's Unequal Treatment." *Boston College Law Review* 410 (July 2002): 883–912.

Herman, Judith, M.D., Diana Russell, Ph.D., and Karen Trocki, Ph.D. "Long-term Effects of Incestuous Abuse in Childhood." *American Journal of Psychiatry* 143 (1986): 1293–1296.

Hodges, Heather. "*Dean v. The District of Columbia*: Goin' to the Chapel and We're Gonna Get Married." *American Journal of Gender & the Law* 5 (1996): 93–146.

Hohengarten, William M. "Note: Same-Sex Marriage and the Right to Privacy." *Yale Law Journal* 103 (April 1994): 1495–1531.

Jaber, Lutfi, G. Halpern, and M. Shohot. "The Impact of Consanguinity Worldwide." *Community Genetics* 1 (1998): 12–17.

Jackson, Robert H. *The Struggle for Judicial Supremacy.* New York: Alfred A. Knopf, 1941.

Jeffrey, Julie Roy. *Frontier Women: Civilizing the West? 1840–1880.* Rev. ed. New York: Hill and Wang, 1998.

Johnson, Greg. "Vermont Civil Unions: The New Language of Marriage." *Vermont Law Review* 25 (fall 2000): 15–59.

Karst, Kenneth L. "The Freedom of Intimate Association." *Yale Law Journal* 89 (1980): 624–692.

Katz, Leo. *Bad Acts and Guilty Minds: Conundrums of the Criminal Law.* Chicago: University of Chicago Press, 1987.

Koppelman, Andrew. "1997 Survey of Books Relating to the Law: II. Sex, Law, and Equality: Three Arguments for Gay Rights." *Michigan Law Review* 95 (1997): 1636–1667.

"Forum: Sexual Morality and the Possibility of Same-Sex Marriage: Is Marriage Inherently Heterosexual?" *American Journal of Jurisprudence* 42 (1997): 51–95.

"*Romer v. Evans* and Invidious Intent." *William and Mary Bill of Rights Journal* 6 (1997): 89–146.

"Why Discrimination Against Lesbians and Gay Men is Sex Discrimination." *New York University Law Review* 69 (1994): 197–287.

Leonard, Arthur. "The Case for Same Sex Marriage." (book review) *Cornell Law Review* 82 (1997): 572–593.

Lupu, Ira. "Untangling the Strands of the Fourteenth Amendment." *Michigan Law Review* 77 (April 1979): 981–1077.

Lusky, Louis. "Footnote Redux: A *Caroline Products* Reminiscence." *Columbia Law Review* 82 (1982): 1093–1105.

Macedo, Steven. "The New Natural Lawyers." *The Harvard Crimson*, October 28, 1993.

MacKinnon, Catherine. *Only Words.* Cambridge: Harvard University Press, 1993.

Feminism Unmodified Discourses on Life and Law. Cambridge: Harvard University Press, 1982.

Marcosson, Samuel. "The Lesson of the Same-Sex Marriage Trial: The Importance of Pushing Opponents of Gay Rights to Their Second Tier of

Defense." *University of Louisville Journal of Family Law* 36 (fall 1996/1997): 721–753.

Michelman, Frank. "The Supreme Court 1968 Term – Forward: On Protecting the Poor Through the Fourteenth Amendment." *Harvard Law Review* 83 (1969): 7–52.

Mill, John Stuart, and Harriet Taylor Mill. *Essays on Sex Equality.* Ed. Alice S. Rossi. Chicago: University of Chicago Press, 1970.

Minnow, Martha. "The Free Exercise of Families." *University of Illinois Law Review* 1991 (1991): 925–947.

Monaghan, Henry. "Of 'Liberty' and 'Property.'" *Cornell Law Review* 62 (1977): 405–444.

Morant, Blake D. "The Teachings of Martin Luther King, Jr. and Contract Theory: An Intriguing Comparison." *Alabama Law Review* 50 (fall 1998): 64–113.

Perry, Michael. *The Constitution, the Courts, and Human Rights.* New Haven: Yale University Press, 1982.

Podhoretz, Norman. "How the Gay-Rights Movement Won." *Commentary* 5 (1996): 32–40.

Polikoff, Nancy D. "We Will Get What We Ask For: Why Legalizing Gay and Lesbian Marriage Will Not 'Dismantle the Legal Structure of Gender in Every Marriage.'" *University of Virginia Law Review* 79 (October 1993): 1535–1549.

Posner, Richard. "Ask, Tell." Review of *GayLaw: Challenging the Apartheid of the Closet*, by William Eskridge. *The New Republic*, October 11, 1999, 52–58.

"1997 Survey of Books Relating to the Law: II. Sex, Law, and Equality: Should There Be Homosexual Marriage? And If So, Who Should Decide?" *Michigan Law Review* 95 (1997): 1578–1585.

Rawls, John. *A Theory of Justice.* Belknap Press of Harvard University Press, 1971.

Regan, Milton C., Jr. "Reason, Tradition, and Family Law: A Comment on Social Constructionism." *Virginia Law Review* 79 (1993): 1515–1533.

Rosenberg, Gerald. *The Hollow Hope: Can Courts Bring About Social Change?* Chicago: University of Chicago Press, 1991.

Schacter, Jane S. "Book Review: Skepticism, Culture and the Gay Civil Rights Debate in a Post-Civil-Rights Era." *Harvard Law Review* 110 (1997): 684–731.

Schroeder, Theodore A. "Fables of the Deconstruction: The Practical Failures of Gay and Lesbian Theory in the Realm of Employment Discrimination." *Journal of Gender & the Law* 6 (1998): 334–367.

Schultz, David, and Stephen E. Gottlieb. "Legal Functionalism and Social Change: A Reassessment of Rosenberg's *The Hollow Hope: Can Courts Bring About Social Change?" Journal of Law and Politics* 12 (1996): 63–99.

Schwartz, Bernard. *The Ascent of Pragmatism: The Burger Court in Action*. Reading, MA: Addison Wesley, 1990.

Segal, Jeffery, and Harold J. Spaeth. *Majority Rule or Majority Will: Adherence to Precedent on the U.S. Supreme Court*. New York: Cambridge University Press, 1999.

Siegel, Lee. "The Gay Science." *The New Republic*, November 9, 1998, 30–42.

Silverstein, Helena. "Revisiting the Logic of Equal Protection: Insights from *Baehr v. Lewin*." Prepared delivery at the 1998 Annual Meeting of the Western Political Science Association, Los Angeles, California, March 19–21, 1998.

Smith, Miriam. "Social Movements and Equality Seeking: The Case of Gay Liberation in Canada." *Canadian Journal of Political Science* 31 (1998): 285–309.

Stoddard, Thomas B. "Bleeding Heart: Reflections on Using the Law to Make Social Change." *New York University Law Review* 72 (1997): 967–991.

Strasser, Mark. "Domestic Relations and the Great Slumbering Baehr: On Definitional Preclusion, Equal Protection and Fundamental Interests." *Fordham Law Review* 64 (December 1995): 921–986.

Legally Wed: Same-Sex Marriage and the Constitution. Ithaca: Cornell University Press, 1997.

Sullivan, Andrew. "State of the Union." *The New Republic*, May 8, 2000, 18–23.

"Three's a Crowd." *The New Republic*. June 17, 1996, 10–12.

Sunstein, Cass. "Homosexuality and the Constitution." *Indiana Law Journal* 70 (1994): 1–28.

One Case at a Time: Judicial Minimalism and the Supreme Court. Cambridge: Harvard University Press, 1999.

Terrell, Timothy. "'Property', 'Due Process', and the Distinction between Definition and Theory in Legal Analysis." *Georgetown Law Journal* 70 (1982): 861–941.

Tribe, Laurence. "The Puzzling Persistence of Process-Based Constitutional Theories." *Yale Law Journal* 89 (1980): 1063–80.

Tribe, Laurence, and Michael Dorf. "Levels of Generality in the Definition of Rights." *University of Chicago Law Review* 57 (fall 1990): 1057–1108.

Trosino, James. "American Weddings: Same-sex Marriage and the Miscegenation Analogy." *Boston University Law Review* 73 (1993): 93–120.

Tushnet, Mark. *Taking the Constitution Away from the Courts*. Princeton: Princeton University Press, 1999.

"Following the Rules Laid Down, A Critique of Interpretivism and Neutral Principles." *Harvard Law Review* 96 (1983): 781–827.

"And Only Wealth Will Bring You Justice – Some Notes on the Supreme Court. 1972 Term." *Wisconsin Law Review* 1974 (1974): 177–197.

"Two Notes on the Jurisprudence of Privacy." *Constitutional Commentary* 8 (1991): 75–86.

Twiss, Benjamin R. *Lawyers and the Constitution: How Laissez-Faire Came to the Supreme Court.* Princeton: Princeton University Press, 1942.

Waaldijk, Kees. "Civil Developments: Pattern of Reform in the Legal Positions of Same-Sex Partners in Europe." *Canadian Journal of Family Law* 17 (2000): 62–88.

Waite, Linda, and Maggie Gallagher. *The Case for Marriage.* New York: Doubleday, 2000.

Wardle, Lynn D. "*Loving v. Virginia* and the Constitutional Right to Marry, 1790–1990." *Howard Law Journal* 41 (1998): 289–347.

   "The Potential Impact of Homosexual Parenting on Children." *University of Illinois Law Review* 1997 (1997): 833–920.

Wechsler, Herbert. "Toward Neutral Principles of Constitutional Law." *Harvard Law Review* 73 (1959): 1–35.

Westen, Peter. "The Empty Idea of Equality." *Harvard Law Review* 95 (1982): 537–560.

Wheeler, Malcolm. "In Defense of Economic Equal Protection." *Kansas Law Review* 22 (1973): 1–77.

Whittington, Keith E. "Commentaries on Mark Tushnet's *Taking the Constitution Away from the Courts*: Herbert Wechsler's Complaint and the Revival of Grand Constitutional Theory." *University of Richmond Law Review* 34 (2000): 509–519.

   Constitutional Interpretation: Textual Meaning, Original Intent, and Judicial Review. Lawrence: University of Kansas Press, 1999.

Wilkinson, J. Harvie III. "The Supreme Court, the Equal Protection Clause and the Three Faces of Constitutional Equality." *Virginia Law Review* 61 (June 1975): 945–1017.

Wolfe, Naomi. *The Beauty Myth.* New York: William Morrow and Co., 1990.

Wolin, Sheldon. "Democracy, Difference, and Re-Cognition." *Political Theory* 21 (1993): 468–475.

Yaworsky, Michael J. "Rights and Obligation Resulting from Human Artificial Insemination." *A.L.R.* 4th 83 (1991): 295–302.

Young, Gary L., Jr. "Don't Ask Don't Tell: Gays in the Military: The Price of Public Endorsement: A Reply to Dr. Marcosson." *University of Missouri at Kansas City Law Review* 64 (1995): 99–114.

Index

Ackerman, Bruce, 76
Adams v. Howerton, 93–94
Advocate poll on interest of gays and
  lesbians in marriage, 6
Allgeyer v. Louisiana, 75
Allport, Gordon, 54
animus; as a constitutional standard, 17
Arendt, Hannah, 8
attitudinal model, 178, 180, 188–190
Augustine, Saint, 93

Baehr v. Lewin/Miike, 27, 29, 43, 49,
  59–61, 87, 89, 92
Baker v. Carr, 152
Baker v. State, 196–198, 205–206
Ball, Carlos, 30–31
Bell v. Burson, 148–149
Bennett, William, 100
Bickel, Alexander, 151, 162, 173, 182
Blackmun, Justice Harry, 121
Boddie v. Connecticut, 91–92, 149, 187
Bolling v. Sharpe, 119
Bork, Robert, 5, 100, 138–141, 165, 170,
  183, 190, 192
Bowers v. Hardwick, 37–38, 176–178
Bradley, Craig, 24
Bradley, Gerard, 24, 26–27
Brandenburg v. Ohio, 174–175, 178–179
Bratt, Carolyn, 105–106
Brennan, Justice William, 152

Burger, Chief Justice Warren, 120
Brown v. Board of Education, 115, 140,
  163, 181, 195–196, 198
Buchanan, G. Sydney, 33, 159

Carter, Lief, 142
Chambers, David, 101
Chaplinsky v. New Hampshire, 185
Chapman, Steven, 103
Chicago Police Department v. Mosley,
  174
child-rearing: as reason to oppose
  same-sex marriage, 27–34, 96–98;
  studies of same-sex partners as
  child-rearers, 30–31
Christian Science Monitor, 204
Civil Unions, 5, 196–200; contrast to
  marriage 199–200
Clinton, Senator Hillary Rodham, 20–21
Coates v. Cincinnati, 38
Constitutional Underclass, 7
Coolidge, David Ogden, 46–47, 53
court-packing plan, 75
coverture, 57
critical legal studies movement, 183

Dahl, Robert, 196
Defense of Marriage Act ("DOMA"), 5,
  100, 161, 195, 199; State versions of
  DOMA, 161, 199

Destro, Robert, 79–81
Dorf, Michael, 191–192
Douglas, Justice William O., 88, 131,
    143, 145
due process clause, 74; substantive due
    process, 75, 118–123; and fundamental
    rights, 117–118, 123, 125–126
Duncan, Richard, 20, 28, 101
Dworkin, Ronald, 167, 188

Eggebeen, David, 32
Eisenstadt v. Baird, 177
Elshtain, Jean Bethke, 7
Ely, John Hart, 70, 125, 128, 130–132,
    136, 137
Embry, Jessie, 101
Employment Non-Discrimination Act
    ("ENDA"), 161
endorsement: fear of endorsing
    homosexuality as a reason to oppose
    same-sex marriage, 34–39; as a
    constitutional standard,
    36–37
Epstein, Lee 178, 201
Epstein, Richard, 4, 35, 150
equal protection clause: connection
    between rights protected under the
    equal protection clause, 145–148; and
    monopoly power by the government,
    148–151; and the political question
    doctrine, 151–154; pragmatic approach
    to finding covered rights, 141; role of
    precedent in interpreting, 142–145;
    three-tier framework for applying,
    14
Eskridge, William, 22, 28, 30, 36, 52,
    55–58, 100–102, 198
Eugenics movement, 49–50, 79

Farrell, Megan, 60, 87
Finnis, John, 24–26, 93
Fish, Stanley, 184–185
Foley, Dan, 44
Fourteenth Amendment: and protection
    of individuals and minorities, 168–199
    (See individual headings for the major
    clauses of the Fourteenth Amendment.)

freedom of speech; and flag-burning,
    203–204; as an example of principled
    adjudication, 173–176, 184–185, 189;
    as extending beyond dictionary
    definition of speech, 96–98; distinction
    between speech and action, 38–39,
    184–185
fundamental rights, 7, 14–15, 69–70; and
    the Bill of Rights, 128–129; and due
    process, 117–118, 123, 125–126; and
    equal protection, 118–122, 125–126;
    and privileges and immunities,
    123–124; and the right to vote, 129; as
    derived from history and tradition,
    116, 137; as derived from penumbras,
    78, 117, 131; as implicit in ordered
    liberty, 116, 138; as a product of
    reasoned judgment, 116; as
    representation-reinforcing, 130–132;
    distinguished from common law rights,
    73; marriage as a fundamental right,
    73–84; penumbras as origin of, 78,
    117, 131

Garfield, Helen, 136–137
gender discrimination: connection
    between heterosexism and patriarchy,
    51–61; theory that discrimination
    against gays and lesbians is gender
    discrimination, 15, 41–61; 'formal'
    version of that theory, 41–51
General Accounting Office's estimate of
    the number of federal laws that would
    be affected by same-sex marriage, 19
George, Robert, 24, 26–27
Gilligan v. Morgan, 154
Gillman, Howard, 188–189
Glendon, Mary Ann, 8
Grad, Frank, 94
Grano, Joseph, 170–171
Griffin, Steven, 160
Griswold v. Connecticut, 77–78, 86, 88,
    117, 133, 145–146

Hafen, Bruce, 73, 147
Harlan, Justice John, 132
Harper v. Virginia Board of Elections, 118,
    120

Hawaii: constitution of, 44–45; public reaction to possibility of same-sex marriage, 195
Hohengarten, William, 94–95
Holmes, Justice Oliver Wendell, 23

incest: analogy to homosexuality, 105–109; and common law, 107; and genetic defects, 105–106; and sexual exploitation of children, 106–109; and the Bible 108; in Sweden, 108
intermediate scrutiny, 15

Jackson, John, 164
Jackson, Justice Robert, 171
Jeffords, Senator James, 161, 198
Jeffrey, Julie Roy, 102
Jim Crow Laws, 46–50
Johnson, Greg, 197–198, 205–206
Jones v. Hallahan, 20
judicial review: and judicial minimalism, 179–180; and levels of generality, 190–192; and principled adjudication, 173–193, 190–192; and the attitudinal model, 178, 180, 188–190; as anti-democratic, 159–193; as disguised ideology, 183; efficacy of, 200–208; 'overturning' via constitutional amendment, 203–204; weak and strong discretion, 188–199

Kant, Emmanuel, 25
Karst, Kenneth, 85, 107
Katz, Pamela, 37
Knight, Jack, 201
Kobylka, Joseph, 178
Koppelman, Andrew, 10, 38, 41– 42, 45, 50

Law, Sylvia, 51
Lochner v. New York, 75, 118, 151
Loving v. Virginia, 46–51, 78–83, 98, 163, 187, 198, 201–203
Lupu, Ira, 117, 120

Macedo, Steven, 25
MacKinnon, Catherine, 51
Marcosson, Samuel, 28, 30

marriage: and nature, 98–99; as a common law right, 73; as an expression of love and commitment, 146; as a 'primary right' 86–93; as the right to bear and raise children in a traditional family environment, 93–96; 'complimentary' nature of, 53; contrast to civil unions, 199–200; definition of, 19–21, 96; evolving nature of, 21–23; precedent and the right to marry, 144; traditionally heterosexual nature of, 20–23; Waite and Gallagher's analysis of the benefits of marriage, 5–6
Marshall, Justice Thurgood, 71, 82, 86, 90
Massachusetts v. Murgia, 148
Massaro, Tony, 55–56
Maynard v. Hill, 74, 81
McCann, Michael, 206
Mclaughlin v. Florida, 50
Meyer v. Nebraska, 75–76, 81, 86, 88
Michelman, Frank, 151
Mill, John Stuart, 99
Moore v. City of East Cleveland, 89, 116, 187
Myrdal, Gunnar, 47

natural law, 24–27, 136
Nietzsche, Friedrich, 22

originalism, 138–141, 165–168

Pea, Janice Farrell, 30–31
Pennoyer v. Neff, 74
Perry, Michael, 136–137
Pierce v. Society of Sisters, 89
Plessy v. Ferguson, 143
political questions, 151–154
polygamy, 99–105; and abusive conduct, 102–103; congressional attempts to ban, 103–104; distinctions from same-sex marriage, 104–105; ruling by the Supreme Court, 104; stereotypes regarding, 101–103
positivism, 135
Posner, Richard 28, 115, 160, 163, 175–176, 178, 194

Powell, Justice Lewis, 116, 121
Pruett, Kyle, 29

rational basis review: application to the
  same-sex marriage ban, 19–40;
  definition of, 15–19; 'second order'
  rational basis, 71
Rawls, John, 168
Regan, Milton, C., 108
Regents of the University of California v.
  Bakke, 199
Rehnquist, Justice William, 121
Religious Freedom Restoration Act
  (RFRA), 172–173
Reynolds v. United States, 104
Roe v. Wade, 123, 144, 206
Romer v. Evans, 16–18, 27, 32, 38
Roosevelt, President Franklin D., 75, 164
Rosenberg, Gerald, 195–196

Saenz v. Roe, 124
Safire, William, 100
same-sex marriage; *passim*; in other
  nations, 5; as a fundamental right,
  73–84
San Antonio Independent School District v.
  Rodriguez, 122–123, 149
Scalia, Justice Antonin, 190–191
Schacter, Jane, 196
Schroeder, Theodore, 43
Shahar v. Bowers, 146
Shapiro v. Thompson, 118, 124, 132
Silverstein, Gordon 204–205
Singer v. Hara, 20
Skinner v. Oklahoma, 77, 81, 86, 88, 118
sodomy; and Georgia statute, 176–178;
  trend toward removing legal bans, 56
Sosna v. Iowa, 150–151
special rights, 3, 7–8, 63, 110, 128, 207
stare decisis, 142–145; reasons for
  ignoring, 143–144; reasons for
  following, 142–43

Stevens, Justice, John Paul, 36
Stewart, Justice Potter, 99, 121
Stoddard, Thomas, 203
Strasser, Mark, 38, 85, 96
strict scrutiny, 14; and fundamental
  rights, 14; and suspect class analysis,
  14, 61–63, 71; and wealth, 120–122,
  152
substantive due process, 75, 118–123
Sullivan, Andrew, 21–22, 23, 195, 200
Sunstein, Cass, 37, 48, 52, 161, 179–180,
  194–195, 203

Terrell, Timothy, 148
three-tier framework for equal
  protection, 14
Tocqueville, Alexis de, 160
Tribe, Laurence 191–192
Trosino, James, 36
Turner v. Safley, 82–83, 90–91, 142–147,
  187
Tushnet, Mark, 161, 164–165, 172,
  185–188

United States v. Kras, 149–150
USDA v. Moreno, 16–17

Volokh, Eugene 189

Wardle, Lynn, 30–31, 42–43, 73, 86
Warren, Chief Justice Earl, 118
Weber v. Aetna Casualty and Security,
  149
Wechsler, Herbert, 180–190
Westen, Peter, 127
Whittington, Keith, 139–143, 166–168,
  194
Wilkinson, J. Harvie, 152, 154
Will, George, 100

Zablocki v. Redhail, 81–83, 89–90, 92, 99,
  142, 187